Entertaining Is Easy
With Surefire Recipes

HOME FOR THE HOLIDAYS…nothing offers folks as much comfort and joy at such special times. And an attractive spread of home-cooked foods makes each occasion more fulfilling and more vivid.

That's why we're pleased to present *Taste of Home's Holiday & Celebrations 2007*. This timeless treasury is packed with 262 easy recipes to make Christmas, Thanksgiving, Easter and any other celebrations throughout the year memorable!

'Tis the Season. The Christmas season is a flurry of activity. Take the worry out of what to make for every holiday happening with this chapter's merry array of 111 recipes, including Prosciutto-Stuffed Mushrooms, Herbed Standing Rib Roast and Raspberry-Cream Chocolate Torte. Don't forget to check out the 20 recipes for festive cookies and candies, such as Almond Crunch Toffee, Butter Pecan Roll-Ups and Creme de Menthe Truffles. We even offer menu ideas for an intimate Christmas Eve dinner and a casual wintertime buffet.

Giving Thanks. Our Thanksgiving menu featuring Maple-Butter Turkey with Gravy, Mushrooms au Gratin and Persimmon Squash Pie is just the thing for folks who favor traditional fare but want to add a tasty twist. In addition to your favorite pumpkin pie, try a selection of sugar-and-spice sweets, such as Caramel Apple Trifle, Icebox Spice Cookies and Ginger Pound Cake. Plus, there are 12 delicious ideas for succulent stuffing and gravy!

Easter Gatherings. Celebrate the arrival of spring with a dinner featuring any number of light-and-lively entrees, including Raspberry-Chipotle Glazed Ham, Spinach Chicken Crepes and Rosemary-Rubbed Lamb Chops. Then bring out a fresh, fruity lemon dessert like Tangy Lemon Nut Tart, Fluted Lemon Cake and Lemon Mascarpone Cheesecake.

Special Celebrations. Occasions throughout the year also call for special celebrations. Get the year going by hosting a New Year's Day brunch or Mardi Gras celebration. Family, food and fun are the focus of our festive game night. In the heat of summer, enjoy a patriotic Fourth of July and some sizzling grilled goodies. When fall comes calling, you just can't resist the appeal of tasty apple recipes or the spirited fun of a haunted Halloween party.

Can-Do Decorating Ideas. There are dozens of ideas for stunning table toppers (see page 117 for a Cornucopia Centerpiece), delightful decorating secrets (such as the Ice Candles on page 105) and fun food crafts (turn to page 93 for Applesauce Cinnamon Ornaments).

With perfect party menus, unforgettable fare and simple decorating ideas, *Taste of Home's Holiday & Celebrations Cookbook 2007* will make entertaining easy for you…and memorable for your family!

WOULD YOU like to see one of your family-favorite recipes featured in a future edition of this timeless treasury? See page 256 for details!

Taste of Home's
HOLIDAY & Celebrations
COOKBOOK 2007

Vice President, Executive Editor/Books: Heidi Reuter Lloyd
Senior Editor/Books: Mark Hagen
Project Editor: Julie Schnittka
Art Director: Gretchen Trautman
Senior Layout Designer: Julie Wagner
Layout Designer: Emma Acevedo
Craft Editor: Jane Craig
Editorial Assistant: Barb Czysz
Proofreaders: Linne Bruskewitz, Jean Steiner,
Julie Blume Benedict

Taste of Home Test Kitchen
Food Director: Diane Werner
Test Kitchen Manager: Karen Scales
Senior Recipe Editor: Sue A. Jurack
Recipe Editors: Mary King, Christine Rukavena
Contributing Copy Editor: Kristine Krueger
Senior Home Economist: Annie Rose
Contributing Home Economists: Anne Addesso,
Jackie Josetti, Lorri Reinhardt

Taste of Home Photo Studio
Senior Food Photographer: Rob Hagen
Food Photographers: Lori Foy, Dan Roberts, Jim Wieland
Set Stylists: Julie Ferron, Stephanie Marchese, Dolores Schaefer,
Grace Natoli Sheldon, Jennifer Bradley Vent
Senior Food Stylists: Sarah Thompson, Joylyn Trickel
Photo Studio Coordinators: Suzanne Kern, Kathy Swaney
Creative Director: Ardyth Cope

Senior Vice President, Editor in Chief: Catherine Cassidy
President, Food & Entertaining: Suzanne M. Grimes
President and Chief Executive Officer: Mary G. Berner

Taste of Home Books
©2007 Reiman Media Group, Inc.
5400 S. 60th Street, Greendale WI 53129
International Standard Book Number (10): 0-89821-559-5
International Standard Book Number (13): 978-0-89821-559-5
International Standard Serial Number: 1535-2781
All rights reserved. Printed in U.S.A.

Cover photo of Herbed Standing Rib Roast (p. 10) and
Poached Pears with Mixed Greens (p. 14) by Dan Roberts.
Food styled by Joylyn Trickel. Set styled by Stephanie Marchese.

'Tis the Season

With all the hustle and bustle surrounding the Christmas season, the last thing you need to worry about is what to make for your holiday happenings. Whether you're hosting an intimate Christmas Eve dinner, a gathering for family and friends on Christmas Day or a casual wintertime buffet, this chapter has you covered. You'll also find appealing appetizers, breads, side dishes and sweets to round out every merry menu.

'TIS THE Season

Dazzling Christmas Dinner

CREATE magical memories this holiday season with a Christmas Day dinner that friends and family won't soon forget.

Guests will realize this is no ordinary event when you set a stunning Herbed Standing Rib Roast on the table.

This impressive, yet easy-to-prepare entree is the perfect choice for an elegant holiday dinner.

Rich and comforting, Sun-Dried Tomato Scalloped Potatoes is a yummy Yuletide side with a tasty twist.

Special occasions call for an extraordinary salad, such as lovely Poached Pears with Mixed Greens. (Recipes shown at right.)

REGAL ROAST

(Top to bottom)

Poached Pears with Mixed Greens (p. 14)

Sun-Dried Tomato Scalloped Potatoes (p. 12)

Herbed Standing Rib Roast (p. 10)

COUNTDOWN TO CHRISTMAS DINNER

A Few Weeks Before:

- Prepare two grocery lists—one for non-perishable items to purchase now and one for perishable items to purchase a few days before Christmas Day.
- Order a 6- to 7-pound bone-in rib roast.
- Assemble items for the Evergreen Christmas Candles (page 15).

Two to Three Days Before:

- Buy remaining grocery items, including the rib roast.
- Combine the dry rub ingredients for the Herbed Standing Rib Roast; store in an airtight container.
- Make croutons for Flavorful French Onion Soup. Let cool; place in a re-sealable plastic bag.
- Prepare sauce for Sun-Dried Tomato Scalloped Potatoes. Cover; chill.

Christmas Eve:

- Set the table.
- Make the spinach mixture for Spinach-Cheese French Bread. Cover and chill.
- Wash and dry the greens for Poached Pears with Mixed Greens.
- Prepare Flavorful French Onion Soup; cover and refrigerate.
- Cook the beans for Festive Bean 'n' Pepper Bundles. Drain and soak in ice-cold water; drain and rinse well. Make zucchini rings and julienne the red peppers. Assemble the bundles; cover and refrigerate.
- Make the Creamy Chocolate Cake Roll, including Chocolate Raspberry Sauce. Cover and refrigerate.

Christmas Day:

- In the morning, poach the pears for the salad and make the dressing. Store covered at room temperature in separate containers.
- Assemble the Sun-Dried Tomato Scalloped Potatoes. Cover and refrigerate.
- For the Herbed Standing Rib Roast, add olive oil to the dry rub ingredients; rub over the roast. Bake as directed.
- Just before guests arrive, assemble the Spinach-Cheese French Bread. Bake and slice.
- Remove the Sun-Dried Tomato Scalloped Potatoes from the refrigerator 30 minutes before baking. Bake as directed alongside the roast.
- Reheat the Flavorful French Onion Soup; sprinkle with croutons and cheese. Serve as the first course.
- When you remove the roast and potatoes from the oven, increase the oven temperature to 350°. Drizzle the Festive Bean 'n' Pepper Bundles with butter. Bake as directed.
- Let the cooked roast stand for 15 minutes before carving. Meanwhile, prepare the au jus.
- Set out the Sun-Dried Tomato Scalloped Potatoes.
- Slice the poached pears and assemble the salad.
- For dessert, reheat the Chocolate Raspberry Sauce. Serve with slices of Creamy Chocolate Cake Roll.

Festive Bean 'n' Pepper Bundles

(Pictured at right)

This is a beautiful, interesting way to prepare vegetables for Christmas dinner. The flavor pairs well with a variety of entrees.
—Judith Krucki, Lake Orion, Michigan

  1 **pound fresh green beans, trimmed**
  1 **pound fresh wax beans, trimmed**
  2 **tablespoons chicken bouillon granules**
1/2 **teaspoon garlic powder**
  3 **medium zucchini**
  2 **medium sweet red peppers, julienned**
1/4 **cup butter, melted**

In a large saucepan, combine the beans, bouillon and garlic powder; cover with water. Bring to a boil. Cook, uncovered, for 8-10 minutes or until crisp-tender; drain.

Cut zucchini into 1/2-in. slices. Hollow out centers, leaving 1/4-in. rings; discard the centers. Thread beans and peppers through squash rings.

Place in a greased 15-in. x 10-in. x 1-in. baking pan; drizzle with butter. Cover and bake at 350° for 15-20 minutes or until zucchini is crisp-tender. **Yield:** 12-15 servings.

MAKING ZUCCHINI RINGS

TO MAKE zucchini rings for the Festive Bean 'n' Pepper Bundles (above), use an apple corer. Slice a medium zucchini in half widthwise, and then push the corer into the center of each half. Slice the zucchini into 1/2-in. slices.

Herbed Standing Rib Roast

(Pictured on page 6 and on cover)

We're a meat-and-potatoes family, so this roast is right up our alley. It really is the highlight of an elegant dinner for special guests. Leftovers are great for sandwiches, too.
—*Carol Stevens, Basye, Virginia*

3 tablespoons grated onion
2 tablespoons olive oil
4 garlic cloves, minced
2 teaspoons celery seed
1 teaspoon coarsely ground pepper
1 teaspoon paprika
1/4 teaspoon dried thyme
1 bone-in beef rib roast (6 to 7 pounds)
2 large onions, cut into wedges
2 large carrots, cut into 2-inch pieces
2 celery ribs, cut into 2-inch pieces
1/4 cup red wine *or* beef broth
Assorted herbs and fruit, optional

In a bowl, combine the first seven ingredients; rub over roast. Place the onions, carrots and celery in a large roasting pan; place roast over vegetables.

Bake, uncovered, at 325° for 1-3/4 to 2-1/2 hours or until meat reaches desired doneness (for medium-rare, a meat thermometer should read 145°; medium, 160°; well-done, 170°).

Remove roast to a serving platter and keep warm; let stand for 15 minutes before slicing. Meanwhile, for au jus, strain and discard vegetables. Pour drippings into a measuring cup; skim fat. Add wine or broth to roasting pan, stirring to remove any browned bits. Stir in drippings; heat through. Serve with roast. Garnish platter with herbs and fruit if desired. **Yield:** 10-12 servings.

SAUCES FOR PRIME RIB

THE term "au jus" (French for "with juice") is often used to describe the serving of meat (like prime rib) with the natural juices that were produced as drippings while the meat was roasting. For the best au jus, use homemade beef stock or good quality purchased beef broth.

Prime rib can also be served with zesty horseradish sauce. Here's an easy recipe to try: In a small bowl, beat 1/2 cup heavy whipping cream until stiff peaks form. Fold in 1/4 cup fresh grated horseradish root, 1/2 teaspoon Dijon mustard and 1/4 teaspoon salt. Cover the sauce and refrigerate it 15 minutes before serving.

Flavorful French Onion Soup

(Pictured at right)

To complement the standing rib roast, our Test Kitchen home economists created this satisfying soup. Serve it as a first course to get mouths watering!

1/4 cup butter, cubed
2-1/2 pounds onions, thinly sliced
   3 tablespoons brown sugar
   1 teaspoon pepper
   3 tablespoons all-purpose flour
   8 cups beef broth
   1 cup dry red wine *or* additional beef broth
1/4 cup A.1. steak sauce

HOMEMADE CROUTONS:
   3 cups cubed French bread
   2 tablespoons olive oil
   2 tablespoons butter, melted
1/2 teaspoon dried oregano
1/2 teaspoon dried basil
1/4 teaspoon salt
1/4 teaspoon pepper
3/4 cup shredded Swiss cheese

In a Dutch oven or soup kettle, melt butter. Add the onions, brown sugar and pepper; cook over low heat until lightly browned, about 1 hour.

Sprinkle onions with flour; stir to blend. Gradually stir in broth. Add wine or additional broth and steak sauce. Bring to a boil. Reduce heat; cover and simmer for 45 minutes.

Meanwhile, in a large bowl, toss bread cubes with oil and butter. Combine the oregano, basil, salt and pepper; sprinkle over bread and toss to coat. Transfer to an ungreased 15-in. x 10-in. x 1-in. baking pan. Bake at 375° for 10-12 minutes or until golden brown. Garnish soup with croutons and Swiss cheese. **Yield:** 11 servings (about 2-1/2 quarts).

Sun-Dried Tomato Scalloped Potatoes

(Pictured on page 7)

My family was tired of my traditional scalloped potatoes. So when I came across this recipe featuring a pesto and sun-dried tomato sauce, I knew I had to try it. I'm so glad I did...and so is my family!
—Jamie Milligan, Kimberley, British Columbia

1 jar (7 ounces) oil-packed
   sun-dried tomatoes, drained
   and patted dry
1/2 cup grated Parmesan cheese
2 tablespoons chopped fresh
   basil
2 tablespoons chopped fresh
   parsley
1 garlic clove, peeled
1/4 teaspoon salt
7 cups sliced peeled potatoes
2 cups (8 ounces) shredded
   cheddar cheese
1 cup chicken broth

Place the first six ingredients in a food processor; cover and process until blended. In a greased 3-qt. baking dish, layer half of the potatoes, tomato mixture and cheese. Repeat layers. Pour broth over the top.

Cover and bake at 325° for 1-1/2 hours. Uncover; bake 15 minutes longer or until potatoes are tender. Let stand for 10 minutes before serving. **Yield:** 10 servings.

POTATO POINTER

FOR 7 cups sliced peeled potatoes, you need roughly 3 pounds (about 9 medium) russet potatoes.

Creamy Chocolate Cake Roll

(Pictured at right)

The beauty of this dessert is that it looks elegant yet is simple to make. It earns rave reviews, especially when served with the chocolate raspberry sauce.
—Cathryn White, Newark, Delaware

  5 eggs, *separated*
  1 cup confectioners' sugar
  1 teaspoon vanilla extract
  1/4 cup all-purpose flour
  1/4 cup baking cocoa
  2 tablespoons sugar

CREAM FILLING/FROSTING:
  1 package (8 ounces) cream cheese, softened
  1/3 cup sugar
  1 package (3.4 ounces) instant vanilla pudding mix
  1 teaspoon vanilla extract
  1 quart heavy whipping cream

CHOCOLATE RASPBERRY SAUCE:
  1-1/2 cups semisweet chocolate chips
  1/2 cup seedless raspberry jam
  1/4 cup heavy whipping cream
  1 teaspoon almond extract

Place egg whites in a small mixing bowl; let stand at room temperature for 30 minutes. Line a greased 15-in. x 10-in. x 1-in. baking pan with waxed paper; grease the paper and set aside.

In a large mixing bowl, beat egg yolks on high speed for 5 minutes or until thick and lemon-colored. Gradually beat in confectioners' sugar. Stir in vanilla. Sift flour and cocoa together twice; gradually add to yolk mixture and mix well (batter will be very thick).

Beat egg whites on medium speed until soft peaks form. Gradually add sugar, 1 tablespoon at a time, beating on high until stiff peaks form. Gradually fold into batter. Spread evenly into prepared pan.

Bake at 375° for 12-15 minutes or until cake springs back when lightly touched. Cool for 5 minutes. Invert onto a kitchen towel dusted with baking cocoa. Gently peel off waxed paper. Roll up cake in the towel jelly-roll style, starting with a short side. Cool completely on a wire rack.

In a large mixing bowl, beat the cream cheese, sugar and pudding mix until smooth. Beat in vanilla. Gradually beat in cream until thick.

Unroll cake; spread 2-1/2 cups filling evenly over cake to within 1/2 in. of edges. Roll up again. Place seam side down on a serving platter. Frost top, sides and ends with remaining filling. Cover and refrigerate for 1 hour.

In a small microwave-safe bowl, combine the chips, jam and cream. Microwave, uncovered, on high for 1-2 minutes or until smooth, stirring every 30 seconds. Stir in extract. Serve with cake. Refrigerate leftovers. **Yield:** 10 servings.

Poached Pears with Mixed Greens

(Pictured on page 6 and on cover)

Slices of pretty poached pears add fabulous flavor to an ordinary mixed green salad.
— *Barbara Hahn, Park Hills, Missouri*

2 medium ripe Bartlett pears
1/2 cup dry red wine *or* grape juice
1 tablespoon red wine vinegar
1 teaspoon sugar
1 teaspoon olive oil
1/4 teaspoon salt
1/8 teaspoon cayenne pepper
1/8 teaspoon pepper
8 cups fresh arugula *or* baby spinach
2 cups torn curly *or* Belgian endive
1/4 cup crumbled blue cheese
3 tablespoons chopped walnuts

Peel, core and quarter the pears. Place cut side down in an 11-in. x 7-in. x 2-in. baking dish. Add wine or grape juice. Bake, uncovered, at 350° for 15-20 minutes or until crisp-tender. Drain, reserving 1 tablespoon liquid. Cool pears to room temperature.

For dressing, in a small bowl, whisk the vinegar, sugar, oil, salt, cayenne, pepper and reserved poaching liquid. Thinly slice the pears. In a large salad bowl, combine the arugula, endive and pears. Drizzle with dressing; toss to coat. Sprinkle with blue cheese and walnuts. **Yield:** 10 servings.

Spinach-Cheese French Bread

I found this recipe in a school cookbook many years ago. I once served it as an appetizer on Thanksgiving.
Guests ate so much of it they were almost too full for dinner!
— *Judy Henfey, Cibolo, Texas*

1 small onion, chopped
2 tablespoons butter
1 package (10 ounces) frozen chopped spinach, thawed and squeezed dry
1 cup (4 ounces) shredded part-skim mozzarella cheese
1 cup (4 ounces) shredded cheddar cheese
1 cup chopped fresh mushrooms
1/8 teaspoon salt

1/8 teaspoon pepper
1/8 teaspoon hot pepper sauce
1 loaf (1 pound) French bread, halved lengthwise
1/2 cup grated Parmesan cheese

In a large skillet, saute onion in butter until tender. Remove from the heat. Stir in the spinach, cheeses, mushrooms, salt, pepper and hot pepper sauce. Spoon onto bread halves.

Place on an ungreased baking sheet. Sprinkle with Parmesan cheese. Bake at 350° for 10-15 minutes or until cheese is melted. **Yield:** 10-12 servings.

Evergreen Christmas Candles

(Pictured above)

INVITE guests to gather around your Christmas dinner table with these stunning candle arrangements that provide a warm, welcoming glow.

First, purchase pillar candles in a color that complements your table linens and china. (The ivory-colored candles shown here would work with any decor.)

Instead of traditional candle holders or candlesticks, we set the candles inside square, clear glass vases that were about half the height of the candles.

For the candle wreaths, wire Christmas greens and artificial red berries into a circle. All stems should be facing the same direction.

Place a wreath over each candle so that it rests on top of the vase.

'TIS THE *Season*

An Intimate Christmas Eve Gathering

FOR MANY people, Christmas Eve is a special night when immediate families gather for an intimate dinner before groups of friends and other relatives arrive the next day.

A smaller gathering is a terrific time to prepare individual entree and dessert items, which would be difficult to do when cooking for a crowd.

Two such singular sensations include Crab-Stuffed Chicken Breasts (shown at right) and Lacy Fruit Cups with Sabayon Sauce (see page 19).

Then pass a crystal bowl of Colorful Bean Salad and a basket brimming with wedges of home-made Savory Focaccia. (Recipes are shown at right.)

'TWAS THE NIGHT
BEFORE CHRISTMAS
(Pictured above)

Crab-Stuffed Chicken Breasts (p. 22)

Colorful Bean Salad (p. 20)

Savory Focaccia (p. 20)

CHRISTMAS EVE DINNER AGENDA

A Few Weeks Before:

- Prepare two grocery lists—one for non-perishable items to purchase now and one for perishable items to purchase a few days before Christmas Eve.
- Bake Savory Focaccia and let cool. Freeze in two large, heavy-duty resealable plastic bags.
- Gather items for your Retro Christmas Scene. Make the Lightbulb Place Makers. (See pages 22 and 23.)

Two to Three Days Before:

- Buy remaining grocery items.
- Make the cookie cups Lacy Fruit Cups with Sabayon Sauce. Store in an airtight container at room temperature. Peel and section grapefruit and oranges; cover and refrigerate.

The Day Before:

- Set the table. Also assemble the Retro Christmas Scene.
- Prepare the crab mixture for Crab-Stuffed Chicken Breasts. Cover; refrigerate. Flatten the chicken breasts; cover and chill.
- Make the Pickled Shrimp as directed; cover and refrigerate.
- Prepare Colorful Two-Bean Salad; cover and chill.

Christmas Eve:

- In the morning, thaw one Savory Focaccia. (Keep the other focaccia in the freezer for a future meal.)
- About 2 hours before dinner, assemble the Crab-Stuffed Chicken Breasts; cover and refrigerate.
- Just before guests arrive, drain Pickled Shrimp and set out with toothpicks.
- Remove Colorful Two-Bean Salad from the refrigerator at least 30 minutes before dinner.
- If desired, wrap the focaccia in foil and reheat in a 350° oven for 15-20 minutes. Cut into wedges and serve.
- When ready for dessert, make the sabayon sauce. Divide the fruit among the cookie cups. Top with sauce and serve.

Lacy Fruit Cups with Sabayon Sauce

(Pictured at right)

This fruity dessert from our Test Kitchen is a refreshing change of pace from other heavy holiday desserts.

>   3 tablespoons butter
>   3 tablespoons brown sugar
>   3 tablespoons light corn syrup
>   2 tablespoons plus 2 teaspoons
>   all-purpose flour
> 1/3 cup ground pecans
> 1/4 teaspoon vanilla extract
>   5 egg yolks
> 1/2 cup rose *or* marsala wine
> 1/3 cup sugar
>   2 medium pink grapefruit,
>   peeled and sectioned
>   2 medium blood oranges *or*
>   tangerines, peeled and
>   sectioned
> 3/4 cup fresh raspberries

In a small saucepan, melt butter over low heat. Stir in brown sugar and corn syrup; cook and stir until mixture comes to a boil. Remove from the heat. Stir in flour. Fold in pecans and vanilla.

Drop by tablespoonfuls 3 in. apart onto parchment paper-lined baking sheets. Bake at 325° for 8-10 minutes or until golden brown. Cool for 30-60 seconds. Working quickly, peel cookies off paper and immediately drape over inverted 6-oz. custard cups; cool completely.

In a double boiler over simmering water, constantly whisk the egg yolks, wine and sugar until sauce is thickened and reaches 160°. Divide the grapefruit, oranges and berries among cookie cups; top with sauce. Serve immediately. **Yield:** 8 servings.

Editor's Note: If the cookies become firm before they are draped over custard cups, warm them on the baking sheet for 1 minute to soften.

SABAYON SAUCE SUBSTITUTE

OUR Test Kitchen home economists like how the sweet rose wine in our sabayon balances the tangy fruits in the recipe above. You could also make the sabayon sauce with marsala, which is traditional, or champagne.

Savory Focaccia

(Pictured on page 17)

*Instead of offering store-bought rolls at a holiday dinner,
our home economists suggest serving this tasty herbed focaccia bread.*

1 medium onion, chopped
1/3 cup olive oil, *divided*
1-1/2 teaspoons minced fresh
    rosemary *or* 1/2 teaspoon
    dried rosemary, crushed
1 teaspoon dried basil
1 teaspoon dried oregano
1-1/2 teaspoons active dry yeast
1-1/2 cups warm water (110° to
    115°), *divided*
1/2 teaspoon sugar
1/2 teaspoon salt
1/2 teaspoon garlic powder
3-1/2 to 4 cups all-purpose flour
Cornmeal
Coarse salt

In a small skillet, saute onion in 2 tablespoons oil until tender; cool. Combine the rosemary, basil and oregano; set aside.

In a large mixing bowl, dissolve yeast in 1/4 cup warm water. Add sugar; let stand for 5 minutes. Add 2 tablespoons oil, salt, garlic powder, 2 cups flour and remaining water. Beat until smooth. Stir in enough remaining flour to form a soft dough.

Turn onto a floured surface; knead until smooth and elastic, about 6-8 minutes. Add sauteed onion and half of the herb mixture; knead 1 minute longer. Place in a greased bowl, turning once to grease top. Cover and let rise in a warm place until doubled, about 40 minutes.

Punch dough down. Turn onto a lightly floured surface; divide in half. Roll each portion into a 10-in. circle; let rest for 5 minutes. Grease two baking sheets and sprinkle with cornmeal. Transfer dough to prepared pans; reshape if necessary. Cover and let rise until doubled, about 40 minutes.

Brush with remaining oil. Sprinkle with coarse salt and remaining herb mixture. Bake at 375° for 25-30 minutes or until golden brown. Remove from pans to wire racks. Cut into wedges; serve warm. **Yield:** 2 loaves.

Colorful Bean Salad

(Pictured on page 17)

Green beans and roasted sweet red peppers make this an attractive Christmas side dish.
—Nancy Hudson, Methuen, Massachusetts

3/4 pound fresh green beans,
    trimmed
2-1/4 cups canned white kidney *or*
    cannellini beans, rinsed and
    drained

1/4 cup julienned roasted sweet red peppers
3/4 cup pitted Greek olives, halved
3 tablespoons olive oil
4 teaspoons lemon juice
6 fresh basil leaves, thinly sliced
Salt and pepper to taste

Place green beans in a steamer basket; place in a large saucepan over 1 in. of water. Bring to a boil; cover and steam for 5-6 minutes or until crisp-tender. Cool.

In a large bowl, combine the green beans, kidney beans, red peppers and olives. In a small bowl, combine the oil, lemon juice, basil, salt and pepper. Pour over bean mixture; toss to coat. Serve at room temperature. **Yield:** 6 servings.

Pickled Shrimp

(Pictured at right)

I appreciate this appetizer's ease of preparation, especially during the hectic holiday season. The recipe can easily be doubled for a crowd.
—Kathi Nelson, Yorba Linda, California

1/3 cup olive oil
1/4 cup red wine vinegar
   1 tablespoon tomato paste
1-1/2 teaspoons sugar
1-1/2 teaspoons celery seed
   1 garlic clove, minced
1/2 teaspoon coarsely ground
      pepper
1/4 teaspoon salt
1/4 teaspoon ground mustard
1/8 teaspoon crushed red pepper
      flakes
1/8 teaspoon hot pepper sauce
   1 pound cooked large shrimp,
      peeled and deveined
   1 small onion, thinly sliced and
      separated into rings
   2 bay leaves

In a large resealable plastic bag, combine the first 11 ingredients; add the shrimp, onion and bay leaves. Seal bag and turn to coat; refrigerate for up to 24 hours.

Drain and discard marinade, onion and bay leaves. Serve shrimp with toothpicks. **Yield:** about 1-1/2 dozen.

Crab-Stuffed Chicken Breasts

(Pictured on page 17)

Holiday dinners in my youth meant Mom would be serving these stuffed chicken breasts.
—*Lorna Hudson, Weott, California*

4 tablespoons butter, *divided*
2 teaspoons plus 3 tablespoons all-purpose flour, *divided*
1/2 teaspoon salt
1/8 teaspoon pepper
1/4 cup milk
2 cans (6 ounces *each*) lump crabmeat, drained
2/3 cup chopped fresh mushrooms
1/3 cup grated Parmesan cheese
6 boneless skinless chicken breast halves (6 ounces *each*)
1/2 teaspoon paprika
SAUCE:
3/4 cup marsala wine
2 teaspoons all-purpose flour
1 teaspoon chicken bouillon granules
1 tablespoon water

In a small saucepan, melt 2 tablespoons butter. Stir in 2 teaspoons flour, salt and pepper until smooth; gradually add milk. Bring to a boil; cook and stir for 1-2 minutes or until thickened. Stir in the crab, mushrooms and Parmesan cheese.

Flatten chicken to 1/4-in. thickness. Top each piece with 3 tablespoons crab mixture. Roll up jelly-roll style, starting with a short side; tie with kitchen string.

In a shallow bowl, combine paprika and remaining flour. Add chicken rolls, one at a time, and turn to coat. In a large skillet, brown chicken in remaining butter on all sides.

Add wine. Bring to a boil. Reduce heat; cover and simmer for 15-20 minutes or until a meat thermometer reads 170°.

Remove chicken and keep warm. In a small bowl, combine flour and bouillon; stir in water until blended. Stir into cooking juices. Bring to a boil; cook and stir for 1-2 minutes or until thickened. Cut string off chicken rolls; top with sauce. **Yield:** 6 servings.

LIGHTBULB PLACE MARKERS

IGNITE memorable discussions about Christmases past by using old-fashioned Christmas tree lightbulbs as dazzling place cards.

First paint the lightbulbs in colors that complement your table setting; let dry.

Using an embossing pen, write a dinner guest's name on each bulb. Sprinkle with embossing powder; melt the powder with a heat gun. You can also write the name with a paint pen. Let dry.

Wrap the end of each bulb with narrow, wire-edge ribbon. Coil the ends of the ribbon.

Tie the bulb place card around a folded napkin with another length of matching ribbon.

Retro Christmas Scene

(Pictured above)

DO YOU have an assortment of ornaments from decades ago (such as the Shiny Brites shown here) that you dare not hang on the tree in case they fall and break? Don't keep those beautiful baubles under wraps where no one can enjoy them.

Take holiday guests on a trip down memory lane by displaying those treasured ornaments in a retro-style tablescape.

Deck the dinner table in your finest linens, china and silverware. Then sprinkle artificial snow down the center to create a snowy scene. Place pretty ornaments inside assorted stemware.

Miniature bottle-brush Christmas trees complete the reminiscent, wintry wonderland.

'Tis the Season

Easy & Elegant Christmas Appetizers

DURING the holidays, your list of things to do is longer than ever. So instead of hosting a labor-intensive dinner party, invite family and friends to a simply stunning appetizer affair!

All of the hors d'oeuvres in this chapter are not only delicious, they each have a time-saving element that will have busy cooks singing "Hallelujah!"

Welcome guests in from the cold with wedges of oven-fresh Fantastic Artichoke Pizza—conveniently made with a pre-baked Italian bread shell.

For a bit of elegance on the table, set out a pretty platter of three-ingredient Ham Asparagus Spirals.

Radish-Stuffed Cherry Tomatoes are refreshing, bite-sized goodies that can be prepared in advance ahead. (All recipes are shown at right.)

FAST AND FESTIVE
(Clockwise from top right)

Fantastic Artichoke Pizza (p. 26)

Ham Asparagus Spirals (p. 26)

Radish-Stuffed Cherry Tomatoes (p. 28)

Fantastic Artichoke Pizza

(Pictured on page 25)

It seems I'm always entertaining at the last minute. I keep many of the ingredients for
this rich pizza on hand so I can make it at a moment's notice.
—Alicia Sinner, Zion, Illinois

1 prebaked Italian bread shell
  crust (14 ounces)
1 can (14 ounces) water-packed
  artichoke hearts, rinsed,
  drained and chopped
1 cup (4 ounces) shredded
  Parmesan cheese, *divided*
1 cup (4 ounces) shredded
  part-skim mozzarella cheese,
  divided
1 cup mayonnaise
6 garlic cloves, minced
1/2 cup sliced grape tomatoes

Place crust on an ungreased 14-in. pizza pan. In a small bowl, combine the artichokes, 3/4 cup of each cheese, mayonnaise and garlic; spread over crust.

Top with tomatoes. Sprinkle with remaining cheeses. Bake at 450° for 15-20 minutes or until edges are lightly browned. **Yield:** 16 slices.

Editor's Note: Reduced-fat or fat-free mayonnaise is not recommended for this recipe.

Ham Asparagus Spirals

(Pictured on page 25)

Just three ingredients are all you need to prepare these impressive-looking hors d'oeuvres.
A vegetable appetizer is a welcome addition to the table.
—Rosie Huffer, Westminster, California

20 fresh asparagus spears,
   trimmed
20 thin slices deli ham
 1 package (10.6 ounces)
   refrigerated Italian
   breadsticks and garlic spread

In a large skillet, bring 1/2 in. of water to a boil; add asparagus. Reduce heat; cover and simmer for 2 minutes. Drain and immediately place asparagus in ice water; drain and pat dry.

Wrap a slice of ham around each asparagus spear. Unroll breadstick dough; spread with garlic spread. Cut each breadstick in half lengthwise. Wrap one piece of dough, garlic spread side out, around each ham-wrapped asparagus spear.

Place on an ungreased baking sheet. Bake at 375° for 13-15 minutes or until golden brown. Serve immediately. **Yield:** 20 appetizers.

Dilly Cheese Ring with Spinach Dip

(Pictured at right)

This is my daughter's favorite appetizer. Instead of serving spinach dip with ordinary bread cubes, you bake refrigerated biscuits into a delicious bread ring.
—*Sandra Conti, Agawam, Massachusetts*

1-1/2 cups (12 ounces) sour cream
1 package (10 ounces) frozen chopped spinach, thawed and squeezed dry
3/4 cup chopped green onions
1 can (8 ounces) water chestnuts, drained and chopped
1/2 cup mayonnaise
1 package vegetable soup mix
1/4 cup grated Parmesan cheese
1/4 cup butter, melted
1 teaspoon dill weed
1/4 teaspoon garlic powder
2 tubes (7-1/2 ounces *each*) refrigerated buttermilk biscuits

For dip, combine the first six ingredients in a bowl. Cover and refrigerate until serving.

In a small bowl, combine the Parmesan cheese, butter, dill and garlic powder. Cut each biscuit in half; arrange half of the pieces in an ungreased 10-in. fluted tube pan. Sprinkle with half of the Parmesan mixture. Repeat layers.

Bake at 400° for 20-30 minutes or until golden brown. Cool for 1 minute before inverting onto a serving platter. Serve warm with spinach dip. **Yield:** 12-16 servings (3 cups dip).

Rum Chocolate Fondue

*Chocolate fondue with fresh fruit or cubed angel food cake will satisfy
any sweet tooth. It makes a tasty snack or light dessert.*
—*Jennifer Schwerin, Rockford, Illinois*

1 cup (6 ounces) semisweet
    chocolate chips
1/2 cup light corn syrup
Dash salt
1 to 2 tablespoons rum *or*
    1/2 teaspoon rum extract
1 teaspoon vanilla extract
**Assorted fresh fruit and angel food
    cake cubes**

In a small saucepan, combine chocolate chips, corn syrup and salt. Cook and stir over low heat until chips are melted.

Remove from the heat. Stir in rum or extract and vanilla until blended. Transfer to a small fondue pot and keep warm. Serve with fruit and cake cubes. **Yield:** 1 cup.

Radish-Stuffed Cherry Tomatoes

(Pictured on page 24)

*Christmas appetizer buffets get a refreshing lift with stuffed cherry tomatoes.
Plus, the color is appropriate for the season!*
—*Sandy Marek, Grand Marais, Minnesota*

18 cherry tomatoes
1/2 cup chopped radishes
2 tablespoons chopped
    almonds, toasted
2 tablespoons mayonnaise
1 tablespoon minced fresh
    parsley
1 teaspoon grated onion

Cut a thin slice off the top of each tomato. Scoop out and discard pulp; invert tomatoes onto paper towels to drain. In a small bowl, combine the remaining ingredients. Spoon into tomatoes. Refrigerate until serving. **Yield:** 1-1/2 dozen.

STUFFING CHERRY TOMATOES

1. With a small sharp knife, cut the top off of each tomato. Scoop out the pulp with a small spoon; discard. Place tomatoes, cut side down, on paper towels to drain.

2. Combine all remaining ingredients and spoon into each tomato. Chill until ready to serve.

Fluffy Fruit Dip

(Pictured at right)

We've been making this dip in my family for generations. Serve it throughout the year with whatever fruits are in season.
—*Sue Pence, Alexandria, Virginia*

1/2 cup sugar
2 tablespoons all-purpose flour
1 cup unsweetened pineapple juice
1 tablespoon butter
1 egg, lightly beaten
1 cup heavy whipping cream, whipped
Assorted fresh fruit

In a small saucepan, combine sugar and flour. Gradually whisk in pineapple juice. Add butter. Cook and stir until butter is melted and mixture comes to a boil. Cook and stir for 1-2 minutes or until thickened.

Remove from the heat. Stir a small amount of hot mixture into egg; return all to the pan, stirring constantly. Bring to a gentle boil; cook and stir for 1 minute. Remove from the heat. Cool to room temperature, stirring several times.

Fold in whipped cream. Cover and refrigerate for at least 1 hour. Serve with fruit. **Yield:** about 2-1/2 cups.

Havarti Cheese Puff

Guests always think I spent a great deal of time on this appetizer and have a hard time guessing the simple ingredients. Havarti is a nice change from the more common Brie.
—*Marla Reece, Gainesville, Florida*

1 package (8 ounces) refrigerated crescent rolls
3 tablespoons honey mustard
1 block (8 ounces) Havarti cheese
Assorted crackers

On a large piece of waxed paper, unroll crescent dough. Starting with a short side, fold a third of the dough to the center; repeat with the opposite side. Roll out into a 12-in. x 8-in. rectangle.

Spread mustard generously over all sides of cheese; place in center of dough. Fold dough over cheese; pinch seams to seal completely. Place on an ungreased baking sheet. Bake at 375° for 15-20 minutes or until golden brown. Serve warm with crackers. **Yield:** 12-16 servings.

Curried Swiss-Crab Bites

Guests will gobble up these golden biscuits topped with a cheesy crab mixture.
You can make the filling ahead of time to cut down on last-minute fuss.
—*Ginny Lange, Dalton, Minnesota*

1 tube (12 ounces) refrigerated
   flaky biscuits
1 package (8 ounces) imitation
   crabmeat, chopped
1 cup (4 ounces) shredded
   Swiss cheese
1/2 cup mayonnaise
1 tablespoon finely chopped
   onion
1 teaspoon lemon juice
1/2 teaspoon curry powder

Bake biscuits according to package directions. Meanwhile, in a large bowl, combine the crab, cheese, mayonnaise, onion, lemon juice and curry.

Remove biscuits to a wire rack. Split each biscuit in half horizontally; spread with crab mixture. Place on an ungreased baking sheet. Bake at 400° for 10-12 minutes or until crab mixture is heated through and lightly browned. **Yield:** 20 appetizers.

Chipotle Ham 'n' Cheese Dip

During the busy holiday season, you just can't beat convenient slow cooker recipes like this.
I can visit with guests instead of working away in the kitchen.
—*Lisa Renshaw, Kansas City, Missouri*

2 packages (8 ounces *each*)
   cream cheese, cubed
1 can (12 ounces) evaporated
   milk
8 ounces Gouda cheese,
   shredded
1 cup (4 ounces) shredded
   cheddar cheese
2 tablespoons chopped chipotle
   peppers in adobo sauce
1 teaspoon ground cumin
2 cups diced fully cooked ham
Tortilla chips *or* fresh vegetables

In a 3-qt. slow cooker, combine the first six ingredients. Cover and cook on low for 40 minutes.

Stir in ham; cook 20 minutes longer or until heated through. Serve warm with tortilla chips or vegetables. **Yield:** 7 cups.

Grits 'n' Shrimp Tarts

(Pictured at right)

This deliciously different appetizer showcases two Mississippi staples— grits and shrimp. I know your family will enjoy them as much as mine!
—Elizabeth Latady, Jackson, Mississippi

  1 cup water
1/4 cup quick-cooking grits
  2 ounces cream cheese, softened
1/4 cup shredded cheddar cheese
  3 tablespoons butter, *divided*
1/4 teaspoon garlic salt
1/8 teaspoon salt
Pepper to taste
  1 pound uncooked small shrimp, peeled and deveined
  3 green onions, sliced
  2 packages (2.1 ounces *each*) frozen miniature phyllo tart shells

In a small saucepan, bring water to a boil. Gradually stir in grits. Reduce heat; cover and simmer for 4 minutes. Stir in the cheeses, 1 tablespoon butter, garlic salt, salt and pepper.

In a large skillet, saute shrimp and onions in remaining butter until shrimp turn pink. Fill tart shells with grits; top with shrimp mixture. Refrigerate leftovers. **Yield:** 2-1/2 dozen.

CABBAGE-NIBBLER BOWL

WHEN she wants a unique appetizer for a holiday party, Janice Grandbois of Dyer, Indiana often assembles this eye-catching snack.

To prepare the cabbage bowl, gently peel back the outer leaves on a small head of cabbage. Cut 1/2 in. from the bottom of cabbage so it sits flat. Cut a 3-in. circle in the top; hollow out a third of the cabbage to form a bowl.

For the nibblers, cut 3 small cucumbers and 1 pound thickly sliced deli turkey into 1/4-in. pieces. You'll also need 2 cups cubed cheddar cheese and a pint of grape tomatoes.

Thread the cucumbers, turkey, cheese and tomatoes onto frilly toothpicks. Insert into cabbage, starting at the bottom. Refrigerate until serving. Just before serving, fill cabbage bowl with your favorite dip. This recipe yields 24 servings.

Warm Bacon-Swiss Spread

*My friends and I get together once a month to play cards...and to sample
a selection of appetizers! One of their favorites is this creamy spread.*
—*Susan Skora, Swanton, Ohio*

1 package (8 ounces) cream
  cheese, cubed
3/4 cup shredded Swiss cheese
1/2 cup mayonnaise
1 green onion, chopped
8 bacon strips, cooked and
  crumbled
1/4 cup crushed butter-flavored
  crackers
Assorted crackers

Place cream cheese in a microwave-safe bowl. Microwave, uncovered, on high for 30 seconds to soften. Stir in the Swiss cheese, mayonnaise and onion until blended.

Transfer to an ungreased 9-in. pie plate. Microwave, uncovered, on high for 1-1/2 minutes or until heated through, stirring once. Sprinkle with bacon and cracker crumbs. Serve with crackers. **Yield:** 2 cups.

Editor's Note: This recipe was tested in a 1,100-watt microwave. Reduced-fat or fat-free mayonnaise is not recommended.

Artichoke Crab Appetizer

*Crabmeat is a deliciously different addition in this cold artichoke spread.
Dijon mustard and hot pepper sauce provide a bit of zip.*
—*Nicole Trapp, Cudahy, Wisconsin*

1/4 cup vegetable oil
4 teaspoons Dijon mustard
3 teaspoons red wine vinegar
1 teaspoon white vinegar
1 garlic clove, minced
1/4 teaspoon dried basil
1/8 teaspoon onion powder
1 drop hot pepper sauce
Dash salt and pepper
1 can (14 ounces) water-packed
  artichoke hearts, rinsed,
  drained and chopped
2 cans (6 ounces *each*)
  crabmeat, drained, flaked
  and cartilage removed
2 green onions, chopped
Toasted French bread slices

In a jar with a tight-fitting lid, combine the oil, mustard, vinegars, garlic, basil, onion powder, hot pepper sauce, salt and pepper; shake well.

In a large bowl, combine the artichokes, crab and onions. Add dressing; toss to coat. Refrigerate until serving. Serve with French bread. **Yield:** 2-1/4 cups.

Jamaican Shrimp

(Pictured at right)

Zesty jerk seasoning is a nice complement to sweet mango in this crowd-pleasing appetizer. Although this dish takes time to prepare, it's conveniently made ahead and refrigerated until ready to serve.
—Mary Lou Wayman, Salt Lake City, Utah

- 3 quarts water
- 1 teaspoon salt
- 2 pounds uncooked medium shrimp, peeled and deveined
- 1/3 cup olive oil
- 1/4 cup white wine vinegar
- 3 tablespoons lime juice
- 1 jalapeno pepper, seeded and finely chopped
- 4 teaspoons honey
- 3 teaspoons Caribbean jerk seasoning
- 1 medium mango *or* 2 medium fresh peaches, peeled and cubed
- 1 small red onion, thinly sliced and separated into rings
- 1 medium lime, quartered and sliced

In a large saucepan, bring water and salt to a boil. Add shrimp; boil for 3 minutes or until shrimp turn pink, stirring occasionally. Drain and rinse with cold water; transfer to a large resealable plastic bag.

In a jar with a tight-fitting lid, combine the oil, vinegar, lime juice, jalapeno, honey and jerk seasoning; shake well. Pour 3/4 cup marinade over shrimp. Seal bag and turn to coat; refrigerate for 1-2 hours. Refrigerate remaining marinade.

Just before serving, drain and discard marinade from shrimp. On a large serving platter, layer the shrimp, mango, onion and lime. Drizzle with remaining marinade. **Yield:** 15-20 servings.

Editor's Note: When cutting or seeding hot peppers, use rubber or plastic gloves to protect your hands. Avoid touching your face.

MAKE YOUR MARK WITH MANGO

WHEN BUYING this tropical fruit, look for ones with unblemished green to yellow skin tinged with red. Ripe mangoes will feel fairly firm when gently pressed and have a sweet, fruity aroma.

Keep green mangoes at room temperature out of direct sunlight until ripened. When ripe, they can be refrigerated for 5 days.

Prosciutto-Stuffed Mushrooms

Prosciutto and oregano give these stuffed mushrooms a bit of an Italian twist.
To make them ahead, cover with plastic wrap and refrigerate until ready to bake.
—Nancy Foust, Stoneboro, Pennsylvania

16 large fresh mushrooms
3 tablespoons olive oil, *divided*
1/2 cup finely chopped onion
1 garlic clove, minced
2 tablespoons butter
1 cup dry bread crumbs
4 thin slices prosciutto, chopped
1/4 teaspoon dried oregano
1/4 teaspoon lemon juice
Pepper to taste
1 cup (4 ounces) shredded part-skim mozzarella cheese
3 tablespoons grated Parmesan cheese

Remove stems from mushrooms; finely chop stems. Drizzle caps with 2 tablespoons oil; set aside. In a large skillet, saute the stems, onion and garlic in butter and remaining oil until tender.

Stir in bread crumbs and prosciutto. Cook for 1-2 minutes or until crumbs are lightly browned. Stir in the oregano, lemon juice and pepper. Spoon mixture firmly into mushroom caps.

Place on a foil-lined baking sheet. Sprinkle with mozzarella and Parmesan cheeses. Bake at 400° for 15-20 minutes or until mushrooms are tender and cheese is melted. **Yield:** 16 appetizers.

AN EYE-CATCHING BUFFET TABLE

ALTHOUGH a host of special appetizers may be the star of your party, using other items on your buffet table can add even more visual interest.

Rise to the Occasion. When all of the serving dishes on a buffet are at the same height, the table can look a little flat. Add some height in the following two ways:

- **Undercover Risers.** Before laying down your tablecloth, set down risers, such as phone books, buckets, sturdy boxes, hardcover books, inverted cake pans and clay pots. Be sure the risers are big enough so serving dishes sit steadily.
- **Pretty Pedestals.** Use cake pedestals in varying heights as serving trays. Don't have any? Create your own with inverted cups or glasses and any pretty plates.

Festive Fillers. After you set up the buffet table, there may be areas that could use some filling in. Here are some items you can try weaving around your serving platters and bowls:

- **Seasonal Decorations.** Ornaments are a natural addition to a Christmas table. But also remember other Yuletide items like small wrapped boxes, nativity sets and Christmas villages.
- **Wrapped in Ribbons.** You can purchase Christmas ribbons in varying sizes and colors to tie into your color scheme. Curl loosely and wrap around other elements on your table.
- **Natural Selections.** Fresh and artificial evergreen boughs brighten any holiday table. Also tuck in pinecones, berries and fruits such as pears and apples.

Honey Garlic Ribs

(Pictured at right)

When you want a more "meaty" appetizer for your holiday buffet, reach for these finger-licking-good ribs!
—Lily-Michele Alexis
Louisville, Kentucky

6 pounds pork baby back ribs,
    cut into two-rib portions
2 cups water, *divided*
3/4 cup packed brown sugar
2 tablespoons cornstarch
1 teaspoon garlic powder
1/4 teaspoon ground ginger
1/2 cup honey
1/4 cup soy sauce

Place ribs bone side down in a large roasting pan; pour 1 cup of water over ribs. Cover tightly and bake at 350° for 1-1/2 hours.

In a small bowl, combine the brown sugar, cornstarch, garlic powder and ginger. Stir in the soy sauce, honey and remaining water until smooth. Drain fat from roasting pan; pour sauce over ribs. Bake, uncovered, for 45 minutes or until meat is tender. **Yield:** 24 servings.

Reuben Rolls

This recipe came about one night when I was trying to think of a new and different snack to serve the next day. The empty plate at the party signaled these rolls were a hit!
—*Darlene Abney, Muenster, Texas*

1 package (8 ounces) cream cheese, softened
3 tablespoons spicy brown mustard
1/4 teaspoon prepared horseradish
5 flour tortillas (10 inches), warmed
4 packages (2-1/2 ounces *each*) thinly sliced deli corned beef
15 thin slices Swiss cheese
1 can (14 ounces) sauerkraut, rinsed and well drained

In a small mixing bowl, beat the cream cheese, mustard and horseradish until blended. Spread a heaping tablespoonful of cream cheese mixture over each tortilla.

Layer with eight slices of corned beef, three slices of cheese, another heaping tablespoonful of cream cheese mixture and 1/2 cup sauerkraut. Roll up tightly. Chill for 1 hour. Cut each roll-up into 1/2-in. slices. **Yield:** about 8 dozen.

Cold Pizza Dip

This is my signature recipe. Feel free to use your own favorite pizza toppings on the cream cheese "crust."
—*Jackie Bass, Clinton, Illinois*

2 packages (8 ounces *each*) cream cheese, softened
1 can (8 ounces) pizza sauce
1 jar (4-1/2 ounces) sliced mushrooms, drained
1/4 pound shaved deli ham, chopped
1 can (2-1/4 ounces) sliced ripe olives, drained
25 slices pepperoni, quartered
3 green onions, chopped
1/3 cup chopped green pepper
2 cups (8 ounces) finely shredded part-skim mozzarella cheese
Tortilla chips

Spread cream cheese onto a 14-in. pizza pan. Spread pizza sauce to within 1/2 in. of edges. Sprinkle with mushrooms, ham, olives, pepperoni, onions, green pepper and cheese. Cover and refrigerate for 1 hour or until chilled. Serve with tortilla chips. **Yield:** 4 cups.

Ranch Pizza Pinwheels

(Pictured at right)

I developed this appetizer to mimic a dish at one of my favorite restaurants. I often need to double the recipe because one batch disappears quickly!
—Jennifer Dietz, Fargo, North Dakota

  1 tube (13.8 ounces)
     refrigerated pizza crust
1/4 cup prepared ranch salad
     dressing
1/2 cup shredded Colby-
     Monterey Jack cheese
1/2 cup diced pepperoni
1/4 cup chopped green onions
Pizza sauce, warmed *or* additional
    ranch salad dressing, optional

On a lightly floured surface, roll pizza dough into a 12-in. x 10-in. rectangle. Spread ranch dressing evenly to within 1/4 in. of edges. Sprinkle with cheese, pepperoni and onions. Roll up jelly-roll style, starting with a long side.

    Cut into 1-in. slices. Place cut side down on a greased baking sheet. Bake at 425° for 10-13 minutes or until lightly browned. Serve warm with pizza sauce or additional ranch dressing if desired. Refrigerate leftovers. **Yield:** 1 dozen.

Roasted Onion Spread

Our Test Kitchen home economists roast onions and garlic to mellow their flavor for this rich, buttery spread. It can be made ahead and reheated when needed.

2 medium sweet onions, cut
    into 1/2-inch wedges
1 tablespoon olive oil
1 tablespoon honey
4 garlic cloves, peeled
1/4 teaspoon salt
Assorted crackers

In a large bowl, combine the onions, oil, honey, garlic and salt; toss to coat. Transfer to a greased 13-in. x 9-in. x 2-in. baking dish. Bake, uncovered, at 350° for 65-75 minutes or until onions are tender and golden brown. Cool for 10 minutes.

    Place onion mixture in a blender or food processor; cover and process for 30 seconds or until blended. Transfer to a small bowl. Serve with crackers. Refrigerate leftovers. **Yield:** 3/4 cup.

'Tis the Season

Home-Baked Holiday Breads

CHRISTMAS and oven-fresh goodies just seem to go hand in hand. After all, nothing welcomes family home for the holidays quite like the wonderful aroma of baking bread.

From tasty quick breads and mouth-watering muffins to tender rolls and yummy yeast breads, homemade breads are fit for any occasion.

Wake up tired taste buds at breakfast with an irresistible Chocolate Walnut Ring.

Slices of Cranberry-Nut Poppy Seed Bread make a great midday snack with a mug of coffee or hot chocolate.

Looking to offer something a little different than ordinary rolls at dinner? Guests will love the savory flavors of Parmesan Onion Rye. (All recipes are shown at right.)

OVEN-FRESH FAVORITES
(Clockwise from top left)

Parmesan Onion Rye (p. 42)

Cranberry-Nut Poppy Seed Bread (p. 44)

Chocolate Walnut Ring (p. 40)

Chocolate Walnut Ring

(Pictured on page 39)

This is an adaptation of my wife's recipe. It's terrific for a holiday brunch or as a mid-morning snack.
— Peter Halferty, Corpus Christi, Texas

    3 to 3-1/2 cups all-purpose
      flour
  1/4 cup sugar
    1 package (1/4 ounce) active
      dry yeast
    1 teaspoon ground cinnamon
  1/2 teaspoon salt
  1/2 cup milk
  1/4 cup water
    2 tablespoons butter
    2 tablespoons vegetable oil
    1 egg
    1 egg yolk
FILLING:
  1/2 cup miniature semisweet
      chocolate chips
  1/2 cup chopped walnuts
    3 tablespoons brown sugar
GLAZE:
  2/3 cup confectioners' sugar
  1/8 teaspoon ground cinnamon
  1/4 teaspoon vanilla extract
    3 to 4 teaspoons milk

In a large mixing bowl, combine 1 cup flour, sugar, yeast, cinnamon and salt. In a small saucepan, heat the milk, water, butter and oil to 120°-130°. Add to dry ingredients; beat just until moistened. Add egg and yolk; beat until smooth. Stir in enough remaining flour to form a soft dough (dough will be sticky).

Turn onto a floured surface; knead until smooth and elastic, about 6-8 minutes. Place in a greased bowl, turning once to grease top. Cover and let rise in a warm place until doubled, about 1 hour. Combine the filling ingredients in a small bowl; set aside.

Punch dough down. Turn onto a lightly floured surface. Roll into an 18-in. x 9-in. rectangle; sprinkle with filling to within 1 in. of edges. Roll up tightly jelly-roll style, starting with a long side; seal ends.

Place seam side down on a greased 12-in. pizza pan; pinch ends together to form a ring. With scissors, cut from outside edge two-thirds of the way toward center of ring at 1-in. intervals. Separate strips slightly; twist to allow filling to show. Cover and let rise until doubled, about 40 minutes.

Bake at 350° for 18-22 minutes or until golden brown. Remove to a wire rack to cool completely. Combine the glaze ingredients; drizzle over ring. **Yield:** 18-20 servings.

Maple-Oat Dinner Rolls

(Pictured at right)

Even though I'm in my 80s, I still love to bake for our children, grandchildren and great-grandchildren. These hearty rolls are one of our favorites.
— *Helen Davis, Waterbury, Vermont*

1 package (1/4 ounce) active dry yeast
1/2 cup warm water (110° to 115°), *divided*
1/2 cup warm strong brewed coffee (110° to 115°)
1/2 cup old-fashioned oats
1/4 cup sugar
1/4 cup maple syrup
1 egg
3 tablespoons shortening
1 teaspoon salt
3 to 3-1/2 cups bread flour
1 tablespoon butter, melted

In a large mixing bowl, dissolve yeast in 1/4 cup warm water. Add the coffee, oats, sugar, syrup, egg, shortening, salt, remaining water and 2 cups flour. Beat until smooth. Stir in enough remaining flour to form a soft dough.

Turn onto a floured surface; knead until smooth and elastic, about 6-8 minutes. Place in a greased bowl, turning once to grease top. Cover and let rise in a warm place until doubled, about 1 hour.

Punch down dough. Turn onto a floured surface; divide into four portions. Divide each portion into six pieces; shape each into a ball. Place in a greased 13-in. x 9-in. x 2-in. baking pan. Cover and let rise until doubled, about 30 minutes.

Bake at 350° for 25-30 minutes or until golden brown. Brush rolls with butter. Remove from pan to a wire rack. Serve warm. **Yield:** 2 dozen.

ROLLS ARE READY TO GO

MAKE Maple-Oat Dinner Rolls when you have some time, then let cool. Place in an airtight container with waxed paper between layers; cover. Freeze for up to three months. Thaw at room temperature. To serve the rolls warm, wrap them in foil. Bake at 350° for about 10 minutes.

Parmesan Onion Rye

(Pictured on page 38)

I've been making my own bread for more than 29 years. The addition of poppy seeds and Parmesan cheese makes this rye bread deliciously different.
— David Heppner, Brandon, Florida

1/2 cup chopped onion
1-1/2 teaspoons butter
1 package (1/4 ounce) active dry yeast
1 cup warm water (110° to 115°)
1-1/2 teaspoons honey
1 egg
1/2 cup shredded Parmesan cheese
1 tablespoon poppy seeds
1-1/2 teaspoons kosher salt
1 cup rye flour
2 cups bread flour
1 egg white, lightly beaten
1-1/2 teaspoons water
Additional kosher salt

In a small nonstick skillet coated with nonstick cooking spray, saute onion in butter until tender; set aside.

In a large mixing bowl, dissolve yeast in warm water. Stir in honey; let stand for 5 minutes. Add the egg, Parmesan cheese, poppy seeds, salt, rye flour, 1/2 cup bread flour and onion mixture; beat on medium speed until blended. Stir in enough remaining bread flour to form a firm dough.

Turn onto a lightly floured surface; knead until smooth and elastic, about 6-8 minutes. Place in a greased bowl, turning once to grease top. Cover and let rise in a warm place until doubled, about 1 hour.

Punch dough down. Turn onto a lightly floured surface; shape into a loaf. Place in a greased 9-in. x 5-in. x 3-in. loaf pan. With a sharp knife, make three or four shallow slashes across top of loaf. Cover and let rise until doubled, about 30 minutes.

In a small bowl, beat egg white with water; brush over loaf. Sprinkle with additional kosher salt. Bake at 350° for 35-40 minutes or until lightly browned. Cool for 10 minutes before removing from pan to a wire rack to cool completely. **Yield:** 1 loaf.

MAKING SLASHES

SLASHING or scoring the top of a bread loaf before baking allows steam to vent, helps prevent cracking and gives bread a decorative appearance. Use a sharp knife to make shallow slashes across the top of a loaf.

Buttery Croissants

(Pictured at right)

A traditional roll like this is always welcome at holiday dinners. The recipe makes a big batch, so it's great when you're entertaining.
—Loraine Meyer, Bend, Oregon

1-1/2 cups butter, softened
1/3 cup all-purpose flour
DOUGH:
   1 package (1/4 ounce) active dry yeast
1/4 cup warm water (110° to 115°)
   1 cup warm milk (110° to 115°)
1/4 cup sugar
   1 egg
   1 teaspoon salt
3-1/2 to 3-3/4 cups all-purpose flour

In a small mixing bowl, beat butter and flour until combined; spread into a 12-in. x 6-in. rectangle on a piece of waxed paper. Cover with another piece of waxed paper; refrigerate for at least 1 hour.

In a large mixing bowl, dissolve yeast in warm water. Add the milk, sugar, egg, salt and 2 cups flour; beat until smooth. Stir in enough remaining flour to form a soft dough. Turn onto a floured surface; knead until smooth and elastic, about 6-8 minutes.

Roll dough into a 14-in. square. Remove top sheet of waxed paper from butter; invert onto half of dough. Remove waxed paper. Fold dough over butter; seal edges. Roll into a 20-in. x 12-in. rectangle. Fold into thirds. Repeat rolling and folding twice. (If butter softens, chill after folding.) Wrap in plastic wrap; refrigerate overnight.

Unwrap dough. On a lightly floured surface, roll into a 25-in. x 20-in. rectangle. Cut into 5-in. squares. Cut each square diagonally in half, forming two triangles. Roll up triangles from the wide end; place 2 in. apart with point down on ungreased baking sheets. Curve ends down to form crescent shape.

Cover and let rise until doubled, about 45 minutes. Bake at 375° for 12-14 minutes or until golden brown. Remove to wire racks. Serve warm. **Yield:** about 3 dozen.

Cranberry-Nut Poppy Seed Bread

(Pictured on page 39)

*As a former home economics teacher, I love to experiment with recipes. One day
I decided to add poppy seeds to my family's favorite cranberry bread. They loved it!*
—Sandra Fish, Newberg, Oregon

4 cups all-purpose flour
2 cups sugar
2 teaspoons salt
1 teaspoon baking soda
1/2 teaspoon baking powder
2 eggs
1-1/2 cups orange juice
1/2 cup vegetable oil
3 tablespoons poppy seeds
2 tablespoons grated orange peel
2 cups chopped fresh *or* frozen cranberries
1-1/2 cups chopped nuts

In a large bowl, combine the flour, sugar, salt, baking soda and baking powder. In another bowl, whisk the eggs, orange juice, oil, poppy seeds and orange peel. Stir into dry ingredients just until moistened. Fold in cranberries and nuts.

Spoon into two greased 8-in. x 4-in. x 2-in. loaf pans. Bake at 350° for 60-65 minutes or until a toothpick inserted near the center comes out clean (cover loosely with foil if tops brown too quickly). Cool for 10 minutes before removing from pans to wire racks to cool completely. **Yield: 2 loaves.**

GIFT-WRAPPED BREAD

HERE'S a simply stunning way to present a gift of fresh-baked bread at Christmas. Purchase, wash and dry an inexpensive kitchen towel. Use it to wrap a cooled loaf of bread. Tie with a little bit of ribbon or raffia.

Danish Crispies

(Pictured at right)

This treasured recipe has been in the family for nearly 50 years. The tender, flaky treats make holiday breakfasts even more special.
—*Mrs. F. H. Steele, Clovis, New Mexico*

    1 package (1/4 ounce) active
      dry yeast
  1/4 cup warm water (110° to 115°)
    1 cup warm milk (110° to 115°)
    2 cups sugar, *divided*
  1/2 cup plus 6 tablespoons butter,
      softened, *divided*
1-1/2 teaspoons grated lemon peel
    1 teaspoon salt
  1/2 teaspoon ground mace
    2 eggs
5-1/2 to 6 cups all-purpose flour
    3 teaspoons ground cinnamon

In a large mixing bowl, dissolve yeast in warm water. Add the milk, 1/2 cup sugar, 1/2 cup butter, lemon peel, salt, mace, eggs and 2 cups flour; beat well. Stir in enough remaining flour to form a soft dough.

Turn onto a floured surface; knead until smooth and elastic, about 6-8 minutes. Place in a greased bowl, turning once to grease top. Cover and rise in a warm place until doubled, about 1 hour.

Punch dough down. On a lightly floured surface, roll out dough into a large rectangle, about 1/4 in. thick.

Spread with 2 tablespoons butter. Sprinkle with 1/3 cup sugar. Fold in half lengthwise; roll to 1/4-in. thickness. Spread with 2 tablespoons butter; sprinkle with 1/3 cup sugar.

Fold in half widthwise; roll to an 18-in. x 10-in. rectangle. Spread with remaining butter. Combine the cinnamon and remaining sugar; sprinkle half over dough to within 1/4 in. of edges. Roll up tightly, starting with a short side; pinch to seal. Cut into 1/2-in. slices.

Place on greased baking sheets (four to six slices per sheet). Cover with waxed paper and flatten with palm of hand. Sprinkle with remaining cinnamon-sugar. Let stand in a warm place for 30 minutes. Bake at 400° for 12-15 minutes. Immediately remove from pans to wire racks. **Yield:** about 1-1/2 dozen.

Moist Pumpkin Scones

After sampling a pumpkin scone at a coffeehouse, I was inspired to look for a recipe to try at home. The glaze nicely complements the pumpkin flavor.
—*Amy McCavour, Gresham, Oregon*

4-1/2 cups all-purpose flour
1/2 cup packed brown sugar
4 teaspoons baking powder
3 teaspoons pumpkin pie spice
1 teaspoon ground cinnamon
1/2 teaspoon baking soda
1/2 teaspoon salt
1 cup cold butter
2 eggs
1-1/4 cups canned pumpkin
3/4 cup milk, *divided*
GLAZE:
2 cups confectioners' sugar
3 tablespoons milk
1/4 teaspoon pumpkin pie spice

In a large bowl, combine the first seven ingredients. Cut in butter until mixture resembles coarse crumbs. In another bowl, whisk the eggs, pumpkin and 1/2 cup milk. Stir into dry ingredients just until moistened.

Turn onto a floured surface; knead 10 times. Divide dough in half. Pat each portion into an 8-in. circle; cut each into eight wedges. Separate wedges and place 1 in. apart on ungreased baking sheets. Brush with remaining milk.

Bake at 400° for 12-15 minutes or until golden brown. Remove to wire racks; cool for 10 minutes. Combine the glaze ingredients; drizzle over scones. Serve warm. **Yield:** 16 scones.

Caraway Rye Bread

This hearty yeast bread earned me a first-place ribbon at our state fair a few years ago!
—*Dolores Mason, Romney, West Virginia*

2 packages (1/4 ounce *each*) active dry yeast
1-1/2 cups warm water (110° to 115°)
2/3 cup honey
3 tablespoons butter, softened
1 tablespoon caraway seeds
1 tablespoon finely grated carrot
1 teaspoon salt
2-3/4 cups rye flour
2 to 3 cups all-purpose flour
Melted butter

In a large mixing bowl, dissolve yeast in warm water. Add the honey, butter, caraway seeds, carrot, salt, rye flour and 1 cup all-purpose flour. Beat until smooth. Stir in enough remaining all-purpose flour to form a soft dough.

Turn onto a floured surface; knead until smooth and elastic, about 6-8 minutes. Place in a greased bowl, turning once to grease top. Cover and let rise in a warm place until doubled, about 1-1/4 hours.

Punch dough down. Turn onto a lightly floured surface; divide in half. Shape into loaves. Place in two greased 8-in. x 4-in. x 2-in. loaf pans. Cover and let rise until doubled, about 45 minutes.

Bake at 350° for 40-50 minutes or until golden brown. Cool for 10 minutes before removing from pans to wire racks. Brush with melted butter. Cool. **Yield:** 2 loaves.

Cranberry Upside-Down Muffins

(Pictured at right)

Fresh cranberries are readily available here, so I cook with them often. The sweet-tart taste of these pretty muffins adds a festive touch to special-occasion suppers.
—Michele Briasco-Brin
Fall River, Massachusetts

1-3/4 cups fresh *or* frozen
    cranberries
  3/4 cup sugar
  1/8 teaspoon ground nutmeg
BATTER:
1-3/4 cups all-purpose flour
  1/3 cup sugar
    2 teaspoons baking powder
  1/4 teaspoon salt
    1 egg
  3/4 cup milk
  1/4 cup vegetable oil
  1/2 teaspoon lemon extract
  1/3 cup chopped walnuts

In a small saucepan, combine cranberries and sugar. Cover and cook over low heat until juice forms. Uncover; cook and stir over medium heat for 10 minutes or until berries pop. Stir in nutmeg; cool slightly. Spoon into 12 paper-lined muffin cups; set aside.

In a large bowl, combine the flour, sugar, baking powder and salt. In another bowl, whisk the egg, milk, oil and lemon extract; stir into dry ingredients just until moistened. Stir in walnuts. Spoon over cranberry mixture.

Bake at 400° for 18-22 minutes or until a toothpick comes out clean. Cool for 10 minutes before removing from pan to a wire rack. Carefully remove paper liners and serve muffins warm, cranberry side up. **Yield:** 1 dozen.

Family Traditions

AT Christmastime, I get busy baking my traditional tea rings. I shape these breads into wreaths or candy canes and decorate them with icing, walnuts and red and green maraschino cherries. Then I give them away to family and friends for a tasty gift from my kitchen. —*Jeanette Pontarolo*
Ft. Laramie, Wyoming

Fruited Zucchini Bread

Green flecks of zucchini and red maraschino cherries make this moist quick bread
a must for the Christmas season. Keep one loaf and give the other away.
—*Mary Rigsby, Springfield, Oregon*

3 cups all-purpose flour
2 cups sugar
2 teaspoons ground cinnamon
1 teaspoon salt
1 teaspoon baking soda
1/2 teaspoon baking powder
3 eggs
3/4 cup vegetable oil
2 teaspoons vanilla extract
2 cups shredded zucchini
1 can (8 ounces) crushed
    pineapple, drained
1 cup chopped pecans
1/2 cup raisins
1/2 cup chopped dates
1/2 cup chopped maraschino cherries, patted dry

In a large bowl, combine the flour, sugar, cinnamon, salt, baking soda and baking powder. In another bowl, whisk the eggs, oil and vanilla. Stir into dry ingredients just until moistened. Fold in the zucchini, pineapple, pecans, raisins, dates and cherries.

Pour into two greased 9-in. x 5-in. x 3-in. loaf pans. Bake at 350° for 55-60 minutes or until bread pulls away from sides of pans and a toothpick inserted near the center comes out with a few moist crumbs. Cool for 10 minutes before removing from pans to wire racks to cool completely. **Yield:** 2 loaves.

Raspberry-Filled Poppy Seed Muffins

Every bite of these golden muffins is packed with poppy seeds, lemon flavor and raspberry preserves.
—*Carolyn Schmeling, Brookfield, Wisconsin*

2-1/4 cups all-purpose flour
1-1/4 cups sugar
2 teaspoons baking powder
1/4 teaspoon salt
1/8 teaspoon baking soda
3 eggs
1/2 cup vegetable oil
1/2 cup buttermilk
3/4 cup chopped pecans
2 tablespoons grated lemon
    peel
2 teaspoons poppy seeds
3 tablespoons seedless
    raspberry preserves

GLAZE:
3/4 cup confectioners' sugar
1/4 cup lemon juice

In a large bowl, combine the flour, sugar, baking powder, salt and baking soda. In another bowl, whisk the eggs, oil and buttermilk. Stir into dry ingredients just until moistened. Fold in the pecans, lemon peel and poppy seeds.

Fill greased or paper-lined muffin cups with a rounded tablespoonful of batter. Drop 1/2 teaspoon of preserves in the center of each; top with remaining batter.

Bake at 350° for 15-20 minutes or until a toothpick comes out clean. Combine glaze ingredients. Poke holes in warm muffins; drizzle with glaze. Cool for 5 minutes before removing from pans to wire racks. Serve warm. **Yield:** 1-1/2 dozen.

Tropical Butterhorn Trees

(Pictured at right)

Coconut turns ordinary butterhorn rolls into a tropical treat! After one taste, folks request the recipe.
—*Carolyn Faust, Caldwell, Texas*

3 to 3-1/2 cups all-purpose flour
1/4 cup sugar
1 package (1/4 ounce) active dry yeast
1 teaspoon salt
1/2 cup sour cream
6 tablespoons butter, softened
1/4 cup water
2 eggs

FILLING:
2 tablespoons butter, softened
3/4 cup flaked coconut, toasted
1/2 cup sugar
2 teaspoons grated orange peel

GLAZE:
1/4 cup sugar
1/4 cup sour cream
2 tablespoons orange juice
2 tablespoons butter
1/4 cup flaked coconut, toasted

In a large mixing bowl, combine 1-1/2 cups flour, sugar, yeast and salt. In a small saucepan, heat the sour cream, butter and water to 120°-130°; add to dry ingredients. Beat on medium speed for 2 minutes. Add eggs and 1/2 cup flour; beat 2 minutes longer. Stir in enough remaining flour to form a firm dough.

Turn onto a lightly floured surface; knead until smooth and elastic, about 5-7 minutes. Place in a greased bowl, turning once to grease top. Cover and let rise in a warm place until doubled, about 1 hour.

Punch dough down. Turn onto a lightly floured surface; divide in half. Roll each portion into a 12-in. circle; spread each with 1 tablespoon butter. Combine the coconut, sugar and orange peel; sprinkle over butter. Cut each circle into 12 wedges.

For one tree, roll up one wedge from the wide end. Place point side down near the top center of a greased baking sheet. Roll up two wedges; place in the second row with sides touching. Repeat, adding one roll per row, until tree has four rows. Roll up another wedge and center below last row for the trunk. Repeat for second tree, using 11 more wedges and a second baking sheet. Roll up remaining two wedges; place one on each baking sheet.

Cover and let rise in a warm place until doubled, about 40 minutes. Bake at 350° for 18-22 minutes or until golden brown. Remove to wire racks.

For glaze, in a small saucepan, combine the sugar, sour cream, orange juice and butter. Bring to a boil; cook and stir for 3 minutes. Spoon or brush over warm rolls; sprinkle with coconut. **Yield:** 2 trees (11 rolls each) plus 2 extra rolls.

Sugar 'n' Spice Pinwheel Rolls

The family is thrilled when my grandmother, mother and I make these
biscuit-like rolls. They have just the right amount of sweetness.
—Mary Ann Marino, West Pittsburg, Pennsylvania

2 cups all-purpose flour
3 tablespoons sugar
1 teaspoon baking powder
1/2 teaspoon salt
1/3 cup plus 1 tablespoon cold
    butter, *divided*
1/2 cup milk
1/2 cup chopped pecans
1/3 cup packed brown sugar
2 tablespoons raisins, chopped
3/4 teaspoon ground cinnamon
1/2 teaspoon ground allspice
EGG WASH:
1 egg yolk
1 tablespoon milk

In a large bowl, combine the flour, sugar, baking powder and salt. Cut in 1/3 cup butter until mixture resembles coarse crumbs. Stir in milk just until moistened.

Turn dough onto a lightly floured surface; knead gently for 1-2 minutes or until smooth. Roll into a 12-in. x 10-in. rectangle. Melt remaining butter; brush over dough to within 1/2 in. of edges.

Combine the pecans, brown sugar, raisins, cinnamon and allspice; sprinkle over dough to within 1/2 in. of edges. Roll up jelly-roll style, starting with a long side; pinch seam to seal. Cut into 12 slices. Place cut side up on a greased baking sheet; press down lightly.

Beat egg yolk and milk; brush over rolls. Bake at 425° for 12-14 minutes or until golden brown. Remove from pan to a wire rack. Serve warm. **Yield:** 1 dozen.

Raisin English Muffin Bread

Batter breads like this are great to make because they don't require kneading.
I slice the loaf and store it in the freezer for a quick breakfast.
—Julie Valdez, Walnut Hill, Florida

Yellow cornmeal
1 cup warm milk (110° to 115°)
1/2 cup raisins
1 tablespoon active dry yeast
1/4 cup warm water (110° to 115°)
1-1/2 teaspoons sugar
1 teaspoon salt
1 teaspoon ground cinnamon
2-1/2 to 2-2/3 cups all-purpose
    flour

Grease an 8-in. x 4-in. x 2-in. loaf pan; sprinkle with cornmeal and set aside. Place warm milk in a small bowl; add raisins and set aside.

In a large mixing bowl, dissolve yeast in warm water. Add the sugar, salt, cinnamon, reserved milk mixture and 1-1/2 cups flour. Beat until smooth, about 3 minutes. Stir in enough remaining flour to form a soft dough. Do not knead. Spoon into prepared pan; sprinkle with cornmeal.

Cover and let rise in a warm place until doubled, about 45 minutes. Bake at 375° for 28-33 minutes or until golden brown. Cool for 10 minutes before removing from pan to a wire rack to cool completely. Serve slices of bread toasted. **Yield:** 1 loaf.

Cardamom Braids

(Pictured at right)

I came across this recipe in 1983 and have been making it for Christmas ever since. One year, I gave away 20 loaves!
—Rita Bergman, Olympia, Washington

6 cups all-purpose flour, *divided*
2 packages (1/4 ounce *each*) active dry yeast
1-1/2 teaspoons ground cardamom
1 teaspoon salt
1-1/2 cups plus 2 tablespoons milk, *divided*
1/2 cup butter, cubed
1/2 cup honey
2 eggs
2 tablespoons sugar

In a large mixing bowl, combine 2 cups flour, yeast, cardamom and salt. In a small saucepan, heat 1-1/2 cups milk, butter and honey to 120°-130°. Add to dry ingredients; beat just until moistened. Add eggs; beat until smooth. Stir in enough remaining flour to form a firm dough (dough will be sticky).

Turn onto a floured surface; knead until smooth and elastic, about 6-8 minutes. Place in a greased bowl, turning once to grease top. Cover and let rise in a warm place until doubled, about 45 minutes.

Punch dough down. Turn onto a lightly floured surface; divide in half. Divide each portion into thirds. Shape each into a 14-in. rope. Place three ropes on a greased baking sheet and braid; pinch ends to seal and tuck under. Repeat with remaining dough. Cover and let rise until doubled, about 30 minutes.

Brush with remaining milk and sprinkle with sugar. Bake at 375° for 20-25 minutes or until golden brown. Remove from pans to wire racks to cool. **Yield:** 2 loaves.

'Tis THE Season

Festive Yuletide Sides

ALTHOUGH the main course tends to take center stage at holiday dinners, great cooks know that nothing completes the meal quite like splendid side dishes.

But if you're looking to add a little variety to your table, why not offer one or two deliciously different dishes alongside the old standbys?

Present Christmas guests with the eye-catching color and appealing flavor of Four-Cheese Rice Casserole, Fruited Holiday Vegetables and Roasted Asparagus with Feta. (All recipes are shown at right.)

Or turn the page for even more mouth-watering vegetables, potatoes, salads and soups that won't ever take a backseat at your Yuletide dinners.

TASTY TRIMMINGS
(Top to bottom)

Four-Cheese Rice Casserole (p. 54)

Fruited Holiday Vegetables (p. 56)

Roasted Asparagus with Feta (p. 54)

Four-Cheese Rice Casserole

(Pictured on page 53)

My husband and I developed this recipe to avoid making a broccoli and rice casserole that we had relied on for years. Now his folks won't let us in the door at the holidays without this dish in hand.
—Gretchen Kavanaugh, Oklahoma City, Oklahoma

  1 medium sweet onion, chopped
1/4 cup butter, cubed
  4 cups cooked long grain rice
  2 packages (10 ounces *each*)
     frozen chopped spinach,
     thawed and squeezed dry
  3 cups (12 ounces) shredded
     part-skim mozzarella cheese,
     divided
1-1/2 cups shredded Parmesan
     cheese, *divided*
  2 packages (8 ounces *each*)
     cream cheese, softened
  1 carton (15 ounces) ricotta
     cheese
3/4 cup milk
1/2 teaspoon garlic powder
1/2 teaspoon beau monde
     seasoning

In a small skillet, saute onion in butter until tender. In a large bowl, combine the rice, spinach, 1-1/2 cups mozzarella, 1 cup Parmesan and the onion mixture.

In a large mixing bowl, beat the cream cheese, ricotta, milk, garlic powder and beau monde seasoning until smooth. Add to the rice mixture and mix well.

Spoon into a greased 13-in. x 9-in. x 2-in. baking dish. Sprinkle with remaining mozzarella and Parmesan. Bake, uncovered, at 325° for 40-45 minutes or until heated through and cheese is melted. **Yield:** 12 servings.

Editor's Note: This recipe was tested with Spice Islands beau monde seasoning. It is a blend of salt, onion powder and celery seed.

Roasted Asparagus with Feta

(Pictured on page 52)

Pretty and festive, this simple-to-make side dish is delicious right out of the oven.
—Phyllis Schmalz, Kansas City, Kansas

  2 pounds fresh asparagus,
     trimmed
  1 tablespoon olive oil
Kosher salt to taste
  2 medium tomatoes, seeded
     and chopped
1/2 cup crumbled feta cheese

Arrange asparagus in an ungreased 13-in. x 9-in. x 2-in. baking dish. Drizzle with oil and sprinkle with salt.

Bake, uncovered, at 400° for 15-20 minutes or until tender. Transfer to a serving dish; sprinkle with tomatoes and feta cheese. Serve immediately. **Yield:** 6 servings.

Cold Plum Soup

(Pictured at right)

When my husband and I were first married, we dined at an inn that served plum soup. After experimenting with different recipes, I came up with my own version!
—Carol Klein, Franklin Square, New York

2 cans (15 ounces *each*) plums
1 cup water
1/2 cup sugar, *divided*
1 cinnamon stick (3 inches)
1/4 teaspoon white pepper
Dash salt
1 tablespoon cornstarch
1/2 cup heavy whipping cream
1/2 cup dry red wine *or* grape
   juice
1 cup (8 ounces) sour cream
1/3 cup creme de cassis *or*
   cranberry-raspberry juice
2 tablespoons lemon juice
1 teaspoon grated lemon peel
Sour cream, optional

Drain plums, reserving juice. Pit plums; puree in a blender with juice. Transfer to a Dutch oven. Stir in the water, 1/4 cup sugar, cinnamon stick, pepper and salt. Bring to a boil. Reduce heat; cover and simmer for 10 minutes.

In a small bowl, combine cornstarch and remaining sugar; stir in cream and wine or grape juice until smooth. Gradually add to plum mixture until blended. Bring to a boil; cook and stir for 2 minutes or until thickened, stirring constantly. Remove from the heat; discard cinnamon stick. Stir in the sour cream, creme de cassis or cranberry-raspberry juice and lemon juice.

Strain half of the soup through a fine mesh strainer over a 1-1/2-qt. bowl. Repeat. Stir in lemon peel. Cover and refrigerate overnight. Garnish with sour cream if desired. **Yield:** 13 servings (2-1/2 quarts).

SOUR CREAM SNOWFLAKE

FOR a special touch, garnish individual servings of Cold Plum Soup with a sour cream snowflake.

Spoon sour cream into a resealable plastic bag; cut off a small piece of one corner. Gently squeeze out the sour cream and make a design of your choice. Don't fret about it looking "perfect." After all, no two snowflakes are alike!

Fruited Holiday Vegetables

(Pictured on page 52)

Mom and I made a great team in the kitchen, cooking and baking for hours at a time.
I treasure this holiday favorite from her the most.
— Paula Marchesi, Lenhartsville, Pennsylvania

1 large rutabaga, peeled and cubed
3 small red potatoes, cubed
3 medium sweet potatoes, peeled and cubed
4 teaspoons cornstarch
1/2 cup cold water
1/2 cup orange juice
1 cup prepared mincemeat
1/4 cup butter, melted
1/4 cup packed dark brown sugar
1/4 cup dark corn syrup
1/4 teaspoon ground ginger
1/4 teaspoon ground cinnamon
1-3/4 cups frozen unsweetened peach slices, thawed and chopped
1 medium tart apple, chopped
1 tablespoon lemon juice
1/2 cup chopped pecans

Place rutabaga in a Dutch oven; cover with water. Bring to a boil. Reduce heat; cover and simmer for 15 minutes. Add red potatoes and enough additional water to cover. Return to a boil. Reduce heat; cover and simmer for 5 minutes.

Add sweet potatoes and enough additional water to cover. Bring to a boil. Reduce heat; cover and simmer 15 minutes longer or until vegetables are tender.

Meanwhile, in a small saucepan, combine cornstarch and cold water until smooth. Gradually stir in the orange juice. Bring to a boil; cook and stir for 1-2 minutes or until thickened. Stir in the mincemeat, butter, brown sugar, corn syrup, ginger and cinnamon; heat through.

In a large bowl, combine the peaches, apple and lemon juice. Drain vegetables; stir in fruit mixture. Transfer to a greased 4-qt. baking dish. Add mincemeat; stir gently. Sprinkle with pecans. Bake, uncovered, at 325° for 30-35 minutes or until fruit is tender. **Yield:** 12 servings.

Broccoli Mushroom Bake

With lots of cheese, this casserole never lasts long on the dinner table.
Even people not fond of broccoli can't deny this dish's goodness.
— Karen Mohr, Austin, Texas

3 tablespoons butter, *divided*
2 tablespoons all-purpose flour
1-1/2 teaspoons Italian seasoning
1/2 teaspoon garlic powder
1/2 teaspoon pepper
1 cup milk

2-1/2 cups (10 ounces) shredded cheddar cheese
1 package (3 ounces) cream cheese, softened
2 packages (10 ounces *each*) frozen broccoli cuts, thawed and drained
1/2 pound fresh mushrooms, chopped
1/2 cup seasoned bread crumbs

In a large saucepan, melt 2 tablespoons butter. Stir in the flour, Italian seasoning, garlic powder and pepper until blended. Gradually add milk. Bring to a boil; cook and stir for 1-2 minutes or until thickened. Reduce heat to low; stir in the cheeses until smooth (sauce will be thick). Fold in the broccoli and mushrooms.

Spoon into a greased shallow 2-qt. baking dish. Melt remaining butter; toss with bread crumbs. Sprinkle over vegetable mixture. Bake, uncovered, at 350° for 30-35 minutes or until golden brown. **Yield:** 8 servings.

Cranberry Rice Pilaf

(Pictured at right)

Juicy cranberries and crunchy pine nuts easily dress up rice in this special side. The subtle flavors make it an appropriate accompaniment to many entrees.
—*Carmel Patrone, Longport, New Jersey*

     3/4 cup chopped celery
     1/2 cup chopped onion
       2 tablespoons butter
       1 tablespoon olive oil
       1 cup uncooked long grain rice
   2-1/2 cups chicken broth
     1/2 cup chopped fresh mushrooms
     1/2 cup dried cranberries
     1/2 teaspoon garlic powder
     1/2 teaspoon curry powder
Salt and pepper to taste
       2 tablespoons minced fresh
         parsley
       3 tablespoons pine nuts, toasted

In a large saucepan, saute celery and onion in butter and oil until tender. Add rice; cook and stir for 5 minutes or until lightly browned.

Add the broth, mushrooms, cranberries, garlic powder, curry powder, salt and pepper. Bring to a boil. Reduce heat; cover and simmer for 20 minutes or until liquid is absorbed and rice is tender.

Remove from the heat. Stir in parsley; sprinkle with pine nuts. **Yield:** 4-5 servings.

Brussels Sprouts and Apples

Don't shy away from trying this deliciously different dish featuring brussels sprouts and apples.
—Mary Lohse, Chatfield, Minnesota

1 **pound fresh brussels sprouts, trimmed and halved**
2 **medium tart apples, cut into 1-inch chunks**
1 **small red onion, cut into wedges**
2 **tablespoons butter, melted**
2 **tablespoons vegetable oil**
1 **teaspoon sugar**
1 **teaspoon salt**
1 **teaspoon Italian seasoning**
1/4 **teaspoon pepper**

Place 1 in. of water in a large saucepan; add brussels sprouts. Bring to a boil. Reduce heat; cover and simmer for 5-6 minutes or until crisp-tender. Drain. Stir in the remaining ingredients.

Arrange in a single layer in a greased 15-in. x 10-in. x 1-in. baking pan. Bake, uncovered, at 425° for 15-20 minutes or until sprouts and apples are tender, stirring occasionally. **Yield:** 5 servings.

Southwestern Squash Medley

Canned green chilies give mild-flavored squash a little zip in this flavorful side dish.
It's prepared in the microwave, leaving your oven free for other foods.
—Martha Schaub, Lake Leelanau, Michigan

4 **cups sliced zucchini (about 2 medium)**
4 **cups sliced yellow summer squash (about 3 small)**
1 **medium onion, chopped**
2 **tablespoons water**
1 **cup (8 ounces) sour cream**
1 **can (4 ounces) chopped green chilies, drained**
1 **jar (2 ounces) diced pimientos, drained**
1/4 **teaspoon salt**
2 **cups (8 ounces) shredded Monterey Jack cheese**
1-1/2 **cups crushed cheese-flavored tortilla chips**

1/4 **teaspoon paprika**
Additional sour cream, optional

In a 2-qt. microwave-safe dish, combine the zucchini, yellow squash, onion and water. Cover and microwave on high for 7-8 minutes, stirring once; drain well. In a bowl, combine the sour cream, chilies, pimientos and salt; stir in cheese.

In an 11-in. x 7-in. x 2-in. microwave-safe dish, layer half the squash mixture, half the sour cream mixture and half the tortilla chips. Repeat layers. Sprinkle with the paprika.

Microwave, uncovered, at 70% power for 7-9 minutes or until heated through, turning dish once. Garnish with additional sour cream if desired. **Yield:** 8 servings.

Editor's Note: This recipe was tested in a 1,100-watt microwave.

Glazed Pearl Onions

(Pictured at right)

As a young girl, my mom always gave me the job of making the glazed onions for Christmas dinner. It's an easy, elegant recipe.
—Jennifer Tunen, Delaware, Ohio

6 cups water
2 pounds pearl onions
1/3 cup butter, cubed
1/4 cup sugar

In a large saucepan, bring water to a boil. Add pearl onions; boil for 3 minutes. Drain and rinse in cold water; peel.

In a large skillet over medium heat, melt butter. Add onions; cook for 6-8 minutes or until tender, stirring occasionally. Sprinkle with sugar. Cook 18-20 minutes longer or until onions are golden brown, stirring occasionally. Serve with a slotted spoon. **Yield:** 6 servings.

PEELING PEARL ONIONS

1. In a Dutch oven or large kettle, bring 6 cups water to a boil. Add pearl onions; boil for 3 minutes.

2. Drain and rinse in cold water; peel with a paring knife.

Gingered Carrots 'n' Parsnips

Guests at my Christmas table are surprised to hear that this tasty side dish has just five ingredients. Speedy recipes like this sure come in handy around the holidays.
—*Lucille Drake, Sherburne, New York*

4 medium carrots, peeled and julienned
4 medium parsnips, peeled and julienned
2 tablespoons chopped candied ginger, *divided*
2 tablespoons butter
1/4 teaspoon salt

Place carrots and parsnips in a steamer basket; place in a large saucepan over 1 in. of water. Bring to a boil; cover and steam for 6-8 minutes or until crisp-tender.

In a large skillet, saute 1 tablespoon ginger in butter for 1 minute. Add the carrots, parsnips and salt; toss to coat. Sprinkle with remaining ginger. **Yield:** 6 servings.

Cranberry Gelatin Salad

This vibrant cranberry gelatin is great for a buffet. It's loaded with nuts, celery, raspberries and oranges so it appeals to everyone.
—*Katherine Newman, Cedarburg, Wisconsin*

1 package (3 ounces) cranberry gelatin
1 package (3 ounces) cherry gelatin
1 package (3 ounces) raspberry gelatin
1 teaspoon ground cinnamon
1 can (8 ounces) crushed pineapple
3/4 cup *each* cherry, cranberry and orange juice
1 can (16 ounces) jellied cranberry sauce, cut into slices
1 cup red wine *or* grape juice
1 can (11 ounces) mandarin oranges, drained

1 package (10 ounces) frozen sweetened raspberries, thawed
1/2 cup finely chopped celery
1/2 cup chopped pecans *or* walnuts

In a large mixing bowl, combine the gelatins and cinnamon; set aside. Drain the pineapple, reserving juice; set the pineapple aside.

In a large saucepan, combine the cherry, cranberry and orange juices; add reserved pineapple juice. Bring to a boil. Pour over gelatin mixture; beat until dissolved.

Stir in cranberry sauce and wine or grape juice until smooth. Stir in the oranges, raspberries, celery, nuts and pineapple. Pour into a 13-in. x 9-in. x 2-in. dish. Chill for 6 hours or overnight or until firm. Cut into squares. **Yield:** 12-15 servings.

Lemon-Garlic Penne With Crab

(Pictured at right)

Our Christmas Eve supper isn't the same without seafood pasta. I love lots of garlic, but you can use less to suit your family's tastes.
—Chrissy Fessler, Hazleton, Pennsylvania

2 cups uncooked penne pasta
5 garlic cloves, minced
1/4 cup butter, cubed
2 tablespoons olive oil
1 can (14-1/2 ounces) chicken broth
2 cans (6 ounces *each*) lump crabmeat, drained
3 tablespoons lemon juice
1/2 cup minced fresh parsley, *divided*
Lemon wedges

Cook pasta according to package directions. Meanwhile, in a large skillet, cook and stir garlic in butter and oil over medium heat for 2 minutes or until garlic is golden (do not brown). Add the broth, crab and lemon juice. Bring to a boil. Reduce heat; simmer, uncovered, for 12-15 minutes or until sauce is reduced by half.

Drain pasta; toss with crab sauce and 1/4 cup parsley. Garnish with lemon wedges and remaining parsley. **Yield:** 5 servings.

Mexican Christmas Eve Salad

I traditionally prepare this on Christmas Eve to share at a posada party (Mexican Christmas celebration).
The unique combination of ingredients makes this salad interesting, yet tasty.
—*Josey Jacobsen, Lander, Wyoming*

1 can (20 ounces) unsweetened
   pineapple chunks, drained
1 can (15 ounces) sliced beets,
   drained
2 medium navel oranges,
   peeled and sectioned
1 large apple, sliced
1 medium banana, sliced
1 medium jicama, peeled and
   julienned
2 to 3 cups torn romaine
1/2 cup dry roasted peanuts
1/2 cup pomegranate seeds
1 medium lime, cut into wedges
DRESSING:
  1/2 cup olive oil
  1/4 cup red *or* white wine vinegar
  2 tablespoons sugar
Dash salt

On a large platter, arrange the pineapple, beets, oranges, apple, banana and jicama over romaine. Sprinkle with peanuts and pomegranate seeds. Garnish with lime.

In a jar with a tight-fitting lid, combine the dressing ingredients; shake well. Drizzle over salad. Serve immediately. **Yield:** 8-10 servings.

Family Traditions

TO HONOR our Mexican culture on Christmas Eve, my family attends a "posada" (meaning lodging or shelter). The celebration commemorates Joseph and Mary's cold, long journey from Nazareth to Bethlehem.
—*Josey Jacobsen*
Lander, Wyoming

Potato Puff

(Pictured at right)

This wonderfully rich potato casserole complements a variety of main courses. I've shared the recipe with so many people that I can almost recite it by heart!
—Donna Cline, Pensacola, Florida

2 pounds potatoes, peeled and
   quartered
3 eggs, *separated*
1 cup milk
3/4 teaspoon salt
1/2 teaspoon dried basil
1/4 teaspoon white pepper
1-1/2 cups (6 ounces) shredded
   Monterey Jack cheese, *divided*

Place potatoes in a large saucepan and cover with water. Bring to a boil. Reduce heat; cover and cook for 15-20 minutes or until tender. Drain and mash.

In a bowl, combine the egg yolks, milk, salt, basil and pepper. Gradually stir into mashed potatoes. Fold in 1 cup cheese. In a small mixing bowl, beat egg whites on high speed until stiff peaks form; fold into potato mixture.

Spoon into a greased 1-1/2-qt. baking dish. Sprinkle with remaining cheese. Bake, uncovered, at 350° for 40-45 minutes or until golden brown. **Yield:** 8 servings.

Corn Pudding

Corn pudding is a specialty on the Eastern shore of Maryland, where I grew up. This recipe from a friend is a mainstay at our Christmas meals.
—Amanda Beheler, Attica, Indiana

2/3 cup sugar
3 tablespoons cornstarch
2 eggs
1 cup evaporated milk
3 teaspoons vanilla extract
1/8 teaspoon ground cinnamon
1 can (14-3/4 ounces) cream-
   style corn

In a large bowl, combine sugar and cornstarch. Whisk in the eggs, milk, vanilla and cinnamon until smooth. Stir in corn.

Pour into a greased 9-in. square baking pan. Bake, uncovered, at 350° for 45-50 minutes or until a knife inserted near the center comes out clean. **Yield:** 8 servings.

Roasted Root Vegetable Medley

Pair this assortment of vegetables with a meaty entree for a mouth-watering winter meal.
—*Mindy Ilar, St. Albans, West Virginia*

3 medium carrots, cut into
  1/2-inch chunks
2 medium red onions, cut into
  wedges
2 large potatoes, peeled and cut
  into 3/4-inch cubes
2 medium sweet potatoes,
  peeled and cut into 1/2-inch
  cubes
2 tablespoons olive oil
1/2 teaspoon salt

1/2 teaspoon garlic powder
3 to 4 medium fresh beets, peeled and quartered
1/4 cup thinly sliced green onions

Place the carrots, red onions and potatoes in two greased 15-in. x 10-in. x 1-in. baking pans. In a small bowl, combine the oil, salt and garlic powder. Drizzle evenly over vegetables; toss to coat.

Place beets in pans (do not stir). Bake, uncovered, at 425° for 40-45 minutes or until vegetables are tender. Sprinkle with green onions. **Yield:** 10 servings.

Elegant Green Beans

Mushrooms and water chestnuts give new life to ordinary green bean casserole.
Every time I make it for friends, I'm asked to share the recipe.
—*Linda Poe, Sandstone, Minnesota*

1 can (8 ounces) sliced water
  chestnuts, drained
1 small onion, chopped
1 jar (4-1/2 ounces) sliced
  mushrooms, drained
6 tablespoons butter, *divided*
1/4 cup all-purpose flour
1 cup milk
1/2 cup chicken broth
1 teaspoon soy sauce
1/8 teaspoon hot pepper sauce
Dash salt
1 package (16 ounces) frozen
  French-style green beans,
  thawed

1/2 cup shredded cheddar cheese
1 cup crushed french-fried onions

In a small skillet, saute the water chestnuts, onion and mushrooms in 2 tablespoons butter for 4-5 minutes or until crisp-tender; set aside.

In large skillet, melt the remaining butter; stir in flour until smooth. Stir in the milk, broth, soy sauce, hot pepper sauce and salt. Bring to a boil; cook and stir for 2 minutes or until thickened. Remove from the heat; stir in green beans and cheese.

Spoon half of the bean mixture into a greased 1-1/2-qt. baking dish. Layer with water chestnut mixture and remaining bean mixture. Bake, uncovered, at 350° for 45 minutes. Top with french-fried onions. Bake 5 minutes longer or until heated through. **Yield:** 8 servings.

Spiced Mixed Fruit

(Pictured at right)

Delicious fresh fruit is hard to come by around Christmas. So this recipe calling for dried and canned fruits is fantastic. This sweet side is a nice change from the usual savory dishes.
—Barb Biedenstein, Centennial, Colorado

2 packages (8 ounces *each*)
   mixed dried fruit
1 can (15 ounces) fruit cocktail,
   undrained
1 cup raisins
1 cup apple cider *or* juice
1/2 cup brandy *or* additional
   apple cider *or* juice
4-1/2 teaspoons chopped candied
   ginger
1-1/2 teaspoons ground cardamom
1-1/2 teaspoons ground allspice
2 medium apples, chopped
1 cup fresh *or* frozen
   cranberries

In a 3-qt. baking dish, combine the first eight ingredients. Cover and bake at 350° for 35-40 minutes or until the fruit is softened.

   Stir in apples and cranberries. Bake, uncovered, for 15-20 minutes or until apples are tender. Serve warm or at room temperature. **Yield:** 6-1/2 cups.

'Tis the *Season*

Gift-Wrapping Dessert Party

THE TASK of wrapping all of the Christmas gifts you purchased can seem like a daunting task. So why not make a fun night of it by inviting over a few close friends for a gift-wrapping party?

In addition to their gifts, have each guest bring along wrapping paper, ribbons and bows. (For a Yuletide twist, see "It's a Wrap!" on page 77 for non-traditional gift-wrapping ideas.)

Let guests know you'll supply plenty of tape, scissors, pens and gift tags.

Avoid the temptation to go all out on the food…keep the celebration simple by offering a stunning dessert, such as Chocolate-Mint Present Cake (pictured at right).

PRETTY PRESENTATION
(Pictured above)

Chocolate-Mint Present Cake (p. 68)

Chocolate-Mint Present Cake

(Pictured on page 67)

The flavor of crushed peppermint candies infuses every forkful of this outstanding chocolate cake from our home economists. It's a tasty surprise during the holidays.

1-1/3 cups baking cocoa
2-2/3 cups boiling water
1-1/3 cups butter, softened
3-1/3 cups sugar
    6 eggs
    1 teaspoon vanilla extract
    4 cups all-purpose flour
2-1/2 teaspoons baking soda
    2 teaspoons salt
1/2 teaspoon baking powder
    1 cup crushed peppermint
      candies
FROSTING:
1-2/3 cups butter, softened
  15 cups confectioners' sugar
    1 cup plus 2 tablespoons milk,
      divided
2-1/2 teaspoons peppermint extract
FONDANT:
    1/4 cup shortening
3-3/4 cups confectioners' sugar
    9 tablespoons light corn syrup
Red paste food coloring
    4 pieces ribbon candy (4 inches
      x 1 inch)
Assorted round candies, optional

In a small bowl, combine cocoa and water until smooth; cool completely. In a large mixing bowl, cream butter and sugar until light and fluffy. Add eggs, one at a time, beating well after each. Beat in vanilla. Combine the flour, baking soda, salt and baking powder; add to creamed mixture alternately with cocoa mixture. Beat until smooth. Fold in peppermint candies.

Pour into four greased and floured 9-in. square baking pans. Bake at 350° for 25-30 minutes or until a toothpick inserted near the center comes out clean. Cool for 10 minutes before removing from the pans to wire racks to cool completely.

For frosting, in a large mixing bowl, cream butter. Add confectioners' sugar, 1 cup milk and extract; beat on low until combined. Beat on medium for 1 minute or until frosting achieves spreading consistency, adding remaining milk if necessary.

Place one cake layer on a serving plate; spread with frosting. Repeat three times. Frost sides of cake.

For fondant, in a large mixing bowl of a heavy-duty stand mixer, cream shortening until light and fluffy. Beat in confectioners' sugar until crumbly. Gradually beat in corn syrup on low speed (mixture will be stiff).

Divide in half; tint one portion red and one portion pink. For ribbon, on a work surface dusted with confectioners' sugar, roll out red portion into a 19-in. x 4-in. rectangle; cut in half lengthwise. Carefully arrange over cake, draping ends down the sides. On a work surface dusted with confectioners' sugar, roll out pink portion into a 19-in. x 2-in. rectangle; cut in half lengthwise. Carefully position over red ribbon, draping ends down the sides.

Just before serving, break ribbon candies in half; place over ribbon on top of cake, creating a bow. Decorate with round candies if desired. **Yield:** 24 servings.

Cherry-Swirl Chiffon Cake

(Pictured at right)

This impressive-looking cake elicits oohs and aahs whenever it appears on the table. Use peppermint extract in place of cherry extract if you desire.
—Edna Hoffman, Hebron, Indiana

        8 egg whites
2-1/4 cups cake flour
1-1/2 cups sugar
        3 teaspoons baking powder
        1 teaspoon salt
        5 egg yolks
    3/4 cup water
    1/2 cup vegetable oil
        2 teaspoons cherry extract
    1/2 teaspoon cream of tartar
        6 drops red food coloring
FROSTING:
    2/3 cup sugar
        2 egg whites
    1/3 cup light corn syrup
        2 tablespoons plus 2 teaspoons
            water
    1/4 teaspoon cream of tartar
        1 teaspoon vanilla extract
    1/2 teaspoon cherry extract
      12 drops red food coloring
Crushed cherry hard candies,
    optional

Place egg whites in a large mixing bowl; let stand at room temperature for 30 minutes. Meanwhile, in another mixing bowl, combine the flour, sugar, baking powder and salt. Whisk egg yolks, water, oil and extract; add to dry ingredients. Beat until well blended.

Add cream of tartar to egg whites; beat on medium speed until stiff peaks form. Fold into batter. Remove a third of the batter to a small bowl; tint pink with red food coloring.

Alternately spoon plain and pink batters into an ungreased 10-in. tube pan. Cut through batter with a knife to swirl. Bake on the lowest oven rack at 325° for 60-70 minutes or until top springs back when lightly touched. Immediately invert pan; cool completely, about 1 hour.

For frosting, in a small heavy saucepan over low heat, combine the sugar, egg whites, corn syrup, water and cream of tartar. With a portable mixer, beat on low speed for 1 minute. Continue beating on low over low heat until frosting reaches 160°, about 8-10 minutes. Pour into a large mixing bowl; add extracts. Beat on high until stiff peaks form, about 7 minutes.

Run a knife around sides and center tube of cake pan. Remove cake to a serving plate. Frost top and sides. Add drops of food coloring to frosting at base of cake; with a spatula, blend color up toward top of cake. Sprinkle with candies if desired. **Yield:** 12 servings.

Editor's Note: A stand mixer is recommended for beating the frosting after it reaches 160°.

Mint Dip with Brownies

(Pictured at far right, bottom)

My sister shared the simple, refreshing dip recipe with me many years ago.
It also tastes terrific with fresh strawberries.
—Carol Klein, Franklin Square, New York

1 **package fudge brownie mix (8-inch square pan size)**
3/4 **cup sour cream**
2 **tablespoons brown sugar**
2 **tablespoons green creme de menthe**

Prepare and bake brownies according to package directions. Cool completely on a wire rack. Meanwhile, in a small bowl, combine the sour cream, brown sugar and creme de menthe; cover and refrigerate until serving.

Cut brownies into 1-in. diamonds. Serve with dip. **Yield:** 1 dozen (3/4 cup dip).

Cranberry Cake Roll

This low-fat angel food cake roll is a guilt-free indulgence, which is
much-appreciated during the Christmas season.
—Paige Kowolewski, Topton, Pennsylvania

9 **egg whites**
1-1/2 **teaspoons vanilla extract**
3/4 **teaspoon cream of tartar**
1/4 **teaspoon salt**
1 **cup plus 2 tablespoons sugar**
3/4 **cup cake flour**
FILLING:
2-1/3 **cups fresh *or* frozen cranberries**
1 **cup sugar**
6 **tablespoons water, *divided***
2 **tablespoons cornstarch**

Place egg whites in a large mixing bowl; let stand at room temperature for 30 minutes. Meanwhile, line a greased 15-in. x 10-in. x 1-in. baking pan with waxed paper; grease the paper and set aside.

Add vanilla, cream of tartar and salt to egg whites; beat on medium speed until soft peaks form. Gradually beat in sugar, 2 tablespoons at a time, on high until stiff glossy peaks form and sugar is dissolved. Fold in flour, about 1/4 cup at a time.

Carefully spread into prepared pan. Bake at 350° for 15-20 minutes or until cake springs back when lightly touched. Cool for 5 minutes. Turn cake onto a kitchen towel dusted with confectioners' sugar. Gently peel off waxed paper. Roll up cake in the towel jelly-roll style, starting with a long side. Cool completely on a wire rack.

For filling, in a large saucepan, combine the cranberries, sugar and 1/4 cup water. Bring to a boil. Reduce heat; simmer, uncovered, for 5-6 minutes or until berries pop. Mash berries; strain, reserving juice and discarding pulp. Return juice to the pan. Combine cornstarch and remaining water until smooth; gradually add to cranberry juice. Bring to a boil; cook and stir for 2 minutes or until thickened. Chill.

Unroll cake and spread filling to within 1/2 in. of edges. Roll up again. Cover and refrigerate for 1 hour before serving. Refrigerate leftovers. **Yield:** 12 servings.

Mint Ice Cream Torte

(Pictured at right, top)

Wouldn't it be great to have an impressive dessert on hand for unexpected company over the Christmas season? Try our Test Kitchen's recipe for a from-the-freezer favorite!

20 **cream-filled chocolate sandwich cookies, crushed**
1/4 **cup butter, melted**
10 **mint Andes candies, melted**
1/2 **gallon mint chocolate chip ice cream,** *divided*
1 **jar (11-3/4 ounces) hot fudge ice cream topping**

In a small bowl, combine the cookie crumbs and butter. Press half of the mixture into a greased 9-in. springform pan. Spread melted candies over crust. Top with half of the ice cream.

Place 1/4 cup hot fudge topping in a small bowl; cover and refrigerate until serving. In another bowl, combine remaining topping and crumb mixture; spread over ice cream. Cover and freeze for 2 hours or until firm.

Top with remaining ice cream. Cover and freeze for 8 hours or overnight until firm. Remove from the freezer 5 minutes before serving. Warm reserved fudge topping and use to garnish torte. **Yield:** 12 servings.

CUTTING ICE CREAM CAKE

TO CUT frozen Mint Ice Cream Torte, use a long straight-edged knife. Dip it often into hot water for easier slicing.

Caramel Tassies

(Pictured at far right)

Buttery cookie cups with a caramel filling make a nice addition to a dessert tray.
—Jane Bricker, Scottdale, Pennsylvania

   1 cup butter, softened
   2 packages (3 ounces *each*)
     cream cheese, softened
   2 cups all-purpose flour
FILLING:
   1 package (14 ounces) caramels
 1/4 cup plus 3 tablespoons
     evaporated milk
FROSTING:
   2 tablespoons shortening
   2 tablespoons butter, softened
   1 cup confectioners' sugar
   1 tablespoon evaporated milk

In a large mixing bowl, cream butter and cream cheese. Gradually beat in flour. Cover and refrigerate for 1 hour or until easy to handle.

Roll dough into 1-in. balls; press onto the bottom and up the sides of ungreased miniature muffin cups. Prick bottoms with a fork. Bake at 375° for 15-17 minutes or until golden. Cool for 5 minutes; remove from pans to wire racks.

In a large heavy saucepan over low heat, melt caramels with milk. Remove from the heat; cool slightly. Transfer to a heavy-duty resealable plastic bag; cut a small hole in a corner of the bag. Pipe filling into pastry cups. Cool to room temperature.

For frosting, in a small mixing bowl, beat shortening and butter until smooth. Gradually beat in confectioners' sugar and milk until fluffy. Pipe onto filling. Store in the refrigerator. **Yield**: 4 dozen.

Cherry-Nut Brownie Bars

I created these bars by accident one day, but now I make a point of preparing them often.
—Richell Welch, Buffalo, Texas

   3 cups all-purpose flour
   2 cups sugar
   1 cup baking cocoa
 1/2 teaspoon baking powder
 1/2 teaspoon baking soda
 1/2 teaspoon salt
   2 eggs
   1 cup butter, melted
   3 teaspoons vanilla extract
   1 can (21 ounces) cherry pie
     filling
   1 cup chopped walnuts
 1/2 cup vanilla *or* white chips
   1 tablespoon milk

In a large mixing bowl, combine the first six ingredients. In another bowl, whisk the eggs, butter and vanilla; add to dry ingredients. Beat until well blended (mixture will be thick).

Set aside 1 cup dough for topping. Press remaining dough into a greased 13-in. x 9-in. x 2-in. baking dish. Spread evenly with pie filling. Crumble reserved dough over the top; sprinkle with walnuts.

Bake at 350° for 35-40 minutes or until top is dry and nuts are golden brown. Cool completely on a wire rack.

In a microwave-safe bowl, melt vanilla chips at 70% power; stir in milk until smooth. Drizzle over bars. **Yield:** about 2 dozen.

Fancy
Phyllo Cups

(Pictured at right)

*Phyllo dough is great for making
eye-catching desserts with little work.
Experiment with other preserves
for a tasty twist.*
—Cody Geisler, Minnetonka, Minnesota

 8 sheets phyllo dough (14 inches
   x 9 inches)
1/3 cup butter, melted
1/2 cup confectioners' sugar
1/2 cup vanilla *or* white chips
 2 tablespoons milk
 1 package (8 ounces) cream
   cheese, softened
 1 carton (8 ounces) frozen
   whipped topping, thawed
1/2 cup seedless raspberry
   preserves, room temperature
White chocolate curls, optional

Place one sheet of phyllo dough on a work surface (keep remaining phyllo covered with plastic wrap and a damp towel to prevent it from drying out); brush sheet with butter and dust with confectioners' sugar. Top with a second sheet of phyllo; brush with butter and dust with sugar.

Cut into 12 squares. Place one square on top of a second square, alternating corner points; press into a greased muffin cup. Repeat with remaining 10 squares, filling five more muffin cups. Repeat the process three times with remaining phyllo dough, butter and sugar.

Bake at 350° for 5-6 minutes or until lightly browned. Carefully remove from pans to wire racks to cool.

In a microwave-safe bowl, heat vanilla chips and milk at 70% power until chips are melted; stir until smooth. In a large mixing bowl, beat cream cheese and melted chip mixture until smooth. Fold in whipped topping.

Spoon or pipe into phyllo cups; drizzle with raspberry preserves. Cover and refrigerate until serving. Garnish with chocolate curls if desired. **Yield:** 2 dozen.

Butterscotch Cake

I get lots of compliments and recipe requests whenever I make this delicious, rich cake.
The filling is similar to German chocolate cake.
—Judy Lamon, Louisville, Tennessee

2/3 cup butterscotch chips
1/4 cup water
1/2 cup shortening
3/4 cup sugar
3/4 cup packed brown sugar
3 eggs
2-1/4 cups all-purpose flour
1 teaspoon baking soda
1/2 teaspoon baking powder
1/2 teaspoon salt
1 cup buttermilk
FILLING/TOPPING:
1/2 cup sugar
1 tablespoon cornstarch
1/2 cup evaporated milk
1/3 cup water
1 egg yolk, lightly beaten
1/3 cup butterscotch chips
2 tablespoons butter
1 cup pecans, chopped
1 cup flaked coconut
2 to 3 cups buttercream
frosting

Line two greased 9-in. round baking pans with waxed paper; set aside. In a saucepan, melt butterscotch chips with water over low heat, stirring occasionally. Cool to room temperature.

In a large mixing bowl, cream shortening and sugars. Add eggs, one at a time, beating well after each addition. Beat in butterscotch mixture. Combine the flour, baking soda, baking powder and salt; add to creamed mixture alternately with buttermilk (do not overbeat).

Pour into prepared pans. Bake at 375° for 30-35 minutes or until a toothpick inserted near the center comes out clean. Cool for 10 minutes before removing from pans to wire racks to cool completely.

In a large saucepan, combine sugar and cornstarch. Stir in evaporated milk and water until smooth. Cook and stir over medium heat until thickened and bubbly. Reduce heat; cook and stir 2 minutes longer. Remove from the heat. Stir a small amount of hot filling into egg yolk; return all to the pan, stirring constantly. Bring to a gentle boil; cook and stir 2 minutes longer.

Remove from the heat. Gently stir in chips and butter. Stir in pecans and coconut. Cool to room temperature without stirring.

Place one cake layer on a serving plate; spread with half of the filling. Top with second layer and remaining filling. Frost sides with buttercream frosting. Store in the refrigerator. **Yield:** 12 servings.

BASIC BUTTERCREAM FROSTING

IN a large mixing bowl, cream 1/2 cup softened butter until light and fluffy. Beat in 4-1/2 cups confectioners' sugar and 1-1/2 teaspoons vanilla extract. Add 5 to 6 tablespoons milk until desired consistency is reached. **Yield:** about 3 cups.

Raspberry-Cream Chocolate Torte

(Pictured at right)

This spectacular torte looks and tastes like it came from a European bakery. Although it takes some time to make, each step is actually very easy.
—Mary Beth Jung
Hendersonville, North Carolina

2/3 **cup butter, softened**
1 **cup sugar**
3 **eggs**
2 **teaspoons vanilla extract**
2 **cups all-purpose flour**
3/4 **cup baking cocoa**
1-1/2 **teaspoons baking powder**
1/2 **teaspoon baking soda**
1-1/3 **cups milk**
FILLING:
1 **package (10 ounces) frozen unsweetened raspberries, thawed**
1 **envelope unflavored gelatin**
1 **cup heavy whipping cream**
1/4 **cup confectioners' sugar**
1/2 **teaspoon vanilla extract**
GANACHE:
1/2 **cup semisweet chocolate chips**
3 **tablespoons heavy whipping cream**

In a large mixing bowl, cream butter and sugar. Beat in eggs and vanilla. Combine the flour, cocoa, baking powder and soda; add to creamed mixture alternately with milk.

Line a greased 15-in. x 10-in. x 1-in. baking pan with waxed paper; grease the paper. Spread batter evenly into pan. Bake at 350° for 15-20 minutes or until cake springs back when lightly touched in center. Cool for 10 minutes before removing from pan to a wire rack; carefully remove paper. Cool completely.

For filling, puree raspberries in a food processor. Strain, reserving juice and discarding seeds. Place juice in a small saucepan. Sprinkle with gelatin; let stand for 1 minute. Cook and stir over low heat until gelatin is completely dissolved. Cool to room temperature.

In a small mixing bowl, beat cream until it begins to thicken. Add confectioners' sugar and vanilla; beat until stiff peaks form. Gently fold into raspberry mixture.

Trim edges from cake. Cut into four 7-1/2-in. x 4-1/2-in. rectangles. Place one rectangle on a serving platter; spread with a third of the filling. Repeat layers twice. Top with remaining rectangle.

For ganache, place chocolate chips and cream in a small saucepan. Cook and stir over low heat until chocolate is melted. Cool until thickened, about 10 minutes. Spread over torte. Refrigerate for 2 hours before serving. **Yield:** 8-10 servings.

Mocha Parfait Dessert

I found this recipe in an old cookbook from my Dad. It's wonderful after a big meal.
—*Robin Lamar, North Easton, Massachusetts*

1 package (9 ounces) devil's
food cake mix
1 envelope unflavored gelatin
1 cup milk, *divided*
1/2 cup sugar
4 teaspoons instant coffee
granules
1/8 teaspoon salt
1 cup heavy whipping cream
3/4 cup chopped walnuts,
toasted, *divided*

Prepare and bake cake according to package directions, using a 9-in. round baking pan. Cool the cake for 10 minutes before removing it from pan to a wire rack to cool completely.

In a small bowl, sprinkle gelatin over 1/4 cup milk; let stand for 1 minute. In a small saucepan, combine the sugar, coffee granules, salt and remaining milk. Cook and stir until bubbles form around edge of pan. Add gelatin mixture; stir until dissolved. Transfer to a bowl. Refrigerate until slightly thickened, about 1-1/4 hours.

In a chilled mixing bowl, beat cream until soft peaks form. Fold whipped cream and 1/2 cup walnuts into gelatin mixture.

Line the bottom of a greased 9-in. round pan with waxed paper. Pour gelatin mixture into pan; carefully place cooled cake layer on top. Refrigerate for at least 3 hours.

Just before serving, invert dessert onto a serving platter; gently peel off waxed paper. Garnish with remaining walnuts. **Yield:** 8-10 servings.

Cream Puffs in a Cloud

We entertain family and friends often, and this dessert is always a hit.
—*Donna Austin, Abbotsford, British Columbia*

1 cup water
1/2 cup butter, cubed
2 tablespoons sugar
1/2 teaspoon salt
1 cup all-purpose flour
4 eggs
1 cup confectioners' sugar
3 tablespoons baking cocoa
2 to 3 tablespoons boiling
water
1 pint fudge ripple, chocolate
or vanilla ice cream
Whipped cream in a can

In a large saucepan, bring the water, butter, sugar and salt to a boil. Add flour all at once; stir until a smooth ball forms. Remove from the heat; let stand for 5 minutes. Add eggs, one at a time, beating well after each addition. Continue beating until smooth and shiny.

Drop batter by heaping teaspoonfuls 1 in. apart onto greased baking sheets. Bake at 400° for 20-25 minutes or until golden brown, dry and firm to the touch. Remove to wire racks. Immediately split puffs open; remove tops and set aside. Discard soft dough from inside. Cool puffs.

For glaze, in a bowl, combine the confectioners' sugar, cocoa and boiling water; stir until smooth. Fill each puff with a small scoop of ice cream; replace tops. Drizzle with glaze. Place three or four puffs in each dessert dish; pipe whipped cream around puffs to resemble a cloud. Serve immediately. **Yield:** 12-16 servings.

It's a Wrap!

(Pictured above)

THINK outside the box when wrapping Christmas gifts this holiday season with these clever ideas:

Go Beyond Gift Wrap. On some of our pretty packages, we used white butcher block paper, faux suede and tulle. Other ideas include felt, flannel, dish towels, newspaper, magazine pages and brown paper bags.

Get Rid of Ribbon. Secure a wrapped bottle of wine with a girl's ponytail or wrap a necktie around a box (both ideas shown above.) You can also use twine, raffia, gold wire and upholstery trim. For a little girl, tie on a new jump rope!

Easy Embellishments. Dress up a wrapped gift with inexpensive things like pom-poms or feathers. Other finishing touches include pine sprigs, pinecones, small jingle bells and cinnamon sticks.

You can even add a little extra gift on the outside of the package. Tie on a silver key ring (as we did), a cookie cutter or candy canes.

Cookie & Candy Exchange

IT WOULDN'T be the Christmas season without platters piled high with an assortment of festive cookies and candies.

To ensure you have plenty of pretty tins loaded with merry morsels—and to save yourself valuable time in the kitchen—host a cookie and candy exchange.

If guests ask you for a little inspiration, share the recipes for Cinnamon-Sugar Crackle Cookies, Three-Layer Bars and Butter Pecan Roll-Ups.

Almond Crunch Toffee and Creme de Menthe Truffles are marvelous choices for folks who want to try their hand at candy making for the first time. (All recipes are shown at right.)

SPECIAL SWEETS
(Clockwise from top)

Cinnamon-Sugar Crackle Cookies (p. 81)

Almond Crunch Toffee (p. 82)

Three-Layer Bars (p. 84)

Creme de Menthe Truffles (p. 82)

Butter Pecan Roll-Ups (p. 80)

Butter Pecan Roll-Ups

(Pictured on page 78)

My version of traditional lace cookies are great alone or alongside ice cream.
—Stella Wartmann, Port Charlotte, Florida

6 tablespoons butter, softened
1/2 cup sugar
1/2 cup packed brown sugar
1 egg
1/2 teaspoon vanilla extract
6 tablespoons all-purpose flour
1/8 teaspoon salt
1 cup ground pecans

In a mixing bowl, cream butter and sugars until light and fluffy. Beat in egg and vanilla. Combine flour and salt; gradually add to creamed mixture. Mix well. Stir in pecans.

Drop six teaspoonfuls onto a well-greased baking sheet. Bake at 400° for 4-5 minutes or until edges begin to brown. Cool for 1 minute. Loosen each cookie and curl around a wooden spoon handle. Cool on a wire rack. Repeat with remaining dough. **Yield:** about 6 dozen.

COOKIE AND CANDY EXCHANGE TIMELINE

Four to Six Weeks Before:

- Send out the invitations to 8 to 10 people about 4 weeks in advance. On the invitation, ask each person to bring 8 to 10 dozen of the same cookie, copies of their recipe and large containers in which to take cookies home.
- As guests RSVP, keep track of who is bringing what so there are no duplicates. Remind them to bring copies of their recipe to share.

Two to Three Weeks Before:

- Bake and freeze your cookies.
- Make Applesauce Cinnamon Ornaments if desired (see page 93). Store them in airtight containers.
- Plan your menu. You can simply serve beverages and extra cookies or set out some hot and cold appetizers.

The Day Before

- Make any food you plan on serving. Gather plates and napkins.
- Set up the table where the cookies will be displayed.
- If you made Applesauce Cinnamon Ornaments, use them to decorate your Christmas tree or miniature potted evergreens. You can also package them as party favors.

The Day of the Party

- As guests arrive, have them set their cookies and copies of the recipe on the display table.
- Serve food and beverages, and enjoy the company!
- Near the end of the party, have guests fill their containers with a dozen of each kind of cookie and candy.

Mint-Topped Chocolate Cookies

(Pictured at right)

This recipe from my neighbor combines two of my favorite flavors. A cake mix makes them quick to fix.
—*Jennifer Burns, McMurray, Pennsylvania*

1 package (18-1/4 ounces)
   devil's food cake mix
1/2 cup shortening
2 eggs
1 tablespoon water
Confectioners' sugar
40 chocolate-covered thin mints

In a large mixing bowl, combine the cake mix, shortening, eggs and water. Shape into 1-in. balls; roll in confectioners' sugar.

Place 2 in. apart on ungreased baking sheets. Bake at 350° for 8-10 minutes or until slightly firm to the touch. Place a mint on each cookie; remove to wire racks to cool. **Yield:** 40 cookies.

Editor's Note: These cookies were tested with Necco Thin Mints. They can be found at Walgreens stores.

Cinnamon-Sugar Crackle Cookies

(Pictured on page 79)

I get lots of compliments on these crunchy cookies. They're always part of my Christmas cookie platter.
—*Sarah Miller, Wauconda, Washington*

1 cup shortening
1-3/4 cups sugar, *divided*
2 eggs
2-3/4 cups all-purpose flour
2 teaspoons cream of tartar
1 teaspoon baking soda
1/2 teaspoon salt
4 teaspoons ground cinnamon

In a large mixing bowl, cream shortening and 1-1/2 cups sugar until light and fluffy. Add eggs, one at a time, beating well after each addition. Combine the flour, cream of tartar, baking soda and salt; gradually add to creamed mixture. Cover and chill for 30 minutes or until easy to handle.

In a small bowl, combine cinnamon and remaining sugar; set aside. Shape dough into 1-in. balls; roll in cinnamon-sugar. Place 2 in. apart on ungreased baking sheets. Bake at 400° for 8-10 minutes or until lightly browned. Cool for 2 minutes before removing to wire racks. **Yield:** 4 dozen.

Almond Crunch Toffee

(Pictured on page 79)

This recipe has been my claim to fame since I was 14 years old. You won't be able to stop eating it!
—*Anna Ginsberg, Austin, Texas*

1-1/2 teaspoons plus 1 cup butter, softened, *divided*
1 cup sugar
1/2 cup water
1/4 teaspoon salt
1 cup sliced almonds
1/2 teaspoon baking soda
8 ounces dark chocolate candy bars, chopped
1 cup chopped pecans, toasted
1/4 cup dry roasted peanuts, chopped
3 tablespoons chocolate-covered coffee beans, halved
4 squares (1 ounce *each*) white baking chocolate, chopped

Line a 13-in. x 9-in. x 2-in. pan with foil. Grease the foil with 1-1/2 teaspoons butter; set aside. In a heavy 3-qt. saucepan, melt the remaining butter. Stir in the sugar, water and salt. Cook over medium heat until a candy thermometer reads 240° (soft-ball stage), stirring occasionally.

Stir in almonds. Cook until candy thermometer reads 295° (hard-crack stage), stirring occasionally. Remove from the heat; stir in baking soda. Pour into prepared pan. Sprinkle with chocolate; let stand for 5 minutes. Carefully spread chocolate; sprinkle with pecans and peanuts. Cool on a wire rack for 30 minutes.

Sprinkle with coffee beans; press down lightly. Chill for 1 hour or until chocolate is firm. In a microwave-safe bowl, melt white chocolate; drizzle over candy. Chill 30 minutes longer or until firm. Using foil, lift candy out of pan; discard foil. Break candy into pieces. Store in an airtight container. **Yield:** about 2 pounds.

Creme de Menthe Truffles

(Pictured on page 79)

I found this in a box of recipe clippings and decided to try them. I'm so glad I did! The minty flavor is perfect for Christmas.
—*Mrs. Joe Mattes, Amana, Iowa*

1/2 cup butter, melted
1 cup finely chopped pecans
1/4 cup creme de menthe
4 cups confectioners' sugar
2 cups (12 ounces) semisweet chocolate chips
2 teaspoons shortening

In a large mixing bowl, combine the butter, pecans and creme de menthe. Gradually beat in confectioners' sugar. Cover and refrigerate for 1 hour or until easy to handle.

With hands lightly dusted with confectioners' sugar, shape mixture into 1-in. balls. Place on waxed paper-lined baking sheets. Chill for 30 minutes or until firm.

In a microwave-safe bowl, melt chocolate chips and shortening; stir until smooth. Dip balls in chocolate mixture; let excess drip off. Return to waxed paper; chill until set. Store in an airtight container in the refrigerator. **Yield:** 4-1/2 dozen.

Butterscotch Hard Candy

(Pictured at right)

The old-fashioned flavor of these butterscotch candies appeals to kids of all ages.
—Edna Hoffman, Hebron, Indiana

1 teaspoon plus 1/2 cup butter, softened, *divided*
2 cups sugar
1/4 cup light corn syrup
2 tablespoons water
2 tablespoons white vinegar

Line a 15-in. x 10-in. x 1-in. baking pan with foil. Grease the foil with 1 teaspoon butter; set aside.

In a heavy saucepan, combine the sugar, corn syrup, water, vinegar and remaining butter. Bring to a boil over medium heat, stirring occasionally. Cover and cook for 3 minutes to dissolve any sugar crystals.

Uncover; cook, without stirring, until a candy thermometer reads 300° (hard-crack stage). Remove from the heat. Pour into prepared pan without scraping the saucepan; do not spread mixture. Cool for 1-2 minutes or until candy is almost set. Using a sharp knife, score into 1/2-in. squares; cool completely. Break squares apart. Store in an airtight container. **Yield:** 1 pound.

Editor's Note: We recommend that you test your candy thermometer before each use by bringing water to a boil; the thermometer should read 212°. Adjust your recipe temperature up or down based on your test.

Three-Layer Bars

(Pictured on page 78)

A small taste of these rich bars goes a long way to satisfy a sweet tooth.
—*Phyllis Chaffin, Bluff City, Tennessee*

1/2 cup butter, cubed
1/3 cup baking cocoa
1/4 cup sugar
  1 egg, lightly beaten
  2 cups crushed vanilla wafers
  1 cup flaked coconut
  1 teaspoon vanilla extract
FILLING:
  3 tablespoons cold milk
  3 tablespoons instant vanilla
    pudding mix
1/2 cup butter, softened
  2 cups confectioners' sugar
TOPPING:
  4 squares (1 ounce *each*)
    semisweet chocolate
  1 tablespoon butter

In a large saucepan, combine the butter, cocoa and sugar. Cook and stir over low heat until butter is melted. Stir in egg; cook over low heat for 5 minutes or until mixture reaches 160°. Stir in the wafer crumbs, coconut and vanilla.

Press into an ungreased 8-in. square dish. Let stand for 15 minutes. Meanwhile, in a small bowl, whisk milk and pudding mix for 2 minutes. Let stand for 2 minutes. In a small mixing bowl, cream butter; beat in confectioners' sugar and pudding. Spread over crust. Cover and refrigerate for 15 minutes or until firm.

In a microwave-safe bowl, melt chocolate and butter; cool slightly. Spread over filling. Refrigerate until serving. Cut into bars. **Yield:** about 1-1/2 dozen.

Crunchy Cracker Candy

When I first made this recipe, I thought I'd be stuck with lots of leftovers. But the big batch was quickly gobbled up!
—*Laura Mahaffey, Annapolis, Maryland*

  3 cups Ritz cracker sticks,
    halved
3/4 cup butter, cubed
3/4 cup packed brown sugar
  1 package (11-1/2 ounces) milk
    chocolate chips
  2 tablespoons shortening
  1 cup chopped pecans, optional
  1 cup English toffee bits *or*
    almond brickle chips,
    optional

Place cracker sticks in a greased 15-in. x 10-in. x 1-in. baking pan; set aside. In a large saucepan over medium heat, bring butter and brown sugar to a boil, stirring constantly. Cook and stir for 3-4 minutes or until sugar is dissolved. Pour over crackers; stir to coat.

Bake at 350° for 5 minutes, stirring once. Meanwhile, in a microwave-safe bowl, melt chips and shortening; stir until smooth. Drizzle over cracker sticks; toss to coat.

Sprinkle with pecans and toffee bits if desired; toss to coat. Spread onto waxed paper-lined baking sheets. Cool until set; break apart. Store in an airtight container. **Yield:** 2-1/2 pounds.

Chocolate Gingersnaps

(Pictured at right)

When my daughter, Jennifer, was 15 years old, she created this recipe as a way to combine two of her favorite flavors. They're great with a glass of milk.
— Paula Zsiray, Logan, Utah

1/2 cup butter, softened
1/2 cup packed dark brown sugar
1/4 cup molasses
  1 tablespoon water
  2 teaspoons minced fresh gingerroot
1-1/2 cups all-purpose flour
  1 tablespoon baking cocoa
1-1/4 teaspoons ground ginger
  1 teaspoon baking soda
  1 teaspoon ground cinnamon
1/4 teaspoon ground nutmeg
1/4 teaspoon ground cloves
  7 squares (1 ounce *each*) semisweet chocolate, chopped
1/4 cup sugar

In a large mixing bowl, cream butter and brown sugar until light and fluffy. Beat in the molasses, water and gingerroot. Combine the flour, cocoa, ginger, baking soda, cinnamon, nutmeg and cloves; gradually add to creamed mixture and mix well. Stir in chocolate. Cover and refrigerate for 2 hours or until easy to handle.

Shape dough into 1-in. balls; roll in sugar. Place 2 in. apart on greased baking sheets. Bake at 350° for 10-12 minutes or until tops begin to crack. Cool for 2 minutes before removing to wire racks. **Yield:** 3 dozen.

White Chocolate Fudge

*When the holiday season arrives, friends and family eagerly await
my fantastic fudge. It's a nice alternative to traditional chocolate fudge.*
—*Gioviana Buser, Riverside, California*

1-1/2 teaspoons plus 3/4 cup butter,
  softened, *divided*
3 cups sugar
1 can (5 ounces) evaporated
  milk
1 package (10 to 12 ounces)
  vanilla *or* white chips
1 jar (7 ounces) marshmallow
  creme
1 teaspoon vanilla extract

Line a 13-in. x 9-in. x 2-in. pan with foil. Grease the foil with 1-1/2 teaspoons butter; set aside. In a heavy saucepan, combine the sugar, evaporated milk and remaining butter. Cook and stir over low heat until sugar is dissolved. Bring to a boil over medium heat; boil for 4 minutes, stirring occasionally.

Remove from the heat. Stir in the chips, marshmallow creme and vanilla until smooth. Pour into prepared pan. Cool completely on a wire rack.

Using foil, lift fudge out of pan. Discard foil. Cut fudge into 1-in. squares. Store in an airtight container. **Yield: 3 pounds.**

Grandma's Chocolate Chip Bars

*My grandmother made these delicious bar cookies with a unique meringue topping for
every holiday and birthday gathering. She's now gone, but her wonderful recipe lives on.*
—*Sandy Hartig, New Berlin, Wisconsin*

1 cup shortening
1/2 cup sugar
1/2 cup packed brown sugar
3 egg yolks
1 tablespoon water
1 teaspoon vanilla extract
2 cups all-purpose flour
1 teaspoon baking powder
1/2 teaspoon salt
1/4 teaspoon baking soda
1 cup semisweet chocolate
  chips
TOPPING:
3 egg whites
1 cup packed brown sugar
1 teaspoon vanilla extract
1/8 teaspoon salt
1/4 cup chopped walnuts

In a large mixing bowl, cream shortening and sugars until light and fluffy. Beat in the egg yolks, water and vanilla. Combine the flour, baking powder, salt and baking soda; gradually add to creamed mixture and mix well. Stir in chocolate chips.

Spread into a greased 13-in. x 9-in. x 2-in. baking pan. Bake at 350° for 15 minutes or until top is dry.

Meanwhile, in a large mixing bowl, beat egg whites on medium speed until soft peaks form. Gradually beat in brown sugar, vanilla and salt on high speed until stiff peaks form. Spread over warm crust to within 1 in. of edges. Sprinkle with walnuts. Bake for 25 minutes or until a toothpick comes out clean. Cool on a wire rack. Cut into bars. **Yield: 2 dozen.**

Gingerbread Men

(Pictured at right)

*Christmas and gingerbread men
go hand in hand.
This is a tried-and-true recipe
I'm happy to share with you.*
—Mitzi Sentiff, Alexandria, Virginia

1/2 cup butter, softened
3/4 cup packed dark brown sugar
1/3 cup molasses
1 egg
2 tablespoons water
2-2/3 cups all-purpose flour
2 teaspoons ground ginger
1 teaspoon baking soda
1/2 teaspoon salt
1/2 teaspoon *each* ground
    cinnamon, nutmeg and
    allspice

In a large mixing bowl, cream butter and brown sugar until light and fluffy. Add the molasses, egg and water; beat well. Combine the flour, ginger, baking soda, salt, cinnamon, nutmeg and allspice; add to creamed mixture. Divide dough in half. Refrigerate for 30 minutes or until easy to handle.

On a lightly floured surface, roll out each portion of dough to 1/8-in. thickness. Cut with a floured 4-in. cookie cutter. Place 2 in. apart on greased baking sheets. Reroll the scraps.

Bake at 350° for 8-10 minutes or until edges are firm. Remove to wire racks to cool completely. Decorate as desired. **Yield:** about 2 dozen.

THE MAKING OF GINGERBREAD MEN

SOME SAY the history of gingerbread men began during the reign of England's Queen Elizabeth I, who gifted court visitors with decorated gingerbread likenesses of themselves.

Secret Ingredient Drop Cookies

Cottage cheese is the secret to making these cake-like cookies moist and tender.
With candied cherries, they're a natural for Christmas.
— Dixie Terry, Goreville, Illinois

1/2 cup butter, softened
1 cup sugar
1/2 cup cottage cheese
1 egg
1/2 teaspoon vanilla extract
1/4 teaspoon lemon extract
1-3/4 cups all-purpose flour
1/2 teaspoon baking soda
1/2 teaspoon salt
1/2 cup chopped candied pineapple
22 red *or* green candied cherries, halved

In a large mixing bowl, cream butter and sugar until light and fluffy. Beat in the cottage cheese, egg and extracts. Combine the flour, baking soda and salt; gradually add to creamed mixture and mix well. Stir in pineapple.

Drop by tablespoonfuls 2 in. apart onto greased baking sheets. Top each with a cherry half. Bake at 375° for 10-12 minutes or until lightly browned. Remove to wire racks to cool. **Yield:** 44 cookies.

Special Chocolate Chip Cookies

With oats, vanilla chips, a crunch candy bar and a strawberry drizzle,
each bite of this cookie is packed with wonderful flavor!
— Linda Wheeler Sparks, Severna Park, Maryland

1/2 cup quick-cooking oats
1 Nestle Crunch candy bar (1.4 ounces), broken into pieces
1/4 cup chopped pecans
1 cup butter, softened
3/4 cup packed brown sugar
1/2 cup sugar
2 eggs
3 teaspoons vanilla extract
2 cups all-purpose flour
1 teaspoon baking soda
1/2 teaspoon salt
1 cup semisweet chocolate chips
1 cup vanilla *or* white chips
ICING:
2 cups confectioners' sugar
2 tablespoons milk

2 teaspoons strawberry *or* raspberry extract
1 to 2 drops red food coloring, optional

In a food processor, combine the oats, candy bar and pecans. Cover and process until finely chopped; set aside. In a large mixing bowl, cream butter and sugars until light and fluffy. Add eggs, one at a time, beating well after each addition. Beat in vanilla. Combine the flour, baking soda, salt and reserved oat mixture; gradually add to creamed mixture. Stir in chips.

Drop by tablespoonfuls 2 in. apart onto ungreased baking sheets. Bake at 350° for 11-13 minutes or until lightly browned. Cool for 2 minutes before removing to wire racks to cool completely.

Combine the icing ingredients until smooth; drizzle over cookies. Let stand until set. Store in an airtight container. **Yield:** about 4-1/2 dozen.

Cherry Chocolate Bark

(Pictured at right)

This recipe from my daughter caught my eye because it reminded me of a favorite candy bar of mine as a child. I love the fudge-like texture.
—Judith Batiuk
San Luis Obispo, California

1 tablespoon plus 1/2 cup
   butter, softened, *divided*
2 cups sugar
12 large marshmallows
1 can (5 ounces) evaporated
   milk
Dash salt
1 cup vanilla *or* white chips
1-1/2 teaspoons cherry extract
1 teaspoon vanilla extract
1 cup semisweet chocolate chips
1/3 cup creamy peanut butter
1/4 cup finely chopped dry
   roasted peanuts

Line a 15-in x 10-in. x 1-in. pan with foil. Grease the foil with 1 tablespoon butter; set aside.

In a large heavy saucepan, combine the sugar, marshmallows, milk, salt and remaining butter. Bring to a boil; cook and stir for 5 minutes. Remove from the heat. Stir in the vanilla chips and extracts until smooth. Pour into the prepared pan.

In a microwave-safe bowl, melt chocolate chips; stir until smooth. Stir in peanut butter and peanuts. Drop by tablespoonfuls over first layer; cut through with a knife to swirl. Chill until firm.

Using foil, lift candy out of pan. Discard foil. Break candy into pieces. Store in an airtight container in the refrigerator. **Yield:** about 2 pounds.

Lemon-Glazed Pecan Slices

A tart lemon icing pairs well with these rich bars that resemble pecan pie.
Everyone loves them whenever I take them to work or potlucks.
—Joan Hallford, North Richland Hills, Texas

1/2 cup cold butter
1 cup plus 2 tablespoons
   all-purpose flour, *divided*
2 eggs
1-1/2 cups packed brown sugar
1 teaspoon vanilla extract
1/2 teaspoon baking powder
1/2 teaspoon salt
1 cup chopped pecans
1/2 cup flaked coconut
1-1/2 cups confectioners' sugar
2 tablespoons lemon juice

In a small bowl, cut butter into 1 cup flour until crumbly. Press into a greased 13-in. x 9-in. x 2-in. baking pan. Bake at 350° for 12 minutes.

Meanwhile, in a small mixing bowl, beat the eggs, brown sugar and vanilla until blended. Combine the baking powder, salt and remaining flour; add to egg mixture. Stir in pecans and coconut. Spread over warm crust. Bake for 25 minutes or until set. Cool on a wire rack.

For glaze, combine confectioners' sugar and lemon juice; spread over bars. Let set before cutting. **Yield:** 4 dozen.

Tiny Tim Sandwich Cookies

When I was growing up, my mother and I created special Christmas memories in the
kitchen preparing these cute, bite-size cookies. Vary the food coloring for holidays throughout the year.
—Eudora Delezenne, Port Huron, Michigan

1 cup sugar, *divided*
2 to 3 drops red food coloring
2 to 3 drops green food coloring
1/2 cup butter, softened
1/2 cup shortening
1/4 cup confectioners' sugar
1 teaspoon almond extract
2-1/3 cups all-purpose flour
FROSTING:
2 cups confectioners' sugar
3 tablespoons butter, softened
4-1/2 teaspoons heavy whipping
   cream
3/4 teaspoon almond extract
Red and green food coloring

In a small bowl, combine 1/2 cup sugar and red food coloring; set aside. In another small bowl, combine green food coloring and remaining sugar; set aside.

In a large mixing bowl, cream the butter, shortening and confectioners' sugar. Beat in extract. Gradually add flour. Shape into 1/2-in. balls.

Place 1 in. apart on ungreased baking sheets. Flatten slightly with a glass dipped in reserved colored sugars. Bake at 375° for 8-10 minutes or until edges are lightly browned. Remove to wire racks to cool.

For the frosting, in a small bowl, combine the confectioners' sugar, butter, cream and extract until smooth. Tint half of the frosting red and the other half green. Frost the bottoms of half of the cookies; top with the remaining cookies. **Yield:** 5 dozen.

Peppermint Lollipops

(Pictured at right)

These splendid suckers from our Test Kitchen are a fun and festive treat to share at Christmastime. There are endless color and design options... so let your creative juices flow!

1-1/2 cups sugar
3/4 cup water
2/3 cup light corn syrup
1/2 teaspoon cream of tartar
1/2 teaspoon peppermint oil
Green and red paste food coloring
10 lollipop sticks

Butter 10 assorted metal cookie cutters and place on a parchment paper-lined baking sheet; set aside.

In a large heavy saucepan, combine the sugar, water, corn syrup and cream of tartar. Cook and stir over medium heat until sugar is dissolved. Bring to a boil. Cook, without stirring, until a candy thermometer reads 300° (hard-crack stage).

Remove from the heat. Stir in oil, keeping face away from mixture as odor is very strong. Spoon 1/4 cup sugar mixture into two ramekins or custard cups; tint one green and one red.

Immediately pour remaining sugar mixture into prepared cookie cutters. Drizzle with green and red mixtures; cut through with a toothpick to swirl. Remove cutters just before lollipops are set; firmly press a lollipop stick into each. **Yield:** 10 lollipops.

Editor's Note: This recipe was tested with LorAnn peppermint oil. It can be found at candy and cake decorating supply shops or at www.lorannoils.com. We recommend that you test your candy thermometer before each use by bringing water to a boil; the thermometer should read 212°. Adjust your recipe temperature up or down based on your test.

Orange Gumdrops

I get nothing but rave reviews when I make these gumdrops and usually have
to prepare three batches. My family prefers it to chocolate candies.
—Becky Burch, Marceline, Missouri

1 teaspoon plus 1 tablespoon
    butter, softened, *divided*
1 cup sugar
1 cup light corn syrup
3/4 cup water
1 package (1-3/4 ounces)
    powdered fruit pectin
1/2 teaspoon baking soda
1-1/2 teaspoons orange extract
1 teaspoon grated orange peel
4 drops yellow food coloring
1 drop red food coloring
Additional sugar, optional

Line the bottom and sides of a 9-in. x 5-in. x 3-in. loaf pan with foil. Grease the foil with 1 teaspoon butter; set aside. Grease the bottom and sides of a large heavy saucepan with the remaining butter; add sugar and corn syrup. Cook and stir over medium heat until mixture comes to a boil, about 9 minutes. Cook over medium-high heat until a candy thermometer reads 280° (soft-crack stage), stirring occasionally.

Meanwhile, in another large saucepan, combine the water, pectin and baking soda (mixture will foam slightly). Cook and stir over high heat until mixture boils, about 2 minutes. Remove from the heat; set aside.

When corn syrup mixture reaches 280°, remove from the heat. Return pectin mixture to medium-high heat; cook until mixture begins to simmer. Carefully and slowly ladle corn syrup mixture in a very thin stream into pectin mixture, stirring constantly. Cook and stir 1 minute longer.

Remove from the heat; stir in extract, orange peel and food coloring. Transfer to prepared pan. Let stand until firm, about 2 hours. Cut into squares. Roll in additional sugar if desired. **Yield:** about 6 dozen.

Editor's Note: We recommend that you test your candy thermometer before each use by bringing water to a boil; the thermometer should read 212°. Adjust your recipe temperature up or down based on your test. Both the corn syrup mixture and pectin mixtures are very hot. Use caution when pouring the corn syrup mixture into the pectin mixture to avoid splatters.

Colorful Snowballs

Add festive fun to holiday bake sales with these pretty popcorn balls dotted with red and green M&M's.
—Kristi Smith, Ashland, Wisconsin

1 quart popped popcorn
2 cups crisp rice cereal
20 large marshmallows
1/4 cup butter, cubed
1 cup red and green milk
    chocolate M&M's

In a large greased bowl, combine popcorn and cereal. In a large saucepan over low heat, combine marshmallows and butter. Cook and stir until marshmallows are melted and mixture is smooth. Pour over popcorn mixture. Add M&M's; stir until combined.

When cool enough to handle, shape 1/3 cupfuls into balls with lightly buttered hands. Place on waxed paper-lined baking sheets. Cool. **Yield:** 16 popcorn balls.

Applesauce Cinnamon Ornaments

(Pictured at right)

These non-edible, cinnamon ornaments on the evergreen add a lovely scent to your home during the holidays.

1 cup applesauce
Approximately 3/4 cup ground cinnamon
2 tablespoons ground cloves
1 tablespoon nutmeg
1 tablespoon ground allspice
Green *or* red heavy thread
Straw *or* wooden skewer

In a large bowl, combine the applesauce and spices; mix well until a stiff dough forms, adding additional cinnamon if needed.

On a board dusted with additional cinnamon, roll out each portion of dough to 1/4-in. thickness. Cut into shapes using 1-1/2-in. cookie cutters dipped in cinnamon. Reroll scraps. Place cutouts on parchment paper-lined baking sheets.

Using a straw or wooden skewer, make a small hole in the top of each of the ornaments.

Bake at 200° for 20 to 30 minutes. Remove to paper towels to dry thoroughly. When completely dry and cool, string a ribbon strip or piece of thread through each hole; tie the ends together to form a loop. **Yield:** about 60 (1-1/2 inch) ornaments.

DISPLAYING APPLESAUCE CINNAMON ORNAMENTS

IN ADDITION to hanging Applesauce Cinnamon Ornaments from your Christmas tree, you can use them to decorate miniature potted evergreens (as pictured above). Place the decorated trees on your mantle or on a sideboard.

Bake another batch of the non-edible decorations and package them up as party favors for your holiday guests.

'Tis The Season

Fire-and-Ice Buffet

ADD a little spark to the Christmas season by hosting a fun-filled Fire-and-Ice party!

Enjoy time with friends and family by building a snowman, planning a snowball fight, sledding down a local hill or ice skating on a frozen pond.

(If you live in a warm climate, take a nature walk, go swimming or plan a bike ride.)

Then when you've had your fill of outdoor fun, head inside and sit by a roaring fire (or air conditioner!).

Set up a buffet featuring foods that play upon hot and cold elements, such as "icy" salad greens topped with Balsamic Honey Vinaigrette and "fiery" Pizza Stromboli and Sausage Wild Rice Soup. (Recipes are shown at right.)

CLIMATE CONTROL
(Clockwise from top left)

Balsamic Honey Vinaigrette (p. 96)

Sausage Wild Rice Soup (p. 98)

Pizza Stromboli (p. 96)

Pizza Stromboli

(Pictured on page 94)

As a mother of two, it seems the only time I have to be creative is in the kitchen.
I received a similar recipe from a co-worker but decided to add veggies and spices.
— Denise Tutton, Ridgway, Pennsylvania

1 loaf (1 pound) frozen bread
  dough, thawed
1 block (8 ounces) brick
  cheese, sliced
1 can (8 ounces) pizza sauce
1/4 teaspoon garlic powder, *divided*
1/4 teaspoon dried oregano, *divided*
1 cup (4 ounces) shredded
  part-skim mozzarella cheese
1/2 cup chopped green pepper
1/4 cup chopped onion
1 cup sliced fresh mushrooms
1/2 cup shredded Parmesan cheese
1 package (3 ounces) sliced
  pepperoni
5 ounces sliced deli ham

Place dough in a greased bowl, turning once to grease top. Cover and let rise in a warm place until doubled, about 1 hour.

On a greased baking sheet, roll out dough into a 15-in. x 10-in. rectangle. Layer with brick cheese, pizza sauce, 1/8 teaspoon garlic powder, 1/8 teaspoon oregano, mozzarella cheese, green pepper, onion, mushrooms, Parmesan cheese, pepperoni and ham.

Roll up, jelly-roll style, starting with a long side; pinch seam to seal and tuck ends under. Sprinkle with remaining garlic powder and oregano.

Bake at 350° for 25-30 minutes or until golden brown. Cut into slices. **Yield:** 10 servings.

Balsamic Honey Vinaigrette

(Pictured on page 94)

All gatherings in our family are centered around meals.
The food gives us all a common bond of warmth, tradition and shared sustenance.
— Betsy Sams, Jamesville, New York

1/2 cup olive oil
1/2 cup vegetable oil
1/3 cup balsamic vinegar
2 tablespoons honey
1 tablespoon Dijon mustard
1 tablespoon Italian seasoning
1 teaspoon salt
1 teaspoon garlic powder

1 teaspoon onion powder
1 teaspoon pepper
Mixed salad greens and sliced sweet red pepper

In a jar with a tight-fitting lid, combine the first 10 ingredients; shake well. Combine the greens and red pepper in a large salad bowl; drizzle with vinaigrette and toss to coat. **Yield:** 1-1/4 cups.

Caramel Apple Fondue

(Pictured at right)

I like to serve this warm caramel dip with sliced apples while we're watching football games on Sunday afternoons. It really warms us up.
—Katie Koziolek, Hartland, Minnesota

1/2 cup butter, cubed
2 cups packed brown sugar
1 can (14 ounces) sweetened
   condensed milk
1 cup light corn syrup
2 tablespoons water
1 teaspoon vanilla extract
Apple slices

In a heavy 3-qt. saucepan, combine the butter, brown sugar, milk, corn syrup and water; bring to a boil over medium heat. Cook and stir until a candy thermometer reads 230° (thread stage), about 8-10 minutes. Remove from the heat; stir in vanilla.

Transfer to a fondue pot or 1-1/2-qt. slow cooker; keep warm over low heat. Serve with apple slices. **Yield:** 3-1/2 cups.

Editor's Note: We recommend that you test your candy thermometer before each use by bringing water to a boil; the thermometer should read 212°. Adjust your recipe temperature up or down based on your test.

COOKING CANDY TO THREAD STAGE

CANDY is cooked to a thread stage when a candy thermometer reads between 230° and 233°. Dip a metal spoon into the hot candy mixture. Hold the spoon over cold water. The mixture should fall off the spoon in a fine thread.

Sausage Wild Rice Soup

(Pictured on page 95)

*This recipe makes a big batch, so I often divide leftovers into
a few containers for "freezer meals." Serve it alongside bread and salad.*
— Tonya Schaffer, Huron, South Dakota

9 cups water, *divided*
1 cup uncooked wild rice
2 pounds bulk Italian sausage
2 large onions, chopped
6 garlic cloves, minced
2 teaspoons olive oil
3 cartons (32 ounces *each*)
   chicken broth
1 can (28 ounces) diced
   tomatoes, undrained
1 can (6 ounces) tomato paste
2 teaspoons dried basil
2 teaspoons dried oregano
1 package (6 ounces) fresh baby
   spinach, coarsely chopped
1/2 teaspoon salt
1/2 teaspoon pepper

In a large saucepan, bring 3 cups water to a boil. Stir in rice. Reduce heat; cover and simmer for 55-60 minutes or until tender.

Meanwhile, in a soup kettle, cook sausage over medium heat until no longer pink; drain. Remove and set aside. In the same kettle, saute onions and garlic in oil until tender. Stir in the broth, tomatoes, tomato paste, basil, oregano and remaining water. Return sausage to the pan. Bring to a boil. Reduce heat; simmer, uncovered, for 20 minutes.

Stir in the spinach, salt, pepper and wild rice; heat through. **Yield:** 5 quarts (13 servings).

Italian Turkey Sandwich Loaf

One wedge of this sandwich goes a long way. Each bite is packed with turkey, cheese and vegetables.
—Joan Camello, Holmdel, New Jersey

1 round loaf (1 pound)
   Italian bread
1/4 cup Italian salad dressing
12 fresh baby spinach leaves
1 cup (4 ounces) shredded
   part-skim mozzarella cheese
1/2 pound thinly sliced deli turkey
3/4 cup thinly sliced peeled
   cucumber
1 medium tomato, sliced

Cut a 1-in. slice off top of the bread and set aside. Carefully hollow out the loaf, leaving a 1/2-in. shell (save removed bread for another use). Brush the inside of the bread with salad dressing.

In the bread shell, layer the spinach, 1/2 cup mozzarella cheese, turkey, cucumber, tomato and remaining cheese. Replace bread top; wrap loaf in foil.

Place on a baking sheet. Bake at 350° for 40-45 minutes or until heated through. Let stand for 10 minutes before cutting into wedges. **Yield:** 6 servings.

Hot Chocolate Souffles

(Pictured at right)

These individual chocolate souffles from our home economists are fudgy and delicious. They look impressive but are easy to make.

1 cup butter, cubed
8 squares (1 ounce *each*) bittersweet chocolate, chopped
4 eggs
4 egg yolks
1-1/2 cups plus 2 tablespoons sugar
2 tablespoons all-purpose flour
1/8 teaspoon baking powder
1 cup miniature marshmallows
4-1/2 teaspoons cinnamon-sugar

Grease the bottoms only of twelve 6-oz. ramekins or custard cups; set aside. In a large microwave-safe bowl, melt butter and chocolate; stir until smooth. Set aside.

In a large mixing bowl, beat eggs and yolks on high speed for 3 minutes or until light and fluffy. Gradually add sugar, beating until thick and lemon-colored, about 5 minutes. Beat in chocolate mixture. Combine flour and baking powder; beat into egg mixture just until combined.

Fill prepared ramekins half full; sprinkle with marshmallows. Bake at 400° for 12-15 minutes or until a toothpick inserted near the center comes out with moist crumbs. Sprinkle with cinnamon-sugar; serve immediately. Refrigerate leftovers. **Yield:** 12 servings.

Slow-Cooked Shredded Pork

The tasty pork filling for these sandwiches requires very little work because it's prepared in the slow cooker. The mild, sweet sauce is appealing to all palates.
—Shirleymae Haefner, O'Fallon, Missouri

1 boneless pork loin roast (2 to 3 pounds)
1 large onion, thinly sliced
1 cup beer *or* nonalcoholic beer
1 cup chili sauce
2 tablespoons brown sugar
1 tablespoon prepared horseradish
8 sandwich rolls, split

Cut the roast in half; place in a 5-qt. slow cooker. Top with onion. In a small bowl, combine the beer, chili sauce, brown sugar and horseradish. Pour over pork. Cover and cook on low for 6 to 6-1/2 hours or until meat is very tender.

Remove pork; shred with two forks. Return meat to cooking juices; heat through. Use a slotted spoon to serve on rolls. **Yield:** 8 servings.

Potluck Banana Cake

I found this recipe about 5 years ago and have been making it for family gatherings ever since. The coffee-flavored frosting complements the moist banana cake.
—Kathy Hoffman, Topton, Pennsylvania

1/2 cup butter, softened
1 cup sugar
2 eggs
1 teaspoon vanilla extract
2 cups all-purpose flour
2 teaspoons baking soda
1/2 teaspoon salt
1-1/2 cups mashed ripe bananas (about 3 medium)
1 cup (8 ounces) sour cream
COFFEE FROSTING:
1/3 cup butter, softened
2-1/2 cups confectioners' sugar
2 teaspoons instant coffee granules
2 to 3 tablespoons milk

In a large mixing bowl, cream butter and sugar until light and fluffy. Add eggs, one at a time, beating well after each addition. Stir in vanilla. Combine the flour, baking soda and salt; add to creamed mixture alternately with bananas and sour cream, beating well after each addition.

Pour into a greased 13-in. x 9-in. x 2-in. baking dish. Bake at 350° for 35-40 minutes or until a toothpick inserted near the center comes out clean. Cool completely on a wire rack.

For frosting, in a small mixing bowl, cream butter and confectioners' sugar. Dissolve coffee granules in milk; add to creamed mixture and beat until smooth. Spread over cake. **Yield:** 12-15 servings.

Mulled
Merlot

(Pictured at right)

Our Test Kitchen home economists created this recipe that's sure to warm up your adult holiday guests!

4 cinnamon sticks (3 inches)
4 whole cloves
2 bottles (750 milliliters *each*) Merlot wine
1/2 cup sugar
1/2 cup orange juice
1/2 cup brandy
1 medium orange, thinly sliced

Place cinnamon sticks and cloves on a double thickness of cheesecloth; bring up corners of cloth and tie with string to form a bag.

In a 3-qt. slow cooker, combine the wine, sugar, orange juice, brandy and orange slices. Add spice bag. Cover and cook on high for 1 hour or until heated through. Discard spice bag and orange slices. Serve warm in insulated glasses or mugs. **Yield:** 9 servings.

GLASS BLOCK PEDESTALS

TO GIVE an icy feel to our Fire-and-Ice buffet table (without adding a blast of cold!), we used ordinary glass blocks to display Mulled Merlot (above) and salad greens and Balsamic Honey Vinaigrette (page 94).

You can also place glass blocks on console tables, sideboards and mantles to display holiday decorations and candles.

Bacon Corn Chowder

*My husband loves this soup on cold winter days, which are plentiful
here in Michigan. He's not a fan of veggies, but he gobbles them up in this soup.*
—*Michelle Campbell, Menominee, Michigan*

4 bacon strips, diced
1 small onion, chopped
1 celery rib, chopped
1/4 cup chopped green pepper
4 cups cubed peeled potatoes
2-1/2 cups chicken broth
1 teaspoon salt
1 teaspoon dried thyme
1/4 teaspoon pepper
3 tablespoons all-purpose flour
1 quart half-and-half cream
1 package (16 ounces) frozen
corn, thawed

In a large saucepan, cook bacon over medium heat until crisp. Remove to paper towels; drain, reserving 1 teaspoon drippings.

In the drippings, saute the onion, celery and green pepper until tender. Add the potatoes, broth, salt, thyme and pepper. Bring to a boil. Reduce the heat; cover and cook for 15-20 minutes or until potatoes are tender.

Combine flour and cream until smooth; stir into pan. Add corn. Bring to a boil; cook and stir for 2 minutes or until thickened. Stir in bacon. **Yield:** 8 servings (about 2 quarts).

Beef Brisket Chili

*My son and I concocted this recipe for a chili cook-off at his work.
He proudly came home with a first place ribbon!*
—*Marie Hattrup, The Dalles, Oregon*

1 fresh beef brisket (2 pounds),
cut into 1/2-inch pieces
1 large onion, finely chopped
2 tablespoons vegetable oil
2 cans (16 ounces *each*) kidney
beans, rinsed and drained
1 pound smoked kielbasa *or*
Polish sausage, coarsely
chopped
1 jar (16 ounces) salsa
1 can (14-1/2 ounces) diced
tomatoes, undrained
1 can (8 ounces) tomato sauce
2 cans (4 ounces *each*) chopped
green chilies
2 garlic cloves, minced

1 tablespoon chili powder
1 tablespoon ground cumin
1 teaspoon celery salt
1/4 teaspoon salt
1/8 teaspoon pepper
2 to 3 tablespoons lemon juice
1-1/2 teaspoons grated lemon peel

In a Dutch oven, brown beef and onion in oil in batches; drain. Stir in the beans, kielbasa, salsa, tomatoes, tomato sauce, chilies, garlic and seasonings.

Bring to a boil. Reduce heat; cover and simmer for 3 hours or until meat is tender. Just before serving, stir in lemon juice and peel. **Yield:** 10 servings (2-1/2 quarts).

Editor's Note: This is a fresh beef brisket, not corned beef. The meat comes from the first cut of the brisket.

Tangy Cheese Bites

(Pictured at right)

These hot cheese bites were brought to an election night party I attended years ago. Sharp cheddar and blue cheese give them a slightly tangy favor.
— Patricia Ward, Fullerton, California

  1 loaf (1 pound) unsliced
    Italian bread
3/4 cup butter, cubed
  4 ounces cream cheese, cubed
1-1/2 cups (6 ounces) shredded
    cheddar cheese
1-1/2 cups (6 ounces) crumbled
    blue cheese
  3 egg whites
  1 teaspoon paprika

Cut crust off all sides of bread. Cut into 1-1/2-in. cubes; set aside. In a large saucepan, melt butter. Stir in cream cheese until melted. Remove from the heat; stir in cheddar cheese and blue cheese until melted.

In a small mixing bowl, beat egg whites until stiff peaks form. Fold into cheese mixture. Dip bread cubes into cheese mixture, turning to coat.

Place on greased baking sheets; sprinkle with paprika. Bake at 375° for 12-15 minutes or until bottoms are golden brown. Serve warm. **Yield:** about 4-1/2 dozen.

ICE BUCKET SERVING SUGGESTION

TO PLAY upon the Fire-and-Ice theme, place Tangy Cheese Bites in a clear, acrylic ice bucket and serve with ice tongs (as shown above).

Onion Yeast Bread

This is an old recipe of my mother's. She was often asked to
make it for the annual banquet hosted by our church's youth group.
—Becky Bontrager, Westminster, South Carolina

2 packages active dry yeast
1/2 cup warm water (110° to 115°)
1-1/2 cups warm milk (110° to 115°)
3 tablespoons sugar
2 tablespoons shortening
1 envelope onion soup mix
1 teaspoon salt
4-3/4 to 5-1/4 cups all-purpose flour

In a large mixing bowl, dissolve yeast in warm water. Add the milk, sugar, shortening, soup mix, salt and 3 cups flour; beat until smooth. Stir in enough remaining flour to form a soft dough.

Turn onto a floured surface; knead until smooth and elastic, about 6-8 minutes. Place in a greased bowl, turning once to grease top. Cover and let rise in a warm place until doubled, about 1 hour.

Punch dough down. Turn onto a lightly floured surface; divide in half. Shape into loaves. Place in two greased 8-in. x 4-in. x 2-in. loaf pans. Cover and let rise until doubled, about 30 minutes.

Bake at 375° for 20-25 minutes or until golden brown. Remove from pans to wire racks to cool. **Yield:** 2 loaves.

Coconut Rice Pudding

Our home economists give regular rice pudding a hint of citrus and a mild coconut flavor.
Look for unsweetened coconut milk in the Asian aisle of your grocery store.

1-1/2 cups uncooked medium
  grain rice
2-1/4 cups water
1 tablespoon brown sugar
1 tablespoon butter
2 cinnamon sticks (3 inches)
1 teaspoon salt
1 teaspoon grated lemon peel
2 cups milk
1 can (14 ounces) sweetened
  condensed milk
1 can (14 ounces) unsweetened
  coconut milk
1/2 cup raisins
1/4 teaspoon vanilla extract
1 cup flaked coconut, toasted

In a large saucepan, combine the rice, water, brown sugar, butter, cinnamon, salt and lemon peel. Bring to a boil. Reduce heat; cover and simmer for 15 minutes or until rice is tender and water is absorbed.

Stir in the milk, condensed milk, coconut milk, raisins and vanilla. Bring to a boil. Reduce heat; simmer, uncovered, for 20-25 minutes or until thick and creamy, stirring frequently. Discard cinnamon sticks. Sprinkle coconut over pudding. Serve warm or chilled. **Yield:** 10 servings.

Ice Candles

(Pictured at right)

These lacy-looking candles are easy to make using wax and candle dye...or even old candles! They take a few days to dry so make them well in advance of your party.

Wash and dry the inside of wax-coated paper cartons. (We used half-pint milk cartons and 64-ounce juice cartons.) Place on a cookie sheet.

In a double boiler over low heat, melt clear wax and add candle dye in the color of your choice. (You can also melt candles in the color of your choice; remove and discard the wicks.) Estimate how much wax you'll need to fill each carton half full. Having too much wax is better than not having enough.

Add a few drops of melted wax to the bottom of a carton. Immediately place a taper candle in the color of your choice into the wax. Let the wax set.

Fill the carton half full with pieces of ice in different sizes and shapes. Pour enough melted wax into the carton to cover the ice.

Let stand until the wax is hardened and the ice is melted. Pour out the water; carefully tear the carton away. Let the candle stand a few days to dry completely before using.

Be sure to place the lighted candle on a holder to collect the wax as it melts.

Cider House Punch

Every sip of this hot beverage tastes like apple pie. For the holidays, I like to float clove-studded orange slices in the punch bowl.
—Barbara Kay Hummel, Tucson, Arizona

2 quarts apple cider *or* juice
1 liter ginger ale
2-2/3 cups unsweetened pineapple juice
1 cup cranberry juice
1/2 cup sugar
1 cinnamon stick (3 inches)

In a large kettle, combine all ingredients. Cook over medium heat until heated through, stirring occasionally. Transfer to a 5-qt. slow cooker; keep warm over low heat. Discard cinnamon stick before serving. **Yield:** 18 servings (about 3-1/2 quarts).

GIVING *Thanks*

For folks who favor traditional Thanksgiving
fare but who want to add a tasty twist, try
Maple-Butter Turkey with Gravy, Mushrooms au Gratin
and Persimmon Squash Pie. Or turn to our unique
selection of gravies and hearty stuffing...these
succulent sides won't play second fiddle on your table.
Then add a little spice to cool autumn days with
cakes, pies, cookies and desserts featuring
nutmeg, cinnamon, mace, cloves, ginger and more!

GIVING Thanks

Tasty Turkey Day Dinner

GOLDEN roasted turkey, fluffy mashed potatoes, savory gravy, delectable desserts...no other holiday seems to center on a spread of fabulous food quite like Thanksgiving.

The menu featured here is just the thing for folks who favor traditional fare but want to add a tasty twist.

A slightly sweet, simple-to-prepare glaze flavors Maple-Butter Turkey with Gravy. (We also offer two other turkey recipes for you to try.)

In addition to your standard mashed potatoes, prepare a deliciously different side dish, such as Mushrooms au Gratin.

And a unique fruit gives new life to dessert in Persimmon Squash Pie. (All recipes are shown at right.)

A FEAST FOR THE EYES
(Clockwise from top right)

Maple-Butter Turkey with Gravy (p. 112)

Mushrooms au Gratin (p. 116)

Persimmon Squash Pie (p. 113)

THANKSGIVING DINNER TIMELINE

A Few Weeks Before:

- Prepare two grocery lists—one for non-perishable items to purchase now and one for perishable items to purchase a few days before Thanksgiving Day.
- Order a fresh turkey or buy and freeze a frozen turkey.
- Purchase a container for the Cornucopia Centerpiece (page 117).

Four Days Before:

- Thaw the frozen turkey in a pan in the refrigerator. (Allow 24 hours of thawing for every 5 pounds.)

Two Days Before:

- Buy remaining grocery items, including the fresh turkey if you ordered one.
- Make the Pomegranate Cranberry Relish up to the point of adding the chopped walnuts and grated orange peel.

The Day Before:

- Set the table.
- Purchase flowers for the centerpiece and assemble.
- Prepare the Persimmon Squash Pie; chill.
- Bake Scalloped Apples for 20 minutes. (Don't top with bread crumbs or bake longer.) Cover and refrigerate.
- If using the recipe for Maple-Butter Turkey with Gravy, make the maple butter. Cover and chill.

Thanksgiving Day:

- In the morning, peel and cube the potatoes for Traditional Mashed Potatoes; place in a bowl of cold water and refrigerate.
- Roast the turkey according to one of the following recipes: Maple-Butter Turkey with Gravy (p. 112), Seasoned Roast Turkey (p. 115) or Citrus-Rosemary Rubbed Turkey (p. 116).
- A few hours before guests arrive, prepare the Apple Cranberry Cider in a slow cooker.
- Assemble the Pecan Sweet Potato Casserole; add to the oven during the last 45 minutes of the turkey's baking time.
- Remove Scalloped Apples from the refrigerator 30 minutes before baking. Top with buttered bread crumbs.
- Prepare the Traditional Mashed Potatoes.
- Make Mushrooms au Gratin.
- Let the cooked turkey stand for 20 minutes before carving. Prepare the gravy if desired.
- Bake Scalloped Apples for 15 minutes or until tender and heated through.
- Reheat the Pomegranate Cranberry Relish; stir in the chopped walnuts and grated orange peel.
- Serve slices of Persimmon Squash Pie for dessert.

Pecan Sweet Potato Casserole

(Pictured at right)

This convenient casserole calls for canned sweet potatoes, so preparation time is minimal. The nutty, brown sugar topping adds a bit of crunch.
—Anita Briner, Etters, Pennsylvania

2 cans (40 ounces *each*)
   sweet potatoes, drained
8 eggs
1/2 cup sugar
1/4 cup all-purpose flour
2 teaspoons vanilla extract
1 teaspoon salt
TOPPING:
   1 cup packed brown sugar
   1/3 cup all-purpose flour
   1 cup chopped pecans
   1/4 cup cold butter

In a large mixing bowl, mash the sweet potatoes. Add the eggs, sugar, flour, vanilla and salt; beat until smooth. Transfer to a greased 13-in. x 9-in. x 2-in. baking dish.

In a small bowl, combine the brown sugar, flour and pecans; cut in butter until crumbly. Sprinkle over sweet potato mixture. Bake, uncovered, at 325° for 60-70 minutes or until a knife inserted near the center comes out clean. Refrigerate leftovers. **Yield:** 12 servings.

Apple Cranberry Cider

(Pictured at far right)

This fruity cider can be made ahead, then kept warm in a slow cooker so people can serve themselves.
—Kathy Wells, Brodhead, Wisconsin

3 cinnamon sticks (3 inches), broken
1 teaspoon whole cloves
2 quarts apple cider *or* juice
3 cups cranberry juice
2 tablespoons brown sugar

Place cinnamon sticks and cloves on a double thickness of cheesecloth; bring up corners of cloth and tie with string to form a bag. Place the cider, cranberry juice and brown sugar in a 5-qt. slow cooker; add spice bag. Cover and cook on high for 2 hours or until cider reaches desired temperature. Discard spice bag before serving. **Yield:** 11 cups.

Maple-Butter Turkey with Gravy

(Pictured on page 109)

Thyme, sage and marjoram blend beautifully with apple cider and maple syrup in this recipe from our Test Kitchen. The maple butter can be prepared 1 to 2 days in advance.

2 cups apple cider *or* juice
1/3 cup maple syrup
3/4 cup butter, cubed
2 tablespoons minced fresh thyme *or* 2 teaspoons dried thyme
1 tablespoon minced fresh sage *or* 1 teaspoon dried sage leaves
2 teaspoons dried marjoram
1 teaspoon salt
1 teaspoon pepper
1 turkey (14 to 16 pounds)
2 to 2-1/2 cups chicken broth
3 tablespoons all-purpose flour

For maple butter, in a small heavy saucepan, bring cider and syrup to a boil. Cook until reduced to 1/2 cup, about 20 minutes. Remove from the heat; stir in the butter, thyme, sage, marjoram, salt and pepper. Transfer to a bowl; cover and refrigerate until set.

With fingers, carefully loosen the skin from both sides of turkey breast. Rub 1/2 cup maple butter under turkey skin. Refrigerate remaining maple butter. Skewer turkey openings; tie drumsticks together. Place on a rack in a roasting pan.

Cover with foil and bake at 325° for 2 hours. Brush top with 1/3 cup maple butter. Bake, uncovered, 1 to 1-1/2 hours longer or until a meat thermometer reads 180°, basting occasionally with pan drippings. (Cover loosely with foil if turkey browns too quickly.) Remove turkey to a serving platter and keep warm. Cover and let stand for 20 minutes before carving.

Pour drippings and loosened brown bits into a 4-cup measuring cup. Skim and discard fat. Add enough broth to drippings to measure 3 cups. In a large saucepan, combine flour and broth mixture until smooth. Stir in remaining maple butter. Bring to a boil; cook and stir for 2 minutes or until thickened. Serve with turkey. **Yield:** 14-16 servings (3-1/3 cups gravy).

Persimmon Squash Pie

(Pictured on page 108 and at right)

I created this recipe for our local persimmon festival, using homegrown squash. I like to make two pies and use more toffee bits and pecans for garnish.
—Betty Milligan, Bedford, Indiana

 1 unbaked pastry shell (9 inches)
1/4 cup buttermilk
1/2 cup mashed cooked butternut
     squash
1/2 cup mashed ripe persimmon
     pulp
3/4 cup sugar
1/4 cup packed brown sugar
 3 tablespoons all-purpose flour
1/2 teaspoon ground cinnamon
1/4 teaspoon baking powder
1/4 teaspoon baking soda
1/4 teaspoon salt
 2 eggs
1/4 cup heavy whipping cream
1/4 cup butter, melted
 1 teaspoon vanilla extract
CARAMEL TOPPING:
 30 caramels
 2 tablespoons milk
1/3 cup chopped pecans
1/3 cup English toffee bits *or*
     almond brickle chips

Bake unpricked pastry shell at 450° for 5-6 minutes or until lightly browned; cool on a wire rack. Reduce heat to 350°.

In a blender, combine the buttermilk, squash and persimmon pulp; cover and process until smooth. In a large bowl, combine the sugars, flour, cinnamon, baking powder, baking soda and salt. In a small bowl, combine the eggs, cream, butter, vanilla and squash mixture; stir into dry ingredients just until moistened.

Pour into pastry shell. Bake for 40-45 minutes or until a knife inserted near the center comes out clean.

In a small saucepan, combine caramels and milk. Cook and stir over medium heat until melted and smooth. Pour over hot pie. Sprinkle with pecans and toffee bits. Cool completely on a wire rack. Store in the refrigerator. **Yield:** 8 servings.

Persimmon Pointers

THE PERSIMMON is an exotic fruit with yellow-orange skin, which is at its sweetest when very ripe. To ripen firm fruit, place it in a paper bag at room temperature for 1 to 3 days. When ripe, store in the refrigerator for up to 3 days.

When ready to eat or to use in cooking, cut off the top, scoop out the pulp and discard the seeds.

Pomegranate Cranberry Relish

(Pictured at far right, bottom)

I was inspired to develop this recipe one evening when I was making my usual cranberry relish and my husband was eating a pomegranate. It's so tasty when served alongside chicken or turkey.
—Donna Rivera, Pleasant Hill, California

1 package (12 ounces) fresh *or* frozen cranberries
1 medium navel orange, peeled and sectioned
3/4 cup sugar
3 tablespoons honey
1/2 cup pomegranate seeds
1/2 cup chopped walnuts
2 to 3 teaspoons grated orange peel

In a large saucepan, combine the cranberries, orange, sugar and honey. Cook and stir over medium heat for 15-20 minutes or until berries pop and mixture is thickened. Stir in pomegranate seeds; cook 2 minutes longer.

Remove from the heat; stir in walnuts and orange peel. Serve warm or chilled. **Yield:** 2-1/2 cups.

POMEGRANATE SEED SECRET

THE SEEDS and surrounding juice sacs (arils) are the only parts of the pomegranate that are edible. One medium pomegranate (about 8 ounces) yields roughly 3/4 cup arils.

Traditional Mashed Potatoes

It's just not Thanksgiving without mashed potatoes! In this version, our home economists stir in half-and-half, sour cream and chives.

12 medium potatoes, peeled and cubed
1-1/4 to 1-1/2 cups half-and-half cream
1/3 cup sour cream
1/2 cup butter, cubed
1 teaspoon salt
1/2 teaspoon pepper
1 tablespoon minced chives, optional

Place potatoes in a Dutch oven and cover with water. Bring to a boil. Reduce heat; cover and cook for 15-20 minutes or until tender. Drain; transfer to a large mixing bowl. Add the cream, sour cream, butter, salt and pepper; beat until light and fluffy. Sprinkle with chives if desired. **Yield:** 16-18 servings.

Scalloped Apples

(Pictured at right, top)

When preparing my first Thanksgiving dinner years ago, I wanted to add a special side dish and came up with this recipe. It's been a part of our traditional dinner ever since.
—Kellie Erwin, Westerville, Ohio

10 cups thinly sliced peeled
    Golden Delicious apples
    (about 8)
 1 cup sugar
1/2 teaspoon ground cinnamon
1/2 teaspoon ground cloves
 6 tablespoons butter, *divided*
 2 cups soft bread crumbs
    (about 4 slices)

In a large bowl, combine the apples, sugar, cinnamon and cloves. Transfer to a greased 13-in. x 9-in. x 2-in. baking dish. Dot with 2 tablespoons butter. Bake, uncovered, at 325° for 25 minutes or until apples are crisp-tender.

Meanwhile, in a small skillet, melt remaining butter. Add bread crumbs; cook and stir for 3-5 minutes or until crispy and golden brown. Sprinkle over apple mixture. Bake 10-15 minutes longer or until apples are tender. Serve warm. **Yield:** 8 servings.

Seasoned Roast Turkey

Rubbing the skin with melted butter keeps this simply seasoned turkey moist and tender.
—Nancy Reichert, Thomasville, Georgia

   2 teaspoons salt
   2 teaspoons garlic powder
   2 teaspoons seasoned salt
1-1/2 teaspoons paprika
   1 teaspoon ground ginger
 3/4 teaspoon pepper
 1/2 teaspoon dried basil
 1/4 teaspoon cayenne pepper
   1 turkey (13 to 15 pounds)
 1/4 cup butter, melted

In a small bowl, combine the first eight ingredients. Place turkey, breast side up, on a rack in a roasting pan; pat dry. Brush with butter. Sprinkle with herb mixture.

Bake, uncovered, at 325° for 2-3/4 to 3-1/4 hours or until a meat thermometer reads 180°, basting occasionally with pan drippings. (Cover loosely with foil if turkey browns too quickly.) Cover and let stand for 20 minutes before carving. **Yield:** 13-15 servings.

Mushrooms au Gratin

(Pictured on page 108)

*This easy-to-prepare side dish brings me rave reviews whenever I prepare it
for the holidays. Even when I double the recipe, my family eats every bite.*
— *Tina McFarland, Elko, Nevada*

2 pounds sliced fresh mushrooms
1/4 cup butter, cubed
1/2 cup white wine *or* chicken
   broth
2 tablespoons all-purpose flour
2/3 cup sour cream
1 teaspoon pepper
1/4 teaspoon ground nutmeg
1 cup (4 ounces) shredded
   Gruyere *or* Swiss cheese
2 tablespoons minced fresh
   parsley

In a large skillet, saute mushrooms in butter until tender. Add wine or broth. Bring to a boil. Reduce heat; simmer, uncovered, for 4 minutes.

Combine the flour, sour cream, pepper and nutmeg until smooth; stir into mushrooms. Cook and stir for 1-2 minutes or until bubbly. Transfer to a shallow serving dish. Sprinkle with cheese and parsley. **Yield:** 8 servings.

Citrus-Rosemary Rubbed Turkey

*While recovering from hip surgery, I wrote my family for some of their
favorite recipes to compile into a cookbook. This seasoned turkey is timeless.*
— *Della Stamp, Long Beach, California*

2 tablespoons minced fresh
   rosemary *or* 2 teaspoons
   dried rosemary, crushed
1-1/2 teaspoons grated fresh *or*
   dried orange peel
1-1/2 teaspoons grated fresh *or*
   dried lemon peel
1 teaspoon salt
1 teaspoon onion powder
1 teaspoon garlic powder
1 teaspoon pepper
1/4 cup olive oil
1 turkey (13 to 15 pounds)

In a small bowl, combine the first seven ingredients. Place turkey, breast side up, on a rack in a roasting pan; pat dry. Brush with oil; sprinkle with rosemary mixture.

Bake, uncovered, at 325° for 2-3/4 to 3-1/4 hours or until a meat thermometer reads 180°, basting occasionally with pan drippings. (Cover loosely with foil if turkey browns too quickly.) Cover and let stand for 20 minutes before carving. **Yield:** 13-15 servings.

Cornucopia Centerpiece

(Pictured above)

CORNUCOPIA is a Latin term derived from two words: "cornu" (meaning horn) and "copia" (meaning plenty).

According to Greek mythology, after Zeus accidentally broke off a horn from the goat, Amalthea, he promised that the horn would always be filled with whatever fruits the goat desired.

A symbol of abundance, the horn of plenty is an appropriate centerpiece for Thanksgiving, where friends and family gather to celebrate around a beautiful table overflowing with home-cooked foods, lively conversation and cherished friends and family.

To create the cornucopia shown above, we purchased a metal, cone-shaped container, filled it with floral foam and added water.

Our fresh flower choices included: wheat-like green grass, liatris, Blue Mountain thistle, myrtle, green button mums, dusty miller, green solidaster and eucalyptus pods.

GIVING *Thanks*

Splendid Stuffing and Gravy

POLISH the silver, launder your finest linens and dust off the china…it's time to gather with family and friends for a truly memorable Thanksgiving meal.

Although the turkey takes center stage on the table, gravy and stuffing are the eagerly awaited accompaniments.

Turkey with Festive Fruit Stuffing features a blend of apples, cranberries and raisins, resulting in a moist, tasty side dish that pairs perfectly with poultry.

From the pan drippings, prepare simple yet succulent Herbed Turkey Gravy. This classic sauce is delicious draped over sliced turkey, mashed potatoes and stuffing. (Both of the recipes shown at right.)

SPECIAL SAUCE 'N' STUFFING
(Pictured above)

Herbed Turkey Gravy (p. 122)

Turkey with Festive Fruit Stuffing (p. 120)

Turkey with Festive Fruit Stuffing

(Pictured on page 119)

Apples, cranberries and raisins make every bite of this stuffing moist and fruity.
A dear friend shared the recipe with me years ago.
—Elaine Helmick, Paradise, California

3 celery ribs, chopped
2 medium onions, chopped
3/4 cup butter, *divided*
5 cups unseasoned stuffing cubes
1-1/2 cups chopped peeled tart apples (about 2 medium)
1 cup chopped walnuts
1/2 cup raisins
1/2 cup dried cranberries
1/4 cup egg substitute
1 teaspoon salt
1/4 teaspoon pepper
1 to 2 cups chicken broth
1 turkey (14 pounds)

In a large skillet, saute celery and onions in 1/2 cup butter until tender. Transfer to a large bowl; stir in the stuffing cubes, apples, walnuts, raisins and cranberries. Stir in the egg substitute, salt, pepper and enough broth to reach desired moistness.

Just before baking, loosely stuff turkey with stuffing. Skewer turkey openings; tie drumsticks together. Place breast side up on a rack in a roasting pan. Melt remaining butter; brush over turkey.

Bake, uncovered, at 325° for 3-3/4 to 4-1/4 hours or until a meat thermometer reads 180° for turkey and 165° for stuffing, basting occasionally with pan drippings. (Cover loosely with foil if turkey browns too quickly.)

Cover turkey and let stand for 20 minutes before removing stuffing and carving turkey. If desired, thicken pan drippings for gravy. **Yield:** 14 servings (10 cups stuffing).

STUFFING SECRETS

- To save time on Thanksgiving morning, begin some stuffing preparation the night before. For example, chop and saute vegetables. Cut bread into cubes or measure out store-bought stuffing croutons. Combine seasonings. Store wet ingredients separate from dry ones, and store perishable items in the refrigerator.
- Don't combine all of the stuffing ingredients or stuff the bird until just before baking. Then loosely spoon stuffing into the neck and body cavities.

- If making dressing to stuff a turkey, allow 3/4 cup for each pound of turkey.
- Stuffed poultry requires a longer roasting time. Add 15 to 45 minutes to the time unstuffed poultry takes. The internal temperature must reach 165° for the stuffing and 180° for the turkey.
- Stuffing can also be baked in a casserole as the poultry roasts. To convert a recipe where the stuffing was baked in a bird, reduce the baking time and cook until the temperature is 165°.

Pear Stuffing For Turkey

(Pictured at right)

I find this to be a delicious change from the usual Southern-style dressing served around here. I found the recipe in one of my mother's old cookbooks.
—Mabel Hammock, Thomson, Georgia

1 pound bulk pork sausage
1 large onion, chopped
3 celery ribs, chopped
8 cups soft bread crumbs
2 cups diced peeled ripe pears
  (about 2 medium)
1 cup chicken broth
1/2 teaspoon salt
1/2 teaspoon pepper
1/4 teaspoon rubbed sage
1 turkey (10 pounds)

In a large skillet, cook the sausage, onion and celery over medium heat until meat is no longer pink and vegetables are tender. Remove from the heat. Stir in the bread crumbs, pears, broth, salt, pepper and sage.

Just before baking, loosely stuff turkey with stuffing. Skewer turkey openings; tie drumsticks together. Place breast side up on a rack in a roasting pan.

Bake, uncovered, at 325° for 3 to 3-1/2 hours or until a meat thermometer reads 180° for the turkey and 165° for the stuffing, basting occasionally with pan drippings. (Cover loosely with foil if turkey browns too quickly.)

Cover turkey and let stand for 20 minutes before removing stuffing and carving turkey. If desired, thicken pan drippings for gravy. **Yield:** 10 servings (8 cups stuffing).

Herbed Turkey Gravy

(Pictured on page 119)

Our Test Kitchen shares this traditional gravy recipe.
It works for any roasted meat or poultry. Two cups of gravy serves about 8 people.

Turkey drippings
    1 to 1-1/2 cups chicken broth
1/4 cup all-purpose flour
1/4 teaspoon dried thyme
1/4 teaspoon rubbed sage
1/4 teaspoon pepper

Pour drippings and loosened browned bits into a 2-cup measuring cup. Skim fat, reserving 1/4 cup. Add enough broth to the drippings to measure 2 cups.

In a small saucepan, combine flour and reserved fat until smooth. Gradually stir in the drippings mixture. Stir in the thyme, sage and pepper. Bring to a boil; cook and stir for 2 minutes or until thickened. **Yield:** 2 cups.

MAKING PAN GRAVY

1. Pour pan drippings into a heat-resistant measuring cup along with any browned bits scraped from roasting pan. Skim fat.

2. Reserve 1/4 cup fat and place in a saucepan. Whisk in flour until smooth.

3. Add enough broth or water to reserved pan drippings to equal 2 cups. Gradually stir into the flour mixture. Bring to a boil; cook and stir 2 minutes or until thickened.

Orange Tarragon Gravy

(Pictured at right)

Tarragon adds terrific flavor to this gravy, while orange juice adds a bit of sweetness.
—Shirley Bedzis, San Diego, California

Turkey drippings
- 1/4 cup all-purpose flour
- 1/2 cup orange juice
- 1 teaspoon chicken bouillon granules
- 3/4 teaspoon minced fresh tarragon *or* 1/4 teaspoon dried tarragon
- 1/8 teaspoon white pepper

Pour drippings and loosened browned bits into a 2-cup measuring cup. Skim fat. Add enough water to the drippings to measure 1-1/2 cups.

In a small saucepan, combine flour and orange juice until smooth. Gradually stir in the drippings mixture. Stir in the bouillon, tarragon and pepper. Bring to a boil; cook and stir for 2 minutes or until thickened. **Yield:** 2 cups.

Tangy Cranberry Gravy

My husband and I first tasted this deliciously different gravy at my aunt's house one Thanksgiving. Now I make it throughout the year.
—Lori Staufer, Kalamazoo, Michigan

- 1 can (14-1/2 ounces) beef broth
- Turkey giblets (liver removed)
- 2 tablespoons cornstarch
- 1 tablespoon sugar
- 3/4 cup cranberry juice
- 1 tablespoon cider vinegar
- 1 tablespoon butter

In a small saucepan, bring broth and giblets to a boil. Reduce heat; cover and simmer for 1 hour. Strain and discard giblets; set broth aside.

In another saucepan, combine the cornstarch, sugar, cranberry juice and vinegar until smooth. Gradually stir in broth and butter. Bring to a boil; cook and stir for 2 minutes or until thickened. **Yield:** 1-3/4 cups.

Butternut Squash Dressing

I became a confirmed squash lover when I sampled this dish at a friend's house more than 20 years ago.
The blend of creamy squash and crunchy stuffing makes it a favorite.
—Kimberley Melander, Brush Prairie, Washington

1 medium onion, chopped
2 tablespoons vegetable oil
1 package (12 ounces) frozen
   cooked winter squash, thawed
1 can (10-3/4 ounces) condensed
   cream of chicken soup,
   undiluted
1 can (8 ounces) water chestnuts,
   drained and chopped
3/4 cup sour cream
1 package (6 ounces) corn bread
   stuffing mix, *divided*
3 tablespoons butter, melted

In a large skillet, saute onion in oil until tender. Remove from the heat; stir in the squash, soup, water chestnuts and sour cream. Stir in 1-1/2 cups stuffing mix.

Transfer to a greased 2-qt. baking dish. Sprinkle with remaining stuffing mix; drizzle with butter. Bake, uncovered, at 350° for 30-35 minutes or until heated through and top is golden brown. This dressing is best served as a side dish, rather than stuffed into poultry. **Yield:** 5 cups.

Sweet Potato Dressing

My mother was known for this splendid stuffing. Now I enjoy making it for family and friends.
The savory flavor complements ham and turkey.
—Holly Nissley, Elizabethtown, Pennsylvania

3 celery ribs, chopped
1 large onion, chopped
1 medium parsnip, peeled
   and chopped
1 medium carrot, grated
1/2 cup butter
1 can (40 ounces) sweet
   potatoes, drained and mashed
4 cups seasoned stuffing cubes
1/4 cup orange juice
1/2 cup egg substitute
2-1/2 teaspoons grated orange peel
1/2 teaspoon dried sage leaves

In a Dutch oven, saute celery, onion, parsnip and carrot in butter for 5-7 minutes or until crisp-tender. Remove from the heat; add remaining ingredients and toss gently.

Transfer to a greased 2-qt. baking dish. Cover and bake at 350° for 40-45 minutes or until a thermometer reads 165°. The dressing may be stuffed into poultry if desired. **Yield:** 8 cups.

Cranberry Wild Rice Dressing

(Pictured at right)

Rice dressing is a tasty twist to a traditional Thanksgiving dinner.
—*Shirley Bedzis, San Diego, California*

3 cups chicken broth
1 large onion, chopped
2 celery ribs, thinly sliced
1 cup uncooked brown rice
1/2 cup uncooked wild rice
1 tablespoon minced fresh rosemary *or* 1 teaspoon dried rosemary, crushed
1 teaspoon chicken bouillon granules
1/2 teaspoon salt
1/4 teaspoon white pepper
1 bay leaf
1 cup whole-berry cranberry sauce

In a large saucepan, combine the first 10 ingredients; bring to a boil. Reduce heat; cover and simmer for 45-50 minutes or until rice is tender. Remove from the heat; let stand for 5 minutes. Discard bay leaf. Stir in cranberry sauce.

Spoon into a greased 2-qt. baking dish. Cover and bake at 350° for 30-35 minutes or until heated through. If dressing is stuffed into poultry, bake until a meat thermometer reads 180° for poultry and 165° for dressing. **Yield:** 5 cups.

Creamy Onion Gravy

You don't need to worry about having enough pan drippings from your turkey to make this gravy from our Test Kitchen. Prepare it any time you serve mashed potatoes.

1 medium onion, finely chopped
3 tablespoons butter, *divided*
2 tablespoons all-purpose flour
1/4 teaspoon salt
1/8 teaspoon garlic powder
1/8 teaspoon pepper
3/4 cup buttermilk
1/4 cup water

In a small saucepan, saute onion in 1 tablespoon butter until tender. Transfer to a small bowl; set aside.

In the same pan, melt remaining butter over medium-low heat. Combine the flour, salt, garlic powder and pepper; whisk into butter until smooth. Gradually add buttermilk and water. Bring to a boil; cook and stir for 1-2 minutes or until thickened. Stir in onion. **Yield:** 1-1/4 cups.

Potato Stuffing Casserole

This treasured family recipe provides the goodness of potatoes and stuffing in every forkful.
We look forward to it every Thanksgiving.
—Eleanor Howell, Falmouth, Maine

5 pounds potatoes, peeled and quartered
5 medium onions, finely chopped
4 celery ribs, chopped
1 cup butter
2 tablespoons poultry seasoning
1 tablespoon *each* dried savory, thyme and marjoram
2 teaspoons salt
1/2 teaspoon pepper
1 package (14 ounces) seasoned stuffing cubes
1/2 to 3/4 cup chicken *or* turkey broth

Place potatoes in a Dutch oven and cover with water. Bring to a boil. Reduce heat; cover and cook for 15-20 minutes or until tender.

Meanwhile, in a large skillet, saute onions and celery in butter for 6-8 minutes or until tender. Stir in the seasonings; set aside.

Drain potatoes; mash in a large bowl. Stir in stuffing cubes. Stir in the vegetable mixture and enough broth to reach desired moistness.

Transfer to two greased shallow 2-qt. baking dishes (dishes will be full). Cover and bake at 350° for 30-35 minutes or until heated through. This dressing is best served as a side dish, rather than stuffed into poultry. **Yield:** 17 cups.

Walnut Mushroom Stuffing

I always make a double batch of this stuffing because it seems to disappear faster than the turkey.
The recipe has been in my husband's family for more than 40 years.
—Suzanne Michaelis, Atwater, California

1/2 pound sliced fresh mushrooms
1 medium onion, chopped
3/4 cup butter
2 to 4 teaspoons rubbed sage
1 teaspoon salt
1 teaspoon dried thyme, optional
1/2 teaspoon dried marjoram
1/4 teaspoon pepper
12 cups cubed day-old bread
3/4 cup chopped walnuts
1/2 to 1 cup chicken broth

In a large skillet, saute mushrooms and onion in butter until tender. Stir in the sage, salt, thyme if desired, marjoram and pepper. Transfer to a large bowl. Add the bread cubes, walnuts and enough broth to reach desired moistness; toss to coat.

Spoon into a greased 2-qt. baking dish. Cover and bake at 350° for 30 minutes. Uncover; bake 10-15 minutes longer or until lightly browned. If stuffed into poultry, bake until a meat thermometer reads 180° for poultry and 165° for stuffing. **Yield:** 8 cups.

Tortilla Dressing

(Pictured at right)

This is not your typical holiday stuffing. Tortillas, jalapenos, chili powder and cilantro lend to its Southwestern flavor.
— *Dorothy Bray, Adkins, Texas*

8 corn tortillas (6 inches), cut into 1/4-inch strips
1/4 cup vegetable oil
8 flour tortillas (6 inches), cut into 1/4-inch strips
1 cup crushed corn bread stuffing
1 small onion, diced
1/3 cup diced sweet red pepper
1 jalapeno pepper, seeded and chopped
1 tablespoon minced fresh cilantro
1 tablespoon chili powder
1 teaspoon minced fresh sage *or* 1/4 teaspoon dried sage leaves
1/2 teaspoon ground coriander
1/2 teaspoon ground cumin
1/4 teaspoon salt
1 egg, beaten
1 cup chicken broth

In a large skillet, saute corn tortilla strips in batches in oil for 1 minute or until golden brown. Drain on paper towels.

In a large bowl, combine the corn tortilla strips, flour tortilla strips, stuffing, onion, red pepper, jalapeno, cilantro, chili powder, sage, coriander, cumin and salt. Stir in the egg and broth.

Transfer to a greased 13-in. x 9-in. x 2-in. baking dish. Cover and bake at 325° for 35-45 minutes or until a thermometer reads 160°. This dressing is best served as a side dish, rather than stuffed into poultry. **Yield:** 9 cups.

Editor's Note: When cutting or seeding hot peppers, use rubber or plastic gloves to protect your hands. Avoid touching your face.

Sugar and Spice Sweets

THROUGHOUT history, explorations have been navigated, wars have been raged and fortunes have been squandered...all in the search of spices.

Today, spices are accessible and inexpensive, and the journeys they inspire are strictly the culinary kind in the kitchen.

From nutmeg, cinnamon and mace to cloves, anise and ginger, spices enhance cakes, pies, cookies and desserts all year long...but especially during the cool, crisp days of autumn.

This Thanksgiving, add a twist to your table by offering such sugar-and-spice selections as Sweet Potato Layer Cake, Double-Crust Pear Pie and Gingersnap-Pumpkin Dessert. (All recipes shown at right.)

THANKSGIVING GOODIES

(Top to bottom)

Sweet Potato Layer Cake (p. 130)

Double-Crust Pear Pie (p. 130)

Gingersnap-Pumpkin Dessert (p. 134)

Sweet Potato Layer Cake

(Pictured on page 129)

Crushed pineapple adds moistness and subtle fruity flavor to this tasty layered cake.
—Joyce Walter, Nicholasville, Kentucky

1 package (18-1/4 ounces)
    yellow cake mix
1 can (15 ounces) sweet
    potatoes, drained and mashed
1 cup water
1/2 cup all-purpose flour
2 eggs
1 can (8 ounces) unsweetened
    crushed pineapple, well
    drained
2 tablespoons vegetable oil
1 teaspoon ground cinnamon
1 teaspoon vanilla extract
1/2 teaspoon ground nutmeg

FROSTING:
2 packages (8 ounces *each*) cream cheese, softened
1/2 cup butter, softened
2 teaspoons vanilla extract
7-1/2 cups confectioners' sugar

In a large mixing bowl, combine the first 10 ingredients. Beat on low speed for 2-3 minutes or until blended.

Divide the batter among three greased and floured 9-in. round baking pans. Bake at 350° for 20-25 minutes or until a toothpick inserted near the center comes out clean. Cool for 10 minutes before removing from pans to wire racks to cool completely.

For frosting, in a large mixing bowl, beat the cream cheese, butter and vanilla until fluffy. Gradually beat in confectioners' sugar. Spread between layers and over top and sides of cake. Store in the refrigerator. **Yield:** 12 servings.

Double-Crust Pear Pie

(Pictured on page 128)

Thanksgiving dinner guests will be pleasantly surprised to see this pretty dessert on the table instead of the usual apple pie. The amount of anise flavor is just right.
—Faye Creech, Moore, Oklahoma

2/3 cup sugar
1/4 cup cornstarch
2 teaspoons grated lemon peel
1-1/2 teaspoons crushed aniseed
1-1/2 teaspoons lemon juice
5 cups thinly sliced peeled ripe
    pears (about 5 medium)
Pastry for double-crust pie
    (9 inches)
GLAZE:
1/2 cup confectioners' sugar
2 to 3 teaspoons lemon juice

In a large bowl, combine the sugar, cornstarch, lemon peel, aniseed and lemon juice. Add pears and toss gently.

Line a 9-in. pie plate with bottom pastry; trim even with edge of plate. Add filling. Roll out remaining pastry to fit top of pie; place over filling. Trim, seal and flute edges. Cut slits in top.

Bake at 400° for 40-45 minutes or until filling is bubbly and pears are tender. Cover edges with foil during the last 20 minutes to prevent overbrowning. Combine glaze ingredients; gently spread over hot pie. Cool completely on a wire rack. Store in the refrigerator. **Yield:** 6-8 servings.

White Chocolate Bread Pudding

(Pictured at right)

A delectable white chocolate sauce is the crowning touch on servings of this comforting cinnamon bread pudding.
—*Kathy Rundle, Fond du Lac, Wisconsin*

16 slices cinnamon bread, crusts
    removed and cubed
1 cup dried cranberries
3/4 cup vanilla *or* white chips
3/4 cup chopped pecans
1/4 cup butter, melted
6 eggs
4 cups milk
3/4 cup plus 1 tablespoon sugar,
    divided
1 teaspoon vanilla extract
1/4 teaspoon ground cinnamon
1/4 teaspoon ground allspice
SAUCE:
2/3 cup heavy whipping cream
2 tablespoons butter
8 squares (1 ounce *each*) white
    baking chocolate, chopped

In a greased 13-in. x 9-in. x 2-in. baking dish, layer half of the bread cubes, cranberries, vanilla chips and pecans. Repeat layers. Drizzle with butter.

In a large mixing bowl, beat the eggs, milk, 3/4 cup sugar, vanilla, cinnamon and allspice; pour over bread mixture. Let stand for 15-30 minutes.

Sprinkle with remaining sugar. Bake, uncovered, at 375° for 55-65 minutes or until a knife inserted near the center comes out clean. (Cover loosely with foil during the last 15 minutes if top browns too quickly.)

In a small saucepan, bring cream and butter to a boil. Add chocolate and remove from the heat (do not stir). Let stand for 5 minutes; whisk until smooth. Serve with warm bread pudding. **Yield:** 12 servings (1-1/2 cups sauce).

Glazed Pfeffernuesse

Our Test Kitchen's version of the classic German cookie is nice to have on hand throughout the holiday season.
They stay fresh—and become more intense in flavor—when stored in an airtight container for weeks.

1-1/4 cups butter, softened
1-1/4 cups packed brown sugar
  3/4 cup molasses
  1/2 cup water
    1 teaspoon anise extract
    6 cups cake flour
  1/2 teaspoon baking soda
  1/2 teaspoon salt
1-1/2 teaspoons ground cinnamon
  1/2 teaspoon ground allspice
  1/2 teaspoon ground cloves
  1/4 teaspoon ground nutmeg
  1/4 teaspoon ground mace
  1/8 teaspoon pepper
  1/8 teaspoon ground cardamom
    2 cups finely chopped nuts

GLAZE:
    1 cup confectioners' sugar
    3 tablespoons milk
  1/4 teaspoon vanilla extract
Additional confectioners' sugar

In a large mixing bowl, cream butter and brown sugar. Beat in the molasses, water and extract. Combine the flour, baking soda, salt and spices; gradually add to creamed mixture and mix well. Stir in nuts. Cover and refrigerate for 1 hour.

Roll dough into 1-in. balls. Place 2 in. apart on greased baking sheets. Bake at 375° for 10-12 minutes or until golden brown.

For glaze, in a shallow bowl, combine the confectioners' sugar, milk and vanilla. Place additional confectioners' sugar in another shallow bowl. Dip tops of warm cookies in glaze, then dip in confectioners' sugar. Cool on a wire rack. Store in an airtight container. **Yield:** about 10 dozen.

Editor's Note: This recipe does not use eggs.

Autumn Cake

A dusting of confectioners' sugar is all that's needed on top of this spice cake.
I've given this cake as a gift more times than I can count!
—Joyce Spiegelhoff, Ingelside, Texas

    2 cups sugar
    1 cup vegetable oil
    2 jars (3-1/2 ounces *each*) plum
      with apples baby food
    3 eggs
    2 cups all-purpose flour
1-1/2 teaspoons baking soda
1-1/2 teaspoons ground cinnamon
1-1/2 teaspoons ground cloves
    1 teaspoon salt
    1 cup chopped nuts
Confectioners' sugar, optional

In a large mixing bowl, beat the sugar, oil, baby food and eggs until well blended. Combine the flour, baking soda, cinnamon, cloves and salt; gradually beat into sugar mixture. Fold in nuts.

Spoon into a greased 10-in. fluted tube pan. Bake at 350° for 40-50 minutes or until a toothpick inserted near the center comes out clean. Cool for 10 minutes before removing from pan to a wire rack to cool completely. Dust with confectioners' sugar if desired. **Yield:** 12-16 servings.

Pumpkin Ice Cream

(Pictured at right)

Folks who favor the flavor of pumpkin really need to try this spiced ice cream from our own home economists. But be prepared to make more!

2 cups heavy whipping cream
1-1/2 cups canned pumpkin
1 cup packed brown sugar
1 teaspoon ground ginger
1 teaspoon ground cinnamon
1 teaspoon vanilla extract
1/4 teaspoon salt
1/8 teaspoon ground cloves

In a large bowl, combine all ingredients; stir until the sugar is dissolved. Fill cylinder of ice cream freezer two-thirds full; freeze according to manufacturer's directions.

Refrigerate remaining mixture until ready to freeze. Transfer to a freezer container; freeze for 2-4 hours before serving. **Yield:** about 1 quart.

SPICE SAVVY

STORE SPICES in tightly closed glass or heavy-duty plastic containers in a cool, dry place. Avoid storing them in direct sunlight, over the stove or near other heat sources.

For best flavor, keep ground spices for up to 6 months. They can be used if they are older, but the flavors may not be as intense. Whole spices can be stored for 1 to 2 years.

The following spices are commonly used in baked goods:

Allspice. Available as whole, dried berries or ground. Blend of cinnamon, cloves and nutmeg.

Aniseed. Available as oval, greenish-brown seeds. Licorice-like flavor.

Cardamom. Available as green pods, brownish-black seeds or ground. Sweet, spicy flavor and slightly pungent.

Cinnamon. Available as sticks or ground. Sweet and pungent flavor.

Cloves. Available whole or ground. Pungent, medicinal, sweet flavor.

Ginger. Available as fresh root, crystallized or ground. Pungent, sweet, spicy, hot flavor.

Mace. Available ground. Nutmeg-like flavor.

Nutmeg. Available whole or ground. Sweet, spicy flavor.

Gingersnap-Pumpkin Dessert

(Pictured on page 129)

I've never quite gotten the hang of making a good pie crust. So I came up with this recipe, featuring a cake mix crust. The creamy pumpkin filling is a nice contrast to the crunchy topping.
— Brigitte Mazure, Wheeling, West Virginia

1 package (18-1/4 ounces) yellow cake mix, *divided*
1 cup crushed gingersnap cookies
1/2 cup butter, melted
1 egg, lightly beaten
FILLING:
1 package (8 ounces) cream cheese, softened
2/3 cup packed brown sugar
3 eggs, lightly beaten
1 can (29 ounces) solid-pack pumpkin
1/4 cup milk
2 teaspoons ground cinnamon
2 teaspoons vanilla extract
TOPPING:
1/2 cup crushed gingersnap cookies
1/4 cup sugar
1/2 cup cold butter
1 cup chopped pecans
Additional gingersnap cookies, halved, optional

Set aside 1 cup cake mix for topping. In a small bowl, combine gingersnap crumbs and remaining cake mix; stir in butter and egg. Press onto the bottom of a greased 13-in. x 9-in. x 2-in. baking dish; set aside.

For filling, in a large mixing bowl, beat cream cheese and brown sugar until smooth. Beat in eggs. Add the pumpkin, milk, cinnamon and vanilla; mix well. Pour over crust.

For topping, in a small bowl, combine the gingersnap crumbs, sugar and reserved cake mix; cut in butter until crumbly. Stir in pecans. Sprinkle over filling.

Bake at 325° for 70-75 minutes or until filling is set and a thermometer inserted near the center reads 160°. Cool on a wire rack for 1-1/2 hours. If desired, garnish each serving with a gingersnap half. Store in the refrigerator. **Yield:** 15-18 servings.

Icebox Spice Cookies

When cooled, these slice-and-bake cookies become very crispy. They're wonderful with coffee or milk.
— Caroline Smid, Winnipeg, Manitoba

1-1/4 cups butter, softened
1 cup sugar
1 cup packed brown sugar
2 eggs
3-3/4 cups all-purpose flour
2 teaspoons ground cinnamon
1 teaspoon baking soda
1 teaspoon salt
1 teaspoon ground cloves
1 teaspoon ground allspice

In a large mixing bowl, cream butter and sugars. Add eggs, one at a time, beating well after each addition. Combine the flour, cinnamon, baking soda, salt, cloves and allspice; gradually add to creamed mixture.

Shape into three 6-in. rolls; wrap each in plastic wrap. Refrigerate for at least 2 hours or until firm.

Unwrap dough and cut into 1/4-in. slices. Place 2 in. apart on greased baking sheets. Bake at 350° for 8-10 minutes or until lightly browned around the edges. Cool for 1-2 minutes before removing to wire racks. **Yield:** 6 dozen.

Caramel Apple Trifle

(Pictured at right)

Trifles are terrific desserts because they're made in advance and feed a crowd. This caramel apple version appeals to kids of all ages.
—Joanne Wright, Niles, Michigan

3 tablespoons butter
4 cups chopped peeled apples (about 5 medium)
1 cup chopped walnuts
1/2 cup packed brown sugar
1 teaspoon apple pie spice, *divided*
1 package (8 ounces) cream cheese, softened
1 jar (12-1/4 ounces) caramel ice cream topping, *divided*
1 carton (12 ounces) frozen whipped topping, thawed, *divided*
2 loaves (10-3/4 ounces *each*) frozen pound cake, thawed and cut into 1-inch cubes
Additional apple pie spice, optional

In a large skillet, melt butter over medium heat. Stir in the apples, walnuts, brown sugar and 1/2 teaspoon apple pie spice. Cook and stir for 8-10 minutes or until apples are tender.

In a large mixing bowl, beat cream cheese until smooth. Beat in 1/2 cup caramel topping and remaining apple pie spice. Fold in 2 cups whipped topping.

In a 3-1/2-qt. trifle bowl or glass serving bowl, layer a third of the cake cubes, cream cheese mixture and apple mixture. Repeat layers twice. Dollop with remaining whipped topping and drizzle with remaining caramel topping. Sprinkle with additional apple pie spice if desired. Cover and refrigerate for at least 1 hour before serving. **Yield:** 14 servings.

Pear-Pecan Crisp with Lemon Sauce

"Pear-adise on a plate" is a great way to describe this fruity crisp.
—Lisa Varner, Greenville, South Carolina

5 cups sliced peeled ripe pears
  (about 5 medium)
1 tablespoon sugar
2/3 cup old-fashioned oats
1/3 cup all-purpose flour
1/3 cup packed brown sugar
1/4 teaspoon ground cinnamon
1/4 cup cold butter
1/3 cup chopped pecans
SAUCE:
1/4 cup sugar
2 teaspoons cornstarch
1/2 cup water
1 egg yolk, beaten
1 tablespoon butter
1 tablespoon lemon juice
1/4 teaspoon grated lemon peel

Place pears in a greased 8-in. square baking dish; sprinkle with sugar. In a small bowl, combine the oats, flour, brown sugar and cinnamon. Cut in butter until mixture resembles coarse crumbs; stir in pecans. Sprinkle over pears. Bake at 350° for 30-35 minutes or until bubbly.

Meanwhile, in a small saucepan, combine the sugar, cornstarch and water. Cook and stir over medium-high heat until thickened and bubbly. Reduce heat; cook and stir 2 minutes longer.

Remove from the heat. Stir a small amount of hot mixture into egg yolk; return all to the pan, stirring constantly. Bring to a gentle boil; cook and stir 2 minutes longer. Remove from the heat; stir in the butter, lemon juice and peel. Serve with warm pear crisp. **Yield:** 6 servings.

Ginger Pound Cake

When I need to take a cake to an autumn potluck dinner, this is the recipe I reach for.
The tall cake looks so attractive and tastes great.
—Lucile Cline, Wichita, Kansas

1 cup butter, softened
1-1/2 cups sugar
3/4 cup packed brown sugar
5 eggs
2 tablespoons minced fresh
  gingerroot
2 teaspoons vanilla extract
3 cups all-purpose flour
1 teaspoon baking powder
1/4 teaspoon baking soda
1/4 teaspoon salt
1 cup milk
1/2 cup chopped crystallized
  ginger

In a large mixing bowl, cream butter and sugars until light and fluffy. Add eggs, one at a time, beating well after each addition. Stir in ginger and vanilla. Combine the flour, baking powder, baking soda and salt; add to creamed mixture alternately with milk. Beat just until combined. Stir in crystallized ginger.

Pour into a greased and floured 10-in. tube pan. Bake at 350° for 65-70 minutes or until a toothpick inserted near the center comes out clean. Cool for 10 minutes before removing from pan to a wire rack to cool completely. **Yield:** 12-16 servings.

Maple Ginger Fudge

(Pictured at right)

I combine two fall favorites—maple and ginger—in this sweet fudge.
—Steve Westphal
Milwaukee, Wisconsin

2 teaspoons plus 2 tablespoons
  butter, *divided*
2 cups sugar
2/3 cup heavy whipping cream
2 tablespoons light corn syrup
1/4 teaspoon ground ginger
1/2 teaspoon maple flavoring
1/2 cup chopped walnuts

Line a 9-in. x 5-in. x 3-in. loaf pan with foil and grease the foil with 1 teaspoon butter; set aside. Butter the sides of a small heavy saucepan with 1 teaspoon butter; add the sugar, cream, corn syrup and ginger. Bring to a boil over medium heat, stirring constantly. Reduce heat; cook until a candy thermometer reads 238° (soft-ball stage), stirring occasionally.

Remove from the heat. Add maple flavoring and remaining butter (do not stir). Cool to 110° without stirring. With a portable mixer, beat on low speed for 1-2 minutes or until fudge begins to thicken. With a clean dry wooden spoon, stir in walnuts until fudge begins to lose its gloss, about 5 minutes.

Spread into prepared pan. Refrigerate until firm, about 30 minutes. Using foil, lift fudge out of pan. Discard foil; cut fudge into 1-in. squares. Store in an airtight container in the refrigerator. **Yield:** 1-1/4 pounds.

Editor's Note: We recommend that you test your candy thermometer before each use by bringing water to a boil; the thermometer should read 212°. Adjust your recipe temperature up or down based on your test.

GET TO KNOW GINGER

GINGER POUND CAKE (recipe at left) uses fresh gingerroot and crystallized ginger, both of which can be found in your grocery store's produce department.

Look for fresh gingerroot that has smooth, wrinkle-free skin and a spicy fragrance. Fresh, unpeeled gingerroot should be wrapped in a paper towel, placed in a plastic bag and refrigerated for up to 3 weeks. It can also be tightly wrapped and frozen for up to 2 months.

Crystallized ginger, also known as candied ginger, has been cooked in a sugar syrup until tender, then coated with granulated sugar. Store it in an airtight container in a cool, dark place for up to 3 months.

EASTER
Gatherings

Celebrate the arrival of the Easter season with a sit-down
dinner featuring a sweet-and-spicy spiral-sliced ham,
pasta spinach salad and home-baked bread. Or are
you looking to liven up your ordinary Easter dinner?
Then turn to this chapter's light-and-lively
entrees. Spring is the perfect time to put aside the
heavy desserts you served all winter and to bring out
sunny sweets showcasing fresh, fruity lemon!

Easter Gatherings

Easter Dinner Features Ham

THE wonderful aroma of a ham baking in the oven inevitably calls Easter guests into the kitchen… and triggers requests for a little taste as the regal entree is being carved.

With a sweet berry jam and slightly spicy peppers, Raspberry-Chipotle Glazed Ham is an irresistible main dish for this special spring celebration.

Instead of an ordinary tossed salad, prepare Caramelized Onion-Tortellini Spinach Salad, which pleasantly partners both pasta and greens.

For ease of preparation, you just can't beat Peppery Parmesan Bread. The dough is conveniently prepared in a bread machine, and then baked in the oven. (All recipes shown at right.)

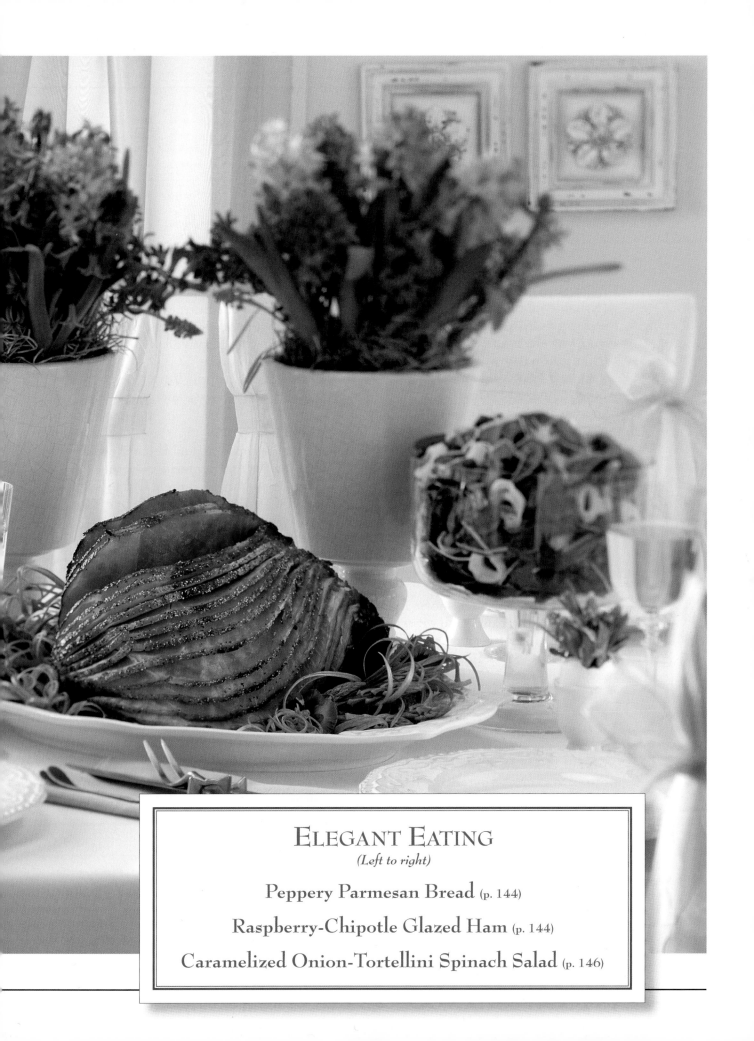

ELEGANT EATING
(Left to right)

Peppery Parmesan Bread (p. 144)

Raspberry-Chipotle Glazed Ham (p. 144)

Caramelized Onion-Tortellini Spinach Salad (p. 146)

EASTER DINNER AGENDA

A Few Weeks Before:
- Prepare two grocery lists—one for non-perishable items to purchase now and one for perishable items to purchase a few days before Easter.
- Order a bone-in fully cooked spiral-sliced ham (9 to 10 pounds).
- Make Peppery Parmesan Bread; cool. Freeze in a heavy-duty resealable plastic bag.
- Purchase the egg cups for Flowering Egg Shells (see page 147) and vases for the centerpiece.

Two to Three Days Before:
- Buy remaining grocery items, including the ham.
- Prepare Pineapple Compote; cover and chill.
- Boil and peel pearl onions for Snap Peas 'n' Pearl Onions. Cover and refrigerate.
- Make sauce for Raspberry-Chipotle Glazed Ham. Store in a covered container; chill.

The Day Before:
- Set the table.
- For Caramelized Onion-Tortellini Spinach Salad, make caramelized onions and cook tortellini. Remove stems from spinach. Store in separate covered containers and refrigerate.

- Purchase flowers for the Flowering Egg Shells and centerpiece vases.
- Assemble Prosciutto-Wrapped Apricots. Cover and store in the refrigerator.
- Thaw the Peppery Parmesan Bread at room temperature.
- Make the Pineapple Torte (do not garnish). Cover loosely and refrigerate.

Easter Day:
- In the morning, assemble the Flowering Egg Shells and centerpiece vases.
- Bake Raspberry-Chipotle Glazed Ham, brushing with sauce and sprinkling with pepper as directed.
- Before guests arrive, bake Prosciutto-Wrapped Apricots.
- If desired, wrap the Peppery Parmesan Bread in foil and reheat in a 350° oven for 10-15 minutes. Slice and set out with butter.
- Make Snap Peas 'n' Pearl Onions.
- Reheat caramelized onions over low heat. Stir in vinegar, salt and pepper; cook as directed. Assemble the salad.
- Serve slices of Raspberry-Chipotle Glazed Ham with sauce.
- If desired, reheat Pineapple Compote and serve alongside ham.
- For dessert, garnish Pineapple Torte; slice and serve.

Pineapple Torte

(Pictured at right)

*This tall, two-layer cake makes quite an
impression at the end of a holiday meal.
A fluffy frosting is the crowning touch.*
—Marie Hattrup, The Dalles, Oregon

1/3 cup butter-flavored shortening
1/3 cup butter, softened
1-3/4 cups sugar
  2 eggs
  1 teaspoon vanilla extract
1/2 teaspoon almond extract
  3 cups cake flour
2-1/2 teaspoons baking powder
  1 teaspoon salt
1-1/4 cups milk
FILLING:
  2 cans (8 ounces *each*) crushed
    pineapple
  2 tablespoons sugar
  1 tablespoon cornstarch
1/4 teaspoon salt
  1 cup milk
  4 egg yolks, beaten
  1 teaspoon grated lemon peel
FROSTING:
 1-1/2 cups sugar
  2 egg whites
  1 tablespoon light corn syrup
1/4 teaspoon cream of tartar
  1 teaspoon vanilla extract
Edible orchids and pansies and
  fresh mint leaves, optional

In a large mixing bowl, cream shortening, butter and sugar. Add eggs,
one at a time, beating well after each.
Beat in extracts. Combine the flour,
baking powder and salt; add to
creamed mixture alternately with milk.

Pour into two greased and floured 9-in. round baking
pans. Bake at 350° for 30-35 minutes or until a toothpick inserted near the center comes out clean. Cool for 10 minutes;
remove from pans to wire racks to cool completely.

Drain pineapple, reserving 1/3 cup juice for frosting; set
pineapple aside. For filling, in a large saucepan, combine the
sugar, cornstarch and salt. Gradually stir in milk until
smooth. Bring to a boil over medium heat, stirring constantly. Remove from the heat. Stir a small amount of hot
filling into egg yolks; return all to the pan, stirring constantly. Bring to a gentle boil; cook and stir for 2 minutes.
Remove from the heat; stir in pineapple and lemon peel.
Transfer to a bowl; cover and refrigerate until chilled.

For frosting, in another large saucepan, combine the sugar, egg whites, corn syrup, cream of tartar and reserved
pineapple juice. With a portable mixer, beat on low speed
over low heat for 1 minute. Continue beating on low over
low heat until frosting reaches 160°, about 8-10 minutes.

Pour into a large mixing bowl; add vanilla. Beat on high
until stiff peaks form, about 7 minutes. Spread filling between cake layers. Spread frosting over the top. Garnish
with flowers and mint if desired. **Yield:** 12 servings.

Editor's Note: Make sure to properly identify flowers before picking. Double-check that they're edible and have not
been treated with chemicals.

Raspberry-Chipotle Glazed Ham

(Pictured on page 141)

Looking to liven up your same-old holiday ham? Try this recipe, which features a sweet and spicy sauce.
—*Mary Lou Wayman, Salt Lake City, Utah*

1 bone-in fully cooked spiral-
  sliced ham (9 to 10 pounds)
2-1/4 cups seedless raspberry jam
3 tablespoons white vinegar
3 chipotle peppers in adobo
  sauce, drained, seeded and
  minced
3 to 4 garlic cloves, minced
1 tablespoon coarsely ground
  pepper

Place ham on a rack in a shallow roasting pan. Bake, uncovered, at 325° for 2 to 2-1/2 hours or until a meat thermometer reads 130°.

In a small saucepan, combine the jam, vinegar, peppers and garlic. Bring to a boil. Reduce heat; simmer, uncovered, for 5 minutes.

Brush some of the sauce over ham. Bake 20 minutes longer or until meat thermometer reads 140°, brushing twice with sauce. Sprinkle pepper over ham. Serve with remaining sauce. **Yield:** 16-20 servings.

Peppery Parmesan Bread

(Pictured on page 140)

I rely on my bread machine to make the dough for this rustic bread.
Serve slices with olive oil for dipping or with butter.
—*Mark Morgan, Waterford, Wisconsin*

3/4 cup plus 2 tablespoons warm
  water (70° to 80°)
1 tablespoon olive oil
1/2 teaspoon hot pepper sauce
1/2 cup freshly grated Parmesan
  cheese
1 tablespoon sugar
1 teaspoon pepper
1/2 teaspoon dried basil
1/2 teaspoon dried oregano
1/2 teaspoon salt
2-1/2 cups bread flour
2-1/4 teaspoons active dry yeast
1 tablespoon cold water

In bread machine pan, place the first 11 ingredients in order suggested by manufacturer. Select dough setting (check dough after 5 minutes of mixing; add 1 to 2 tablespoons of water or flour if needed).

When the cycle is completed, turn dough onto a lightly floured surface. Punch down; knead until smooth and elastic, about 5 minutes. Shape into an 8-in. round loaf. Place on a greased baking sheet. Cover and let rise in a warm place until doubled, about 30 minutes.

Slash top of loaf with a sharp knife; brush with cold water. Bake at 400° for 25-30 minutes or until golden brown. Remove to a wire rack to cool. **Yield:** 1 loaf.

Prosciutto-Wrapped Apricots

(Pictured at right)

Our home economists stuff dried apricots with sweetened Mascarpone cheese, then wrap them with prosciutto before baking. The result is an appealing snack for special occasions.

3/4 cup Mascarpone cheese
2 tablespoons confectioners' sugar
1/8 teaspoon white pepper
1 package (6 ounces) dried pitted Mediterranean apricots
12 thin slices prosciutto

In a small bowl, combine the cheese, confectioners' sugar and pepper. Cut a slit in each apricot; fill with cheese mixture.

Cut each slice of prosciutto in half lengthwise; wrap a piece around each apricot and secure with a toothpick.

Place in an ungreased 15-in. x 10-in. x 1-in. baking pan. Bake, uncovered, at 425° for 15-20 minutes or until heated through. Refrigerate leftovers. **Yield:** 2 dozen.

SUBSTITUTION SECRET

CAN'T FIND prosciutto at your grocery store? Regular bacon can be used instead when making Prosciutto-Wrapped Apricots.

Caramelized Onion-Tortellini Spinach Salad

(Pictured on page 141)

Tender tortellini pairs well with crunchy fresh spinach in this innovative salad from our Test Kitchen home economists. Caramelized onions add a flavorful element.

4 cups thinly sliced sweet onions
3 tablespoons butter
3 tablespoons olive oil
2 teaspoons brown sugar
1 package (19 ounces) frozen cheese tortellini
3 tablespoons balsamic vinegar
1/4 teaspoon salt
1/4 teaspoon pepper
1 package (10 ounces) fresh spinach, stems removed and torn
1/3 cup shredded Parmesan cheese

In a large skillet over medium-low heat, cook onions in butter and oil for 5 minutes or until tender. Add brown sugar; cook over low heat for 20 minutes or until onions are golden brown, stirring frequently. Meanwhile, cook tortellini according to package directions.

Add the vinegar, salt and pepper to onion mixture. Bring to a boil. Reduce heat; cook 1-2 minutes longer or until syrupy.

Drain tortellini and rinse in cold water. In a large serving bowl, combine the tortellini, spinach and Parmesan cheese. Add onion mixture and toss to coat. **Yield:** 12 servings.

Snap Peas 'n' Pearl Onions

Pearl onions add a little "pop" to sugar snap peas in this side dish that goes nicely with a variety of entrees.
—Carol Fischer, Hartland, Wisconsin

4 cups water
1-1/2 cups fresh pearl onions (about 6 ounces)
5 cups fresh *or* frozen sugar snap peas
2 tablespoons butter
2 teaspoons lemon juice
1 teaspoon honey
1/4 teaspoon salt
1/4 teaspoon dill weed
1/8 teaspoon pepper

In a large saucepan, bring water to a boil. Add onions; boil, uncovered, for 3 minutes. Drain and rinse in cold water; peel and set aside.

Add 1 in. of water to a large skillet. Add peas; bring to a boil. Reduce heat. Cover and simmer for 5-6 minutes or until crisp-tender; drain.

Add the onions, butter, lemon juice, honey, salt, dill and pepper. Cook and stir for 2-3 minutes or until well coated. **Yield:** 6 servings.

Flowering Egg Shells

(Pictured at right)

EASTER dinner guests will shell out countless compliments when they catch sight of these flower-filled "vases" made from ordinary eggs.

To hatch these cute cups, crack the narrow end of a raw egg and break away a small portion.

Empty the contents of the egg. Rinse the shell and let dry.

Create a larger opening by breaking away more of the shell. Place a small piece of wet floral foam inside the shell. Fill with water. Insert small, fresh spring flowers (such as grape hyacinth and agapanthus) into the floral foam. Set the flower-filled shell in egg cup.

For our centerpiece (as shown on page 140), we mimicked these miniature flowering egg shells by placing greens and bigger blooms of hyacinth in larger vases.

Pineapple Compote

Our home economists came up with this slightly sweet compote to complement slices of spicy Raspberry-Chipotle Glazed Ham.

6 cups cubed fresh pineapple
2/3 cup pear nectar *or*
   unsweetened pineapple juice
1/3 cup packed brown sugar
1/3 cup raspberry vinegar
1/2 teaspoon ground allspice

In a large saucepan, combine all ingredients. Bring to a boil over medium-low heat. Reduce heat; simmer, uncovered, for 10 minutes or until slightly thickened, stirring frequently. Transfer to a bowl. Serve warm or chilled. **Yield:** 4 cups.

Special Springtime Entrees

WHEN the spring season arrives, cooks leap at the chance to set aside the recipes they've been preparing all winter and to try light 'n' lively dishes.

Whether you need new entree ideas for family dinners or for an Easter celebration, this chapter is blooming with innovative ideas!

Seafood en Croute is a from-the-sea favorite featuring scallops and salmon surrounded by a flaky pastry crust.

Add a little dazzle to Easter dinner by serving Rosemary-Rubbed Lamb Chops.

Is a bright-eyed brunch on tap? Guests will be impressed when you dish out delicious Spinach Chicken Crepes. (All recipes shown at right.)

DELIGHTFUL MAIN DISHES
(Clockwise from top)

Seafood en Croute (p. 150)

Rosemary-Rubbed Lamb Chops (p. 150)

Spinach Chicken Crepes (p. 152)

Seafood en Croute

(Pictured on page 149)

*I'm a busy mom with little time to spend in the kitchen. So when I'm given a recipe like this
that's impressive, easy and tasty, I know I have a winner!*
—Alexandra Armitage, Nottingham, New Hampshire

1 package (17.3 ounces) frozen
   puff pastry, thawed
4 salmon fillets (6 ounces *each*)
1/2 pound fresh sea *or* bay
   scallops, finely chopped
1/3 cup heavy whipping cream
2 green onions, chopped
1 tablespoon minced fresh
   parsley
1/2 teaspoon minced fresh dill
1/4 teaspoon salt
1/8 teaspoon pepper
1 egg white
1 egg, beaten

On a lightly floured surface, roll each pastry sheet into a 12-in. x 10-in. rectangle. Cut each sheet into four 6-in. x 5-in. rectangles. Place a fillet in the center of four rectangles.

In a small bowl, combine the scallops, cream, onions, parsley, dill, salt and pepper. In a small mixing bowl, beat egg white on medium speed until soft peaks form; fold into scallop mixture. Spoon about 1/2 cup over each salmon fillet.

Top each with a pastry rectangle and crimp to seal. Place in a greased 15-in. x 10-in. x 1-in. baking pan; brush with beaten egg. Bake at 400° for 20-25 minutes or until a thermometer reads 160°. **Yield:** 4 servings.

Rosemary-Rubbed Lamb Chops

(Pictured on page 149)

*These lamb chops from our Test Kitchen are a delicious treat.
They're moist, tender and flavorful...making them a perfect choice for company.*

2 frenched racks of lamb
   (1-1/2 pounds *each*)
2 tablespoons olive oil
2 tablespoons Dijon mustard
4 garlic cloves, minced
1 tablespoon minced fresh
   rosemary
1 tablespoon minced fresh
   marjoram
1 teaspoon soy sauce
1/2 teaspoon salt
1/4 teaspoon pepper

With a sharp knife, cut each rack of lamb into individual chops. In a small bowl, combine the remaining ingredients. Rub over both sides of chops; place on a rack in a shallow roasting pan. Cover and refrigerate for 2 hours.

Bake, uncovered, at 400° for 14-16 minutes or until meat reaches desired doneness (for medium-rare, a meat thermometer should read 145°; medium, 160°; well-done, 170°). **Yield:** 4-6 servings.

Gorgonzola Chicken Penne

(Pictured at right)

I came up with this recipe in my attempt to re-create a meal at a European restaurant. The hearty Gorgonzola sauce pairs well with the chicken and pasta.
—*C.W. Steve Stevenson*
Newfoundland, Pennsylvania

> 2 cups uncooked penne pasta
> 2 cups fresh broccoli florets
> 1 tablespoon water
> 1 pound boneless skinless
>   chicken breasts, cut into
>   1-inch cubes
> 9 tablespoons butter, *divided*
> 1 large onion, chopped
> 6 tablespoons all-purpose flour
> 2 cups chicken broth
> 3/4 cup white wine *or* additional
>   chicken broth
> 1-1/2 cups (6 ounces) crumbled
>   Gorgonzola cheese
> Pepper to taste

Cook pasta according to package directions. Meanwhile, place broccoli and water in a small microwave-safe bowl. Cover and microwave on high for 2 to 2-1/2 minutes or until crisp-tender. Set aside.

In a large skillet, saute chicken in 3 tablespoons butter until no longer pink. Remove and keep warm. In the same skillet, saute onion in remaining butter until tender. Stir in flour until blended. Gradually add broth and wine or additional broth. Bring to a boil; cook and stir for 2 minutes or until thickened. Reduce heat to low; stir in cheese until blended.

Drain the pasta and broccoli; add to the onion mixture. Add the chicken; heat through. Season with pepper. **Yield:** 6 servings.

SHOESTRING SWEET POTATOES

ON page 149, Rosemary-Rubbed Lamb Chops (recipe at left) are shown with Shoestring Sweet Potatoes. Here's how to make them:

Peel 3 large sweet potatoes; julienne into 3-in. x 1/4-in. strips. In an electric skillet or deep-fat fryer, heat oil to 375°. Fry potatoes, a few at a time, for 3-4 minutes or until golden brown. Drain on paper towels. (For crispier potatoes, after draining them on paper towels, fry shoestrings 3-4 minutes longer or until deep golden brown. Drain on paper towels.) Sprinkle with salt.

Spinach Chicken Crepes

(Pictured on page 148)

I made this dish at a cooking class several years ago. These spinach- and chicken-filled crepes are topped with a tasty mushroom sauce.
—*Nina De Witt, Aurora, Ohio*

    1 **egg, beaten**
    1 **cup milk**
  3/4 **cup all-purpose flour**
  1/8 **teaspoon salt**
SAUCE:
    2 **cups sliced fresh mushrooms**
  1/2 **cup sliced leek (white portion only)**
    1 **medium carrot, shredded**
  1/2 **cup water**
    2 **tablespoons cornstarch**
  3/4 **cup evaporated milk**
  1/4 **teaspoon salt**
  1/8 **teaspoon pepper**
  1/2 **cup shredded cheddar cheese**
    2 **tablespoons sherry *or* chicken broth**
FILLING:
    1 **package (10 ounces) frozen chopped spinach, thawed and squeezed dry**
    2 **cups cubed cooked chicken**

For crepe batter, in a small mixing bowl, combine egg and milk. Add flour and salt; mix well. Cover and refrigerate for 1 hour.

Heat a lightly greased 6-in. nonstick skillet; pour 2 tablespoons batter into the center of skillet. Lift and tilt pan to coat bottom evenly. Cook until top appears dry; turn and cook 15-20 seconds longer. Remove to a wire rack. Repeat with remaining batter, greasing skillet as needed. When cool, stack crepes with waxed paper or paper towels in between.

For sauce, in a large saucepan, bring the vegetables and water to a boil. Reduce heat; cover and simmer for 5 minutes or until tender. In a small bowl, combine the cornstarch, evaporated milk, salt and pepper until smooth; stir into vegetables. Bring to a boil; cook and stir for 2 minutes or until thickened. Reduce heat to low. Add cheese and sherry or broth; stir until cheese is melted. Remove from the heat.

Combine the spinach, chicken and 1 cup sauce; spread 1/4 cupful down the center of each crepe. Roll up and place in a greased 13-in. x 9-in. x 2-in. baking dish. Spoon remaining sauce over crepes. Cover and bake at 375° for 20-25 minutes or until heated through. **Yield:** 6 servings.

Veal Chops With Mustard-Sage Crust

(Pictured at right)

Our home economists use stone-ground mustard to flavor moist veal chops that simply bake in the oven for a quick-and-easy entree.

4 veal chops (8 ounces *each*)
1/2 teaspoon pepper
1/4 teaspoon salt
1 cup soft bread crumbs
3 tablespoons stone-ground mustard
2 tablespoons minced fresh sage
2 garlic cloves, minced

Sprinkle veal chops on both sides with pepper and salt. Place bread crumbs in a shallow bowl. Combine the mustard, sage and garlic; spread over one side of each chop, then dip into bread crumbs.

Place chops, coated side up, on a rack in a shallow roasting pan. Bake at 450° for 25-30 minutes or until a meat thermometer reads 160°. **Yield:** 4 servings.

Garlic-Lime Sea Bass

I was a chef on a dive boat, and this was one of my favorite ways to serve our fresh catch.
—Peg Nelson, Islamorada, Florida

1 whole garlic bulb
1 teaspoon olive oil
1/4 cup butter, cubed
1 large onion, chopped
2 to 3 tablespoons lime juice
1 tablespoon spicy brown mustard
1/4 teaspoon salt
1/4 teaspoon pepper
4 sea bass *or* grouper fillets (8 ounces *each*)

Remove papery outer skin from garlic (do not peel or separate cloves). Cut top off of bulb. Brush with oil. Wrap in heavy-duty foil. Bake at 425° for 30-35 minutes or until softened. Cool for 10-15 minutes.

Reduce heat to 350°. In a small saucepan, melt butter. Squeeze softened garlic into pan. Stir in the onion, lime juice, mustard, salt and pepper. Cook and stir over medium heat until onion is tender.

Arrange the fillets in an ungreased 11-in. x 7-in. x 2-in. baking dish; top with onion mixture. Bake, uncovered, for 30-35 minutes or until fish flakes easily with a fork. **Yield:** 4 servings.

Artichoke 'n' Fennel Lasagna

This lasagna is so full of different flavors and textures that you'll never miss the meat.
—*Bev Jones, Brunswick, Missouri*

2 cups thinly sliced fennel bulb
  (about 1 large)
2 tablespoons olive oil
1 jar (12 ounces) marinated
  artichoke hearts, drained and
  chopped
1 jar (10 ounces) prepared pesto
1 cup Alfredo sauce
2 cups (8 ounces) shredded
  Italian cheese blend
1 cup (4 ounces) crumbled
  goat cheese
1 cup grated Parmesan cheese
1 jar (26 ounces) meatless
  spaghetti sauce, *divided*
9 lasagna noodles, cooked
  and drained

1 jar (16 ounces) roasted sweet red peppers, drained
2-1/2 teaspoons Italian salad dressing mix

In a large skillet, saute fennel in oil for 10-13 minutes or until tender and lightly browned. Remove from the heat; stir in the artichokes, pesto and Alfredo sauce. Set aside. Combine the cheeses; set aside.

Spread 1 cup spaghetti sauce into a greased 13-in. x 9-in. x 2-in. baking dish. Top with three noodles and the fennel mixture. Layer with three noodles, the cheese mixture and remaining noodles. Combine red peppers and remaining spaghetti sauce; spread over the top. Sprinkle with salad dressing mix.

Cover and bake at 350° for 45 minutes. Uncover; bake 5-10 minutes longer or until bubbly. Let stand for 10 minutes before cutting. **Yield:** 9-12 servings.

Mushroom-Stuffed Pork Tenderloin

Pork tenderloin is filled with a flavorful mushroom stuffing in this pretty entree from our home economists.

1-1/2 cups water
  1/2 ounce dried porcini
    mushrooms
    1 pork tenderloin (1 pound)
  1/2 teaspoon plus 1/8 teaspoon
    salt, *divided*
  1/4 teaspoon plus 1/8 teaspoon
    pepper, *divided*
  1/4 pound bulk pork sausage
2-1/2 cups coarsely chopped fresh
    shiitake mushrooms, *divided*
    1 small onion, chopped
2-1/2 cups soft bread crumbs
    4 teaspoons minced fresh
      parsley, *divided*

3/4 teaspoon minced fresh rosemary *or* 1/4 teaspoon
    dried rosemary, crushed
3/4 teaspoon minced fresh sage *or* 1/4 teaspoon
    rubbed sage
  1 tablespoon butter
  4 teaspoons all-purpose flour
3/4 cup chicken broth

In a small saucepan, bring water and porcini mushrooms to a boil. Remove from the heat; let stand for 30 minutes.

Meanwhile, make a lengthwise slit down the center of the pork to within 1/2 in. of bottom. Open meat so it lies flat; cover with plastic wrap. Flatten to 3/8-in. thickness. Remove plastic wrap; sprinkle with 1/2 teaspoon salt and 1/4 teaspoon pepper. Set aside.

Crumble sausage into a large skillet; add 2 cups shiitake mushrooms and onion. Cook over medium heat until meat is no longer pink. Remove from heat; stir in bread crumbs, 3 teaspoons parsley, rosemary and sage.

Drain porcini mushrooms, reserving liquid. Chop mushrooms; stir into sausage mixture along with 3 tablespoons soaking liquid. Spoon stuffing down center of pork; bring long sides over stuffing to close. Tie at 2-in. intervals with kitchen string; secure ends with toothpicks.

Place on a rack in a shallow roasting pan. Bake, uncovered, at 425° for 30-35 minutes or until a meat thermometer reads 160°. Let stand for 5 minutes before slicing.

For sauce, in a small saucepan, saute remaining shiitake mushrooms in butter until tender. Sprinkle with flour; stir until blended. Gradually add broth and 1/4 cup mushroom soaking liquid. Bring to a boil; cook and stir for 2 minutes or until thickened. Stir in the remaining salt, pepper and parsley. Serve with pork. **Yield:** 4 servings (1 cup sauce).

Baked Pineapple-Pork Kabobs

(Pictured at right)

These tasty kabobs are baked instead of grilled, so you can enjoy them even when the weather doesn't cooperate.
—*Bobbie Keefer, Byers, Colorado*

2 pounds boneless pork loin roast, cubed
1 large green pepper, cut into 1-inch pieces
1 sweet onion, cut into 1-inch pieces
18 medium fresh mushrooms
18 fresh sweet cherries, pitted
18 pineapple chunks
1/2 cup apricot preserves
1/2 cup packed brown sugar
2 tablespoons butter, melted
1 tablespoon unsweetened pineapple juice
1/4 to 1/2 teaspoon ground cloves
Hot cooked rice

Line a 15-in. x 10-in. x 1-in. baking pan with foil and grease the foil. On six metal or soaked wooden skewers, alternately thread the pork, green pepper, onion, mushrooms, cherries and pineapple. Place in prepared pan.

In a small bowl, combine the preserves, brown sugar, butter, pineapple juice and cloves. Brush half of the sauce over kabobs.

Bake at 375° for 15 minutes. Turn kabobs; brush with remaining sauce. Bake 10-15 minutes longer or until meat juices run clear. Serve with rice. **Yield:** 6 servings.

Asparagus Pasta 'n' Salmon

Asparagus and a light lemon dressing make this pasta salad perfect for spring dinners.
—Clara Coulston, Washington Court House, Ohio

1 salmon fillet (1 pound)
1/2 teaspoon salt, *divided*
1/2 teaspoon pepper, *divided*
3 cups uncooked bow tie pasta
1-1/2 pounds fresh asparagus, trimmed and cut into 2-inch pieces
3 medium leeks (white portion only), thinly sliced
2 teaspoons olive oil
2 teaspoons cornstarch
1/2 cup water
1/2 cup chicken broth
3 tablespoons snipped fresh dill *or* 3 teaspoons dill weed
1 tablespoon lemon juice

If grilling the salmon, coat grill rack with nonstick cooking spray before starting the grill. Sprinkle salmon with 1/4 teaspoon each salt and pepper. Grill, covered, over medium heat or broil 4-6 in. from the heat for 12-18 minutes or until fish flakes easily with a fork.

Meanwhile, cook pasta according to package directions. In a large skillet, saute asparagus and leeks in oil until asparagus is crisp-tender. Sprinkle with remaining salt and pepper.

In a small bowl, combine the cornstarch, water, broth, dill and lemon juice until smooth; stir into asparagus mixture. Bring to a boil; cook and stir until thickened and bubbly. Reduce heat; cook and stir 2 minutes longer. Drain the pasta; toss with the asparagus mixture. Serve with salmon. **Yield:** 4 servings.

Beef Tenderloin Supreme

A wine and mushroom gravy gives fantastic flavor to tenderloin slices in this recipe.
—Barb Laabs, Iron Ridge, Wisconsin

4 cups beef broth
2 cups Burgundy wine *or* additional beef broth
1/4 cup tomato paste
4 teaspoons minced fresh parsley
4 teaspoons white wine vinegar
2 teaspoons dried thyme
1 teaspoon pepper
1 beef tenderloin (about 4 pounds), trimmed
2 cups sliced fresh mushrooms
1 medium onion, chopped
6 tablespoons butter
3 tablespoons all-purpose flour

In a large bowl, combine the first seven ingredients. Place beef in a large resealable plastic bag; add half of the marinade. Seal bag and turn to coat. Refrigerate for 8 hours or overnight. Cover and refrigerate remaining marinade for sauce.

Drain and discard marinade. Place tenderloin on a rack in a shallow roasting pan. Bake, uncovered, at 425° for 45-60 minutes or until meat reaches desired doneness (for medium-rare, a meat thermometer should read 145°; medium, 160°; well-done, 170°). Let stand for 10 minutes before slicing.

For sauce, in a large skillet, saute mushrooms and onion in butter until tender. Stir in flour until blended; gradually add the reserved marinade. Bring to a boil; cook and stir for 2 minutes or until thickened. Serve with beef. **Yield:** 12 servings (3 cups sauce).

Roast Pork With Cherry-Almond Glaze

(Pictured at right)

Your pork roast won't dry out during cooking with this sweet cherry glaze. You can also spoon the sauce over slices of baked ham.
—Joan Laurenzo, Johnstown, Ohio

- 1 **boneless whole pork loin roast (3-1/2 pounds)**
- 1 **teaspoon salt**
- 1 **jar (12 ounces) cherry preserves**
- 1/4 **cup cider vinegar**
- 2 **tablespoons light corn syrup**
- 1/4 **teaspoon *each* ground cinnamon, nutmeg and cloves**
- 1/4 **cup slivered almonds**

Sprinkle roast with salt; place on a rack in a shallow roasting pan. Bake, uncovered, at 350° for 30 minutes.

In a small saucepan, bring the preserves, vinegar, corn syrup and spices to a boil. Reduce heat; simmer, uncovered, for 2 minutes. Set aside 3/4 cup for serving. Stir almonds into remaining mixture.

Brush roast with some of the glaze. Bake 35-50 minutes longer or until a meat thermometer reads 160°, brushing frequently with remaining glaze. Let stand for 10 minutes before slicing. Serve with reserved cherry mixture. **Yield:** 10 servings.

Luscious Lemon Desserts

SPRING is the perfect time to put aside the heavy desserts you served all winter and to bring out a sunny selection of sweets featuring fresh, fruity lemon.

When you think lemon desserts, Classic Lemon Meringue Pie is sure to come to mind. Pass plates topped with sky-high pieces and get ready for *mmm*any compliments!

Do you consider fudge to be a sweet saved especially for Christmas? Creamy Lemon Fudge is a lovely, light candy that will be favored by family and friends this Easter season.

For an extra-easy treat, try Tangy Lemon-Nut Tart. It's simple to prepare with refrigerated crescent rolls. (All recipes are shown at right.)

Tart 'n' Tasty
(Clockwise from top left)

Creamy Lemon Fudge (p. 162)

Tangy Lemon-Nut Tart (p. 162)

Classic Lemon Meringue Pie (p. 160)

Classic Lemon Meringue Pie

(Pictured on page 158)

This is the one and only lemon meringue pie recipe you'll ever need.
The flaky and tender from-scratch crust is worth the effort.
—Lee Bremson, Kansas City, Missouri

1-1/3 cups all-purpose flour
  1/2 teaspoon salt
  1/2 cup shortening
    3 tablespoons plus 1/2 cup cold water, *divided*
    2 tablespoons sugar
    1 tablespoon cornstarch
FILLING:
1-1/4 cups sugar
  1/4 cup cornstarch
    3 tablespoons all-purpose flour
  1/4 teaspoon salt
1-1/2 cups water
    3 egg yolks, beaten
    2 tablespoons butter
1-1/2 teaspoons grated lemon peel
  1/3 cup lemon juice
MERINGUE:
    4 egg whites
  3/4 teaspoon vanilla extract
    6 tablespoons sugar

In a small bowl, combine flour and salt; cut in shortening until crumbly. Gradually add 3 tablespoons cold water, tossing with a fork until dough forms a ball. Roll out pastry to fit a 9-in. pie plate. Transfer pastry to pie plate. Trim to 1/2 in. beyond edge of plate; flute edges. Bake at 425° for 12-15 minutes or until lightly browned.

In a small saucepan, combine sugar and cornstarch. Gradually stir in remaining cold water until smooth. Bring to a boil over medium heat; cook and stir for 1 minute or until mixture is thickened and clear. Remove from the heat; set aside to cool.

For filling, in a large saucepan, combine the sugar, cornstarch, flour and salt. Gradually stir in water until smooth. Cook and stir over medium-high heat until thickened and bubbly. Reduce heat; cook and stir 2 minutes longer.

Remove from the heat. Stir a small amount of hot filling into egg yolks; return all to the pan, stirring constantly. Bring to a gentle boil; cook and stir 2 minutes longer. Remove from the heat. Gently stir in butter and lemon peel. Gradually stir in lemon juice just until combined. Pour into the crust.

In a large mixing bowl, beat egg whites and vanilla on medium speed until soft peaks form. Gradually beat in sugar, 1 tablespoon at a time, on high. Beat in reserved cornstarch mixture on high until stiff glossy peaks form and sugar is dissolved. Spread evenly over hot filling, sealing edges to crust.

Bake at 350° for 25 minutes or until meringue is golden. Cool on a wire rack for 1 hour. Refrigerate for at least 3 hours before serving. Refrigerate leftovers. **Yield:** 6-8 servings.

TOPPING A PIE WITH MERINGUE

USE a metal spatula to spread meringue over hot filling. Be sure to seal meringue to edges of the pastry to prevent any shrinkage that may occur while baking.

Lemonade
Layer Cake

(Pictured at right)

*Lemonade concentrate gives both
the cake and frosting fantastic flavor.
I like to garnish this dessert
with lemon slices and mint leaves.*
—Jana Randich, Phoenix, Arizona

  6 tablespoons butter, softened
1-1/3 cups sugar
  3 tablespoons lemonade
     concentrate
  2 tablespoons grated lemon peel
  2 teaspoons vanilla extract
  2 eggs
  2 egg whites
  2 cups all-purpose flour
  1 teaspoon baking powder
1/2 teaspoon baking soda
1/4 teaspoon salt
1-1/4 cups buttermilk
FROSTING:
  1 package (8 ounces) cream
     cheese, softened
  2 tablespoons butter, softened
  2 tablespoons grated lemon peel
  2 teaspoons lemonade
     concentrate
  1 teaspoon vanilla extract
3-1/2 cups confectioners' sugar

In a large mixing bowl, beat butter and sugar until crumbly, about 2 minutes. Beat in the lemonade concentrate, lemon peel and vanilla. Add eggs and egg whites, one at a time, beating well after each addition. Combine the flour, baking powder, baking soda and salt; add to batter alternately with buttermilk.

Pour into two greased and floured 9-in. round baking pans. Bake at 350° for 18-22 minutes or until a toothpick inserted near center comes out clean. Cool 10 minutes before removing from pans to wire racks to cool completely.

For frosting, in a small mixing bowl, beat cream cheese and butter until smooth. Add the lemon peel, lemonade concentrate and vanilla; mix well. Gradually beat in confectioners' sugar until blended.

Spread frosting between layers and over top and sides of cake. Refrigerate for at least 1 hour before serving. Refrigerate leftovers. **Yield:** 16 servings.

Tangy Lemon-Nut Tart

(Pictured on page 159)

I like to top wedges of this tasty tart with whipped cream or ice cream.
Get ready to hand out copies of the recipe!
—*Mary Detweiler, West Farmington, Ohio*

1 can (8 ounces) refrigerated
  crescent rolls
4 eggs
1 cup sugar
2 tablespoons all-purpose flour
4 teaspoons lemon juice
1 tablespoon grated lemon peel
1 cup flaked coconut
1/2 cup chopped blanched
  almonds, hazelnuts *or*
  walnuts
Confectioners' sugar

Separate crescent dough into eight triangles; place in an 11-in. fluted tart pan with a removable bottom with points toward the center. Press dough onto the bottom and up the sides of pan to form a crust; seal perforations. Bake at 350° for 5 minutes.

Meanwhile, in a small mixing bowl, beat the eggs, sugar, flour, lemon juice and peel until blended. Stir in coconut and nuts. Pour over hot crust.

Bake for 20-25 minutes or until lightly browned. Cool on a wire rack. Sprinkle with confectioners' sugar. Refrigerate leftovers. **Yield:** 8 servings.

Creamy Lemon Fudge

(Pictured on page 158)

This is a refreshing change from traditional chocolate fudge. It's a must at our house for Easter.
Pudding mix makes this a breeze to prepare.
—*Darlene Brenden, Salem, Oregon*

1-1/2 teaspoons plus 1/2 cup butter,
  divided
1 package (4.3 ounces)
  cook-and-serve lemon
  pudding mix
1/2 cup milk
3-3/4 cups confectioners' sugar
1 teaspoon lemon extract

Line a 9-in. square pan with foil. Grease the foil with 1-1/2 teaspoons butter; set aside.

In a large heavy saucepan, combine the pudding mix, milk and remaining butter. Cook and stir over medium heat until thickened. Remove from the heat. Beat in confectioners' sugar and extract. Pour into prepared pan; refrigerate until set.

Using foil, lift fudge out of pan. Discard foil; cut fudge into 1-in. squares. Store in the refrigerator. **Yield:** about 1-1/2 pounds.

Chocolaty Lemon Meringue Cups

(Pictured at right)

Tart, homemade lemon curd balances the light meringue cups and rich chocolate ganache in these individual desserts from our home economists.

2 egg whites
1/2 teaspoon vanilla extract
1/4 teaspoon salt
1/4 teaspoon white vinegar
1/2 cup sugar
1/4 cup miniature semisweet chocolate chips
LEMON CURD:
6 eggs
2 cups sugar
1 cup lemon juice (about 4 lemons)
1/2 cup butter, melted
2 tablespoons grated lemon peel
GANACHE:
4 squares (1 ounce *each*) semisweet chocolate, coarsely chopped
1/2 cup heavy whipping cream
1/2 teaspoon vanilla extract

Place egg whites in a small mixing bowl; let stand at room temperature for 30 minutes. Add vanilla, salt and vinegar; beat on medium speed until soft peaks form. Gradually beat in sugar, 1 tablespoon at a time, on high until stiff peaks form. Fold in chocolate chips.

Drop meringue into eight mounds on parchment paper-lined baking sheets. Shape into 3-in. cups with the back of a spoon. Bake at 275° for 45 minutes or until set and dry. Turn oven off; leave meringues in oven for 1-1/2 hours.

Meanwhile, in a large heavy saucepan, combine eggs and sugar. Stir in the lemon juice, butter and lemon peel. Cook and stir over medium-low heat for 15 minutes or until mixture is thickened and reaches 160°. Transfer to a small bowl; refrigerate until chilled.

For ganache, in a small saucepan, melt chocolate with cream over low heat; stir until blended. Remove from the heat; stir in vanilla. Cool slightly.

Just before serving, spoon lemon curd into meringue cups. Drizzle ganache around meringue. **Yield:** 8 servings.

Strawberry Lemon Bavarian

Although I'm a well-seasoned cook, I never tire of simple pleasures.
With few ingredients and easy preparation, this dessert is one of my all-time favorites.
— Dale Lanhardt, Kerrville, Texas

1 envelope unflavored gelatin
3/4 cup cold water
1/2 cup lemonade concentrate
1 package (10 ounces) frozen sweetened sliced strawberries, thawed
1-1/2 teaspoons sugar
1 cup heavy whipping cream, whipped
Fresh strawberries and additional whipped cream, optional

In a small saucepan, sprinkle gelatin over cold water; let stand for 1 minute. Heat over low heat, stirring until gelatin is completely dissolved. Remove from the heat; stir in the lemonade concentrate, strawberries and sugar.

Transfer to a large bowl; cover and refrigerate until partially set, about 50 minutes.

Fold in whipped cream. Spoon into six dessert dishes. Cover and refrigerate for 2 hours or until firm. Garnish with fresh berries and additional whipped cream if desired. **Yield:** 6 servings.

Lemon Pound Cake

If you and your family like lemon, you'll love this impressive-looking cake!
Every bite is both sweet and tart at the same time.
— Traci Wynne, Bear, Delaware

1-1/4 cups butter, softened
1 package (8 ounces) cream cheese, softened
3 cups sugar
6 eggs
3 tablespoons lemon juice
2 teaspoons vanilla extract
1 teaspoon lemon extract
1/2 teaspoon orange extract
2-3/4 cups all-purpose flour
1/8 teaspoon salt

GLAZE:
1 cup confectioners' sugar
1 tablespoon butter, melted
2 tablespoons lemon juice
1 teaspoon grated lemon peel

In a large mixing bowl, cream the butter, cream cheese and sugar until light and fluffy, about 5 minutes. Add eggs, one at a time, beating well after each addition. Stir in lemon juice and extracts. Combine flour and salt; add to creamed mixture just until combined.

Pour into a greased and floured 10-in. tube pan. Bake at 325° for 65-70 minutes or until a toothpick inserted near the center comes out clean. Cool for 10 minutes before removing from pan to a wire rack to cool completely.

In a small bowl, whisk the glaze ingredients; drizzle over cake. **Yield:** 12-16 servings.

Fluted Lemon Cake

(Pictured at right)

My husband says this is the best lemon cake he's ever eaten. Cake mix and lemon gelatin make it a breeze to make.
—Brenda Daugherty, Lake City, Florida

1 package (18-1/4 ounces) yellow cake mix
1 package (3 ounces) lemon gelatin
4 eggs
2/3 cup water
2/3 cup vegetable oil
GLAZE:
1 cup confectioners' sugar
3 tablespoons lemon juice
1 teaspoon grated lemon peel

In a large mixing bowl, combine the cake mix, gelatin, eggs, water and oil. Beat on low speed for 1 minute. Beat on medium for 2 minutes.

Pour into a greased and floured 10-in. fluted tube pan. Bake at 350° for 38-42 minutes or until a toothpick inserted near the center comes out clean. Cool for 10 minutes before removing from pan to a wire rack.

Combine glaze ingredients; drizzle over warm cake. Cool completely before cutting. **Yield:** 12-16 servings.

ZEST SUCCESSFULLY

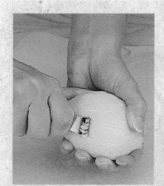

SHREDDED or grated lemon peel, also called lemon zest, can be made using a tool called a zester. Holding the lemon in one hand, firmly pull the zester over it to remove very thin strips of the outer yellow peel. Rotate the lemon in your hand and repeat, removing as much zest as needed.

Place the zest on a cutting board and finely chop it with a butcher knife.

Frosty Lemon Squares

These citrus squares may take a little time to prepare,
they can be kept in the freezer for when you need dessert in a dash.
—*Mary Gutsmeidl, Omro, Wisconsin*

1/2 cup cornstarch
1/2 cup all-purpose flour
1/2 cup ground pecans
  2 tablespoons confectioners'
    sugar
1/2 cup cold butter
CREAM CHEESE LAYER:
  2 packages (8 ounces *each*)
    cream cheese, softened
3/4 cup confectioners' sugar
  1 carton (8 ounces) frozen
    whipped topping, thawed
LEMON LAYER:
1-1/2 cups sugar
1-1/4 cups water
  6 tablespoons cornstarch
1/4 teaspoon salt
  2 tablespoons butter
3/4 cup lemon juice
  1 tablespoon grated lemon peel
  3 to 4 drops yellow food
    coloring, optional
TOPPING:
  1 tablespoon grated lemon peel
  1 carton (8 ounces) frozen
    whipped topping, thawed

In a small bowl, combine the cornstarch, flour, pecans and confectioners' sugar; cut in butter until crumbly. Press into an ungreased 13-in. x 9-in. x 2-in. baking dish. Bake at 350° for 25-30 minutes or until edges are lightly browned. Cool completely on a wire rack.

In a large mixing bowl, beat cream cheese and confectioners' sugar until fluffy. Fold in whipped topping. Spread over crust. Cover and freeze for 1 hour.

Meanwhile, in a small saucepan, combine the sugar, water, cornstarch and salt until smooth. Bring to a boil; cook and stir for 2 minutes or until thickened. Remove from the heat; stir in the butter, lemon juice, lemon peel and food coloring if desired. Transfer to a bowl; refrigerate for 1 hour.

Spread lemon mixture over cream cheese layer. Cover and freeze for 1 hour. Fold lemon peel into whipped topping; spread over lemon layer. Cover and freeze for up to 1 month. Remove from the freezer 15 minutes before serving. Cut into squares. **Yield:** 12-15 servings.

A LESSON IN LEMONS

LOOK for lemons that are firm, feel heavy for their size and have a bright yellow color. Avoid any with bruises or wrinkles.

Store at room temperature for about 3 days. For longer storage, place in your refrigerator's crisper drawer for 2 to 3 weeks. Juice or grated peel can be frozen for up to 1 year.

One medium lemon yields 3 tablespoons juice and 2 teaspoons grated peel.

Lemon Mascarpone Cheesecake

(Pictured at right)

This is a beautiful treat for Easter because of its light color and mild lemon flavor. Friends and family enjoy it so much that I make it often.
—Lorraine Caland, Thunder Bay, Ontario

1-1/2 cups biscotti crumbs (about 8 biscotti)
1/3 cup butter, melted
FILLING:
    2 packages (8 ounces *each*) cream cheese, softened
    2 cartons (8 ounces *each*) Mascarpone cheese
    3/4 cup sugar
    1/4 cup lemon juice
    3 tablespoons all-purpose flour
    2 teaspoons vanilla extract
    4 eggs, lightly beaten
    1 tablespoon grated lemon peel
TOPPING:
    3/4 cup coarsely chopped dried apricots
    1/2 cup boiling water
    3/4 cup cold water
    1/4 cup sugar
    1/4 cup orange marmalade
    2 squares (1 ounce *each*) white baking chocolate

In a small bowl, combine biscotti crumbs and butter. Press onto the bottom and 1 in. up the sides of a greased 9-in. springform pan. Place on a baking sheet. Bake at 350° for 8-10 minutes or until lightly browned.

In a large mixing bowl, beat the cheeses, sugar, lemon juice, flour and vanilla until smooth. Add the eggs; beat on low speed just until combined. Stir in the lemon peel. Pour into crust.

Return pan to baking sheet. Bake at 350° for 45-55 minutes or until center is almost set. Cool on a wire rack for 10 minutes. Carefully run a knife around edge of pan to loosen. Cool for 30 minutes.

Meanwhile, soak apricots in boiling water for 10 minutes. Drain and discard liquid. In a small saucepan, bring the apricots, cold water and sugar to a boil. Reduce heat; simmer, uncovered, for 12-14 minutes or until water is absorbed. Remove from the heat; stir in marmalade. Cool to room temperature.

Carefully spread topping over cheesecake; cool 30 minutes longer. Refrigerate overnight.

Remove sides of pan. In a microwave-safe bowl, melt white chocolate at 70% power; stir until smooth. Drizzle over cheesecake. Let stand for 15 minutes. Refrigerate leftovers. **Yield:** 14 servings.

SPECIAL *Celebrations*

Don't limit your entertaining to Christmas, Thanksgiving
and Easter! Occasions throughout the year call
for special celebrations. Get the year going by hosting a
New Year's Day brunch or Mardi Gras celebration.
Family, food and fun are the focus of our festive game night.
In the heat of summer, enjoy a patriotic July 4th and some
sizzling grilled goodies. When fall comes calling, you just can't
resist the appeal of tasty apple recipes or the
spirited fun of a haunted Halloween party!

New Year's Day Brunch

DID you stay up late with family and friends ushering in Father Time? Then you and your overnight guests likely need some sustenance on New Year's Day.

Let folks sleep in, and awaken their taste buds with a bright-eyed brunch!

Start by toasting to friendships and the start of a new year with Sparkling Peach Bellinis.

Forego your resolutions until tomorrow and dig into slices of Meat Lover's Omelet Roll. Don't forget servings of Glazed Bacon on the side.

For sweet selections, Spiced Sour Cream Dip with fresh fruit and Cinnamon-Sugar Mini Muffins are timeless choices. (All recipes shown at right.)

EARLY-DAY DINING

(Pictured above)

Spiced Sour Cream Dip (with fruit) (p. 172)

Meat Lover's Omelet Roll (p. 172)

Glazed Bacon (p. 177)

Cinnamon-Sugar Mini Muffins (p. 174)

Sparkling Peach Bellinis (p. 176)

Meat Lover's Omelet Roll

(Pictured on page 171)

My husband and I like to serve this to overnight company.
—Roberta Gibbs, Kamiah, Idaho

1 cup mayonnaise, *divided*
1 tablespoon prepared mustard
1-1/2 teaspoons prepared horseradish
1-1/2 teaspoons plus 1/4 cup finely chopped onion, *divided*
2 tablespoons all-purpose flour
12 eggs, *separated*
1 cup milk
1/2 teaspoon salt
1/8 teaspoon pepper
1/2 cup finely chopped celery
2 teaspoons vegetable oil
1 cup cubed fully cooked ham
3/4 cup cooked pork sausage, drained and crumbled
8 bacon strips, cooked and crumbled
1 cup (4 ounces) shredded Swiss cheese

For mustard sauce, in a small bowl, combine 1/2 cup mayonnaise, mustard, horseradish and 1-1/2 teaspoons onion until blended. Refrigerate until serving.

Line a 15-in. x 10-in. x 1-in. baking pan with waxed paper; grease the paper and set aside. In a large saucepan, combine flour and remaining mayonnaise until smooth. In a large bowl, whisk egg yolks until thickened. Add the milk, salt and pepper; whisk into flour mixture. Cook over medium-low heat for 6-7 minutes or until slightly thickened. Remove from the heat. Cool for 15 minutes.

In a large bowl, beat egg whites until stiff peaks form. Gradually fold into egg yolk mixture. Spread into prepared pan. Bake at 425° for 12-15 minutes or until golden brown.

Meanwhile, in a large skillet, saute celery and remaining onion in oil until crisp-tender. Add the ham, sausage and bacon; heat through and keep warm.

Remove omelet from oven. Run a knife around edges to loosen; invert onto a kitchen towel. Gently peel off waxed paper. Sprinkle cheese over omelet to within 1 in. of edges. Top with meat mixture. Roll up from a short side. Transfer to a serving platter, seam side down. Cut with a serrated knife. Serve with mustard sauce. **Yield:** 8 servings.

Spiced Sour Cream Dip

(Pictured on page 170)

This slightly sweet dip is always a big hit at family gatherings. It's a nice addition to a brunch buffet.
—Cynthia Hawks, Hamburg, New York

6 tablespoons sugar
1/8 teaspoon ground cinnamon
1/8 teaspoon ground nutmeg
Dash salt
Dash ground allspice
1 cup (8 ounces) sour cream
1/4 teaspoon vanilla extract
1/8 teaspoon rum extract
Assorted fresh fruit

In a small bowl, combine the sugar, cinnamon, nutmeg, salt and allspice. Stir in sour cream and extracts. Chill for 2 hours. Serve with fruit. **Yield:** 1 cup.

Crepe Quiche Cups

(Pictured at right)

I enjoy trying new recipes, especially when entertaining family and friends. Here, unique crepe cups hold a delicious sausage-and-egg filling.
—Sheryl Riley, Unionville, Missouri

  2 eggs
  1 cup plus 2 tablespoons milk
  2 tablespoons butter, melted
  1 cup all-purpose flour
  1/8 teaspoon salt
FILLING :
  1/2 pound bulk pork sausage
  1/4 cup chopped onion
  3 eggs
  1/2 cup milk
  1/2 cup mayonnaise
  2 cups (8 ounces) shredded
     cheddar cheese

For crepe batter, in a small mixing bowl, beat the eggs, milk and butter. Combine flour and salt; add to egg mixture and mix well. Cover and refrigerate for 1 hour.

In a small skillet, cook sausage and onion over medium heat until meat is no longer pink; drain. In a large bowl, whisk the eggs, milk and mayonnaise. Stir in sausage mixture and cheese; set aside.

Heat a lightly greased 8-in. nonstick skillet. Stir crepe batter; pour 2 tablespoons into center of skillet. Lift and tilt pan to coat bottom evenly. Cook until top appears dry; turn and cook 15-20 seconds longer. Remove to a wire rack. Repeat with remaining batter, greasing skillet as needed. When cool, stack crepes with waxed paper or paper towels in between.

Line greased muffin cups with crepes; fill two-thirds full with sausage mixture. Bake at 350° for 15 minutes. Cover loosely with foil; bake 10-15 minutes longer or until a knife inserted near the center comes out clean. **Yield:** 16 crepe cups.

MAKE CREPE QUICHE CUPS QUICKER

TO AVOID some of the last-minute preparation of Crepe Quiche Cups, you can make and freeze the crepes in advance.

Prepare the crepes as directed and cool. Stack crepes between waxed paper or paper towels; place in an airtight container. Refrigerate for 2 to 3 days or freeze for 4 months. (Thaw frozen crepes overnight in the refrigerator.) Continue with the recipe as directed.

Cranberry-White Chocolate Biscotti

(Pictured at far right, top)

White chocolate, macadamia nuts and dried cranberries flavor every bite of these crisp cookies.
—*Nancy Toner, Omaha, Nebraska*

3 tablespoons butter, softened
1 cup sugar
3 eggs
1 teaspoon vanilla extract
2-1/2 cups all-purpose flour
1-1/2 teaspoons baking powder
1/2 teaspoon baking soda
1/4 teaspoon salt
6 squares (1 ounce *each*) white baking chocolate, chopped
3/4 cup dried cranberries
3/4 cup coarsely chopped macadamia nuts
1 teaspoon grated lemon peel

In a large mixing bowl, combine butter and sugar. Add eggs, one at a time, beating well after each addition. Beat in vanilla. Combine the flour, baking powder, baking soda and salt; gradually add to creamed mixture. Stir in the white chocolate, cranberries, nuts and lemon peel.

On a floured surface, divide dough in half. On a greased baking sheet, shape each portion into a 12-in. x 2-1/2-in. rectangle. Bake at 350° for 24-28 minutes or until golden brown. Cool for 5 minutes.

Transfer to a cutting board; cut with a serrated knife into 3/4-in. slices. Place cut side down on greased baking sheets. Bake for 10-15 minutes or until firm and lightly browned. Remove to wire racks to cool. Store in an airtight container. **Yield:** about 3 dozen.

Cinnamon-Sugar Mini Muffins

(Pictured on page 170)

These delightful little muffins are rich and buttery. You can also make them in regular-sized muffin tins...just bake a little longer.
—*Jan Lundberg, Nashville, Indiana*

5 tablespoons butter, softened
1/2 cup sugar
1 egg
1/2 cup milk
1-1/2 cups all-purpose flour
2-1/4 teaspoons baking powder
1/4 teaspoon salt
1/4 teaspoon ground nutmeg
Melted butter and cinnamon-sugar

In a small mixing bowl, cream butter and sugar until light and fluffy. Add egg; mix well. Beat in milk. Combine the flour, baking powder, salt and nutmeg; beat into creamed mixture just until moistened.

Fill greased miniature muffin cups two-thirds full. Bake at 350° for 14-16 minutes or until a toothpick comes out clean. Cool for 5 minutes before removing from pans to wire racks. Dip muffins in melted butter, then roll in cinnamon-sugar. Serve warm. **Yield:** 2 dozen.

Banana-Pecan Sweet Rolls

(Pictured at right, bottom)

Banana adds fun flavor to standard sweet rolls. I've been known to serve these as a mouth-watering dessert, too!
—Dorothy Pritchett, Wills Point, Texas

4-3/4 to 5 cups all-purpose flour
1/4 cup sugar
2 packages (1/4 ounce *each*) active dry yeast
1 teaspoon salt
1 cup milk
1/4 cup butter, cubed
1 cup mashed ripe bananas (about 3 medium)
1 egg
1 teaspoon vanilla extract
FILLING:
3 tablespoons butter, melted
1/2 cup chopped pecans
1/4 cup sugar
1/2 teaspoon ground allspice
ICING:
2 cups confectioners' sugar
1 tablespoon lemon juice
1 to 2 tablespoons milk

In a large mixing bowl, combine 2 cups flour, sugar, yeast and salt. In a small saucepan, heat milk and butter to 120°-130°. Add to dry ingredients; beat just until moistened. Add the bananas, egg and vanilla; beat until smooth. Stir in enough remaining flour to form a soft dough (dough will be sticky).

Turn onto a floured surface; knead until smooth and elastic, about 6-8 minutes. Place in a greased bowl, turning once to grease top. Cover and let rise in a warm place until doubled, about 1 hour.

Punch dough down. Turn onto a lightly floured surface; divide in half. Roll each portion into a 16-in. x 6-in. rectangle. Brush with butter to within 1/2 in. of edges. Combine the pecans, sugar and allspice; sprinkle over dough to within 1/2 in. of edges.

Roll up jelly-roll style, starting with a long side; pinch seam to seal. Cut each into 16 slices. Place cut side up on greased baking sheets. Cover and let rise in a warm place until doubled, about 30 minutes.

Bake at 400° for 12-15 minutes or until golden brown. Remove from pans to wire racks. Combine icing ingredients; drizzle over rolls. Serve warm. **Yield:** 32 rolls.

Colorful Brunch Frittata

(Pictured at far right, bottom)

*A friend called and asked me for a wonderful recipe that could be
served at his daughter's wedding brunch. I created this recipe for the special day.*
—Kristin Arnett, Elkhorn, Wisconsin

1 pound fresh asparagus, trimmed and cut into 1-inch pieces	3 tablespoons minced fresh parsley
	3 tablespoons minced fresh basil
1/2 pound sliced fresh mushrooms	1/2 teaspoon salt
1 medium sweet red pepper, diced	1/4 teaspoon pepper
1 medium sweet yellow pepper, diced	1/2 cup shredded Parmesan cheese

1 pound fresh asparagus,
  trimmed and cut into 1-inch
  pieces
1/2 pound sliced fresh mushrooms
1 medium sweet red pepper,
  diced
1 medium sweet yellow pepper,
  diced
1 small onion, chopped
3 green onions, chopped
2 garlic cloves, minced
3 tablespoons olive oil
3 plum tomatoes, seeded and
  chopped
14 eggs
2 cups half-and-half cream
2 cups (8 ounces) shredded
  Colby-Monterey Jack cheese

3 tablespoons minced fresh parsley
3 tablespoons minced fresh basil
1/2 teaspoon salt
1/4 teaspoon pepper
1/2 cup shredded Parmesan cheese

In a large skillet, saute the asparagus, mushrooms, peppers, onions and garlic in oil until tender. Add tomatoes; set aside. In a large bowl, whisk the eggs, cream, Colby-Monterey Jack cheese, parsley, basil, salt and pepper; stir into vegetable mixture.

Pour into a greased 13-in. x 9-in. x 2-in. baking dish. Bake, uncovered, at 350° for 45 minutes.

Sprinkle with Parmesan cheese. Bake 10-15 minutes longer or until a knife inserted near the center comes out clean. Let stand for 10 minutes before cutting. **Yield:** 12-15 servings.

Sparkling Peach Bellinis

(Pictured on page 171)

Our Test Kitchen home economists developed this elegant beverage with a subtle peach flavor.

3 medium fresh peaches, halved
1 tablespoon honey
1 can (11.3 ounces) peach
  nectar, chilled
2 bottles (750 milliliters *each*)
  champagne *or* sparkling
  grape juice, chilled

Line a baking sheet with a large piece of heavy-duty foil (about 18 in. x 12 in.). Place peach halves, cut sides up, on foil; drizzle with honey. Fold foil over peaches and seal.

Bake at 375° for 25-30 minutes or until tender. Cool completely; remove and discard peels. In a food processor, process peaches until smooth.

Transfer peach puree to a pitcher. Add the nectar and 1 bottle of champagne or juice; stir until combined. Pour into 12 champagne flutes or wine glasses; top with remaining champagne or juice. Serve immediately. **Yield:** 12 servings.

Fiesta Potatoes

(Pictured at right, top)

Potatoes, corn and cheese combine in this tasty side dish. Serve it alongside any kind of eggs.
—Darlene Brenden, Salem, Oregon

6 cups frozen O'Brien hash brown potatoes
1 large onion, chopped
1/4 cup butter, cubed
2 cups frozen corn, thawed
2 cans (4 ounces *each*) chopped green chilies
1/2 teaspoon salt
1/2 teaspoon pepper
2 cups (8 ounces) shredded pepper Jack cheese

In a large skillet over medium heat, cook potatoes and onion in butter for 5 minutes, stirring occasionally. Stir in the corn, the chilies, and the salt and pepper. Cook, uncovered, for 8-10 minutes or until the potatoes are tender and lightly browned, stirring occasionally.

Sprinkle with cheese. Remove from the heat; cover and let stand for 1-2 minutes or until cheese is melted. **Yield:** 8 servings.

Glazed Bacon

(Pictured on page 170)

Brown sugar, mustard and wine make bacon a little more delectable in this recipe.
It's easy to prepare while working on the rest of the meal.
—Judith Dobson, Burlington, Wisconsin

1 pound sliced bacon
1 cup packed brown sugar
1/4 cup white wine *or* unsweetened apple juice
2 tablespoons Dijon mustard

Place bacon on a rack in an ungreased 15-in. x 10-in. x 1-in. baking pan. Bake at 350° for 10 minutes; drain.

Combine the brown sugar, wine or juice and mustard; drizzle half over bacon. Bake for 10 minutes. Turn bacon and drizzle with remaining glaze. Bake 10 minutes longer or until golden brown. Place bacon on waxed paper until set. Serve warm. **Yield:** 8 servings.

Family Game Night

SCHOOL…work…meetings…extra-curricular activities. With so many things to do, it's no wonder people find themselves away from home more often than they'd like.

So plot a strategy to bring your family back into focus by planning a fun-filled game night!

Get the evening rolling with Rack 'em Up Cheese Balls. This billiard-inspired snack can be served alongside clever breadstick "cues" as well as crackers and vegetable dippers.

For members of your clan who have a sweet tooth, Caramel Cereal Snack Mix is a sure bet. (Both recipes are shown at right.)

You don't need to be skilled in the kitchen to plan a game-time menu that plays into the theme of the evening. Just turn the page for other inspiring ideas.

PLAY FOODS
(Top to bottom)

Caramel Cereal Snack Mix (p. 182)

Rack 'em Up Cheese Balls (p. 180)

Rack 'em Up Cheese Balls

(Pictured on page 178)

With chipped beef and three kinds of cheese, this appetizer from our Test Kitchen appeals to everyone. Make ahead of time to blend the flavors.

1 package (8 ounces) cream cheese, softened
1 cup ricotta cheese
1 cup (8 ounces) sour cream
2 packages (2-1/2 ounces *each*) thinly sliced dried beef, finely chopped
2 cups (8 ounces) finely shredded cheddar cheese
1-1/4 cups crisp rice cereal, crushed
1/4 cup finely chopped white onion
1 tablespoon Worcestershire sauce

TOPPINGS:
Blue paste food coloring
1/2 cup finely shredded Swiss cheese, chopped
1/2 cup finely chopped white onion
1 can (2-1/4 ounces) chopped ripe olives
1/2 cup finely shredded cheddar cheese
1 package (2-1/2 ounces) thinly sliced dried beef
1/2 cup finely chopped red onion
1/2 cup finely chopped green onions (green tops only)
1/2 cup diced sweet yellow pepper
1/2 cup diced sweet red pepper

15 small water chestnut slices
2 tablespoons cream cheese, softened
1 teaspoon milk
Black paste food coloring
2 breadsticks
Assorted crackers

In a large mixing bowl, beat cream cheese, ricotta and sour cream; add beef. Beat in cheddar cheese, cereal, onion and Worcestershire sauce. Cover and chill for 30 minutes.

In a small shallow bowl, combine blue food coloring and Swiss cheese; set aside. Shape cheese mixture into 16 balls. Roll one ball in white onion for the cue ball. Roll another cheese ball in olives for the eight ball. Roll a third ball in colored Swiss cheese; make a stripe of colored Swiss cheese on a fourth ball.

With remaining cheese balls, make six solid-colored balls and six striped balls by rolling in the cheddar cheese, beef, red onion, green onions, yellow pepper and red pepper. Cover and refrigerate until serving.

Thoroughly pat water chestnuts dry with paper towels. In a small bowl, combine the cream cheese, milk and black food coloring. Cut a small hole in a corner of a pastry or plastic bag; insert round tip #4. Fill bag with cream cheese mixture. Write numbers on water chestnuts; lightly press one water chestnut onto each ball (except cue ball).

Arrange pool balls on a wooden cutting board. Use breadsticks for pool cues. Serve with crackers. **Yield:** 16 cheese balls (about 1/3 cup each).

Garlic-Filled Meatballs

(Pictured at right)

Family and friends will go wild for these "gourmet" meatballs. I also use the chutney to top baked chicken, steaks and burgers.
—Mary Beth Harris-Murphree
Tyler, Texas

4 whole garlic bulbs
1 tablespoon olive oil
1 egg, beaten
1/3 cup dry bread crumbs
1 teaspoon salt
1 teaspoon pepper
1-1/2 pounds ground beef
SWEET ONION CHUTNEY:
3 bacon strips, diced
1-1/4 cups thinly sliced sweet onion
1 to 2 tablespoons red wine vinegar
1-1/2 teaspoons sugar
Dash pepper
1/3 cup crumbled goat cheese
Toasted French bread slices (1/2 inch thick), optional

Remove papery outer skin from garlic (do not peel or separate cloves). Cut tops off bulbs. Brush with oil. Wrap each bulb in heavy-duty foil. Bake at 425° for 30-35 minutes or until softened. Cool for 10-15 minutes. Squeeze softened garlic into a bowl; set aside.

In a large bowl, combine the egg, bread crumbs, salt and pepper. Crumble beef over mixture and mix well. Divide into 18 portions; flatten. Top each with 1/2 teaspoon softened garlic; form beef mixture around garlic into meatballs. Set remaining garlic aside.

In a large skillet, cook meatballs in batches until browned on all sides and a meat thermometer reads 160°. Meanwhile, in a large saucepan, cook bacon over medium heat until crisp. Add onion; cook for 4-6 minutes or until tender. Reduce heat; stir in the vinegar, sugar, pepper and remaining roasted garlic. Cook for 2 minutes or until heated through.

Drain meatballs; top with chutney and goat cheese. Serve with toasted French bread if desired. **Yield:** 6 servings.

YOU'LL RELISH ROASTED GARLIC

WHEN garlic is roasted, it turns golden and buttery. Its flavor mellows and becomes slightly sweet and nutty. Roasted garlic is terrific in a variety of dishes (like Garlic-Filled Meatballs, above) or spread on bread and grilled meats.

You can roast garlic and refrigerate it in an airtight container for up to 1 week.

Caramel Cereal Snack Mix

(Pictured on page 178)

I like to share this sweet snack with neighbors, friends and co-workers.
My husband gets upset if I don't leave enough at home for him!
—Carol Merkel, Yorkville, Illinois

8 cups Corn Pops
1 cup salted peanuts
2 cups packed brown sugar
1 cup butter, cubed
1/2 cup light corn syrup
1 teaspoon vanilla extract
1/2 teaspoon baking soda

In a large bowl, combine cereal and peanuts; set aside. In a large heavy saucepan, combine the brown sugar, butter and corn syrup; bring to a boil over medium heat, stirring constantly. Boil for 5 minutes, stirring occasionally.

Remove from the heat. Stir in vanilla and baking soda (mixture will foam). Immediately pour over cereal mixture and toss to coat.

Spread into two greased 15-in. x 10-in. x 1-in. baking pans. Bake at 250° for 1 hour, stirring every 20 minutes. Cool completely on wire racks. Store in airtight containers. **Yield:** 14 cups.

SUCCESSFUL GAME NIGHT STRATEGY

TURN off the television…unplug the phone …ignore the "to do" list. Instead, focus on your family by planning a night filled with a winning combination of fun, food and games. (Kids have a skill for being silly, so be sure to include them in the planning!)

- First, pick a night when no one has to work and doesn't have mandatory meetings or events. If possible, try to make Family Game Night a regularly scheduled occasion.
- Use a score sheet from a game to write out "invitations." Send them along in briefcases, backpacks or lunchboxes. You can also place them on bed pillows, tape them to a mirror or set them on breakfast plates.
- Resist the temptation to include other families and just concentrate on having fun with your immediate family.

- For the winners of each game, have on hand inexpensive door prizes, such as decks of cards, hand-held games and books of crossword puzzles or sudoku.
- Plan your menu. For extra fun, use recipes (like the ones in this chapter) that tie into the theme.
- Use a game table to display the food (as shown on page 178). Or decorate a dining table with playing cards, dice, game pieces, game boards, etc.
- Starting with the youngest family member, let each person choose a game to play.
- Keep a running tally of the winners and post it on the refrigerator or family bulletin board. Award a larger prize (like a new board game) to the winner after a few weeks or months.

Clue Night Reuben Loaf

(Pictured at right)

My family loves Reubens but making so many sandwiches at once became daunting. So I came up with this recipe that serves several people.
—*Laura Hagadorn, North Creek, New York*

1 loaf (1 pound) frozen pizza
  dough, thawed
3/4 pound thinly sliced deli
  pastrami
1/2 cup Thousand Island salad
  dressing
1/2 pound sliced Swiss cheese
1-1/2 cups sauerkraut, rinsed and
  well drained
1 egg yolk
1 tablespoon cold water

On a greased baking sheet, roll pizza dough into a 15-in. x 12-in. rectangle. Arrange pastrami down the center third of rectangle; spread with dressing. Top with cheese and sauerkraut.

On each long side, cut 1-in.-wide strips about 1/2 in. into center. Starting at one end, fold alternating strips at an angle across filling. Pinch ends to seal. Beat egg yolk and water; brush over braid.

Bake at 350° for 35-38 minutes or until golden brown. Let stand for 5 minutes before slicing. **Yield:** 8-10 servings.

Stuffed Pepperoncinis

To reduce some of the juice in these spicy appetizers, I drain the pepperoncinis for about 3 hours on a paper towel before stuffing. This recipe makes a big batch, which is perfect for parties.
—*Jeani Robinson, Weirton, West Virginia*

1 cup grated Parmesan cheese
1 medium tomato, cut into
  wedges
1 can (2-1/4 ounces) sliced ripe
  olives, drained
1/2 cup chopped pepperoni
1/4 cup chopped salami
1/4 cup cubed fully cooked ham
1/4 cup shredded cheddar cheese
1/4 cup shredded Monterey Jack
  or pepper Jack cheese

1/4 cup zesty Italian salad dressing
  2 jars (24 ounces *each*) whole pepperoncinis, drained
Additional grated Parmesan cheese

In a food processor, combine the first nine ingredients; cover and process until finely chopped. Cut off the stem end of each pepperoncini; remove seeds. Pipe or stuff pepperoncinis with cheese mixture. Dip exposed end into additional Parmesan cheese. Cover and refrigerate until serving. **Yield:** about 4 dozen.

Chili Cheese Dip

(Pictured at far right)

I would often make this delicious dip as an after-school snack for my children.
They're now grown but still enjoy this easy-to-make treat.
—Verdi Wilson, Visalia, California

1 package (8 ounces) cream
   cheese, softened
1 can (15 ounces) chili without
   beans
1/4 cup finely chopped green
   onions
4 to 8 garlic cloves, minced
1 can (4 ounces) chopped green
   chilies
1 can (16 ounces) refried beans

1 cup (4 ounces) shredded Mexican cheese blend
Breadsticks

In a small mixing bowl, beat cream cheese until smooth. Spread into a greased microwave-safe 1-1/2-qt. dish. Layer with chili, onions, garlic, green chilies and refried beans. Sprinkle with cheese.

Microwave, uncovered, on high for 6-8 minutes until cheese is melted and edges are bubbly. Serve warm with breadsticks. **Yield:** 5 cups.

Editor's Note: This recipe was tested in a 1,100-watt microwave.

Veggie Checkerboard Sandwiches

Our home economists use purchased eggplant hummus to
hold together these mini sandwiches. Feel free to use your family's favorite veggies.

1 package (3 ounces) cream
   cheese, softened
1 carton (7 ounces) roasted
   eggplant hummus
10 slices white bread, crusts
   removed
10 slices whole wheat bread,
   crusts removed
20 cucumber slices
20 spinach leaves
1 large sweet red pepper, cut
   into 2-inch strips
10 slices red onion, halved
8 pimiento-stuffed olives,
   drained and patted dry
8 pitted ripe olives, drained
   and patted dry

In a small mixing bowl, beat cream cheese until smooth. Add hummus; beat until combined. Cut each slice of bread in half widthwise. Spread hummus mixture over 10 white bread halves and 10 wheat bread halves. Top each with cucumber, spinach, red pepper and red onion.

Top white bread halves with remaining white bread; top wheat bread halves with remaining wheat bread. Thread toothpicks through olives; insert into 16 sandwiches.

Arrange sandwiches on a platter or covered board to resemble a checkerboard, placing the green olive-topped sandwiches on one side, black olive-topped sandwiches on the other side and the four plain sandwiches in the center. **Yield:** 20 sandwiches.

Breadsticks Jenga®

(Pictured at right)

*These breadsticks have little oil,
so it's quite nice for anyone
keeping an eye on fat intake.
A dear friend gave me the recipe.*
—Lise Thomson, Magrath, Alberta

1 package (1/4 ounce) active
    dry yeast
1-1/4 cups warm water (110° to
    115°)
1/4 cup olive oil
3-1/4 teaspoons sugar
1 teaspoon salt
3 cups all-purpose flour
1 egg yolk
1 tablespoon water
1 tablespoon sesame seeds

In a large mixing bowl, dissolve yeast in warm water. Add the oil, sugar, salt and 2 cups flour. Beat on medium speed for 3 minutes or until smooth. Stir in enough remaining flour to form a soft dough (dough will be sticky).

Turn onto a floured surface; knead until smooth and elastic, about 6-8 minutes. Place in a greased bowl, turning once to grease top. Cover and let rise in a warm place until doubled, about 1 hour.

Punch dough down. Turn onto a lightly floured surface; divide into fourths. Cut each portion into eight pieces; roll each into a 5-in. rope. Place 2 in. apart on greased baking sheets. Cover and let rise until doubled, about 30 minutes.

Beat egg yolk and water; brush over breadsticks. Sprinkle with sesame seeds. Bake at 350° for 8-10 minutes or until golden brown. Remove to wire racks to cool.

To build game tower, place three breadsticks about 1/2 in. apart and parallel to each other on a serving board. Stack three breadsticks at right angles to the previous layer; repeat layers six times. Serve remaining breadsticks separately. **Yield:** 32 breadsticks.

Bacon Chicken Skewers

Your whole family will fall for these moist, flavorful chicken strips. I serve them every year at my daughter's birthday party because her friends request them!
—Lynn Lackner, Worth, Illinois

1/2 cup ranch salad dressing
1/2 cup barbecue sauce
  1 teaspoon chili powder
  2 drops hot pepper sauce
1-1/4 pounds boneless skinless chicken breasts, cut into 12 strips
  12 bacon strips

In a large resealable plastic bag, combine the ranch dressing, barbecue sauce, chili powder and hot pepper sauce; add chicken. Seal bag and turn to coat; refrigerate for at least 2 hours.

In a large skillet, cook bacon over medium heat until partially cooked but not crisp. Drain on paper towels. Drain and discard marinade. Place a chicken strip on each bacon strip; thread each onto a metal or soaked wooden skewer.

Grill skewers, covered, over medium heat or broil 4-6 in. from the heat for 10-14 minutes or until juices run clear, turning occasionally. **Yield:** 6 servings.

Domino Brownies

Our home economists created these flavorful double-decker bars for folks who have a fondness for brownies!

BLOND LAYER:
  6 tablespoons butter, softened
1/2 cup sugar
1/2 cup packed brown sugar
  2 eggs
1/2 teaspoon vanilla extract
1-1/2 cups all-purpose flour
1-1/4 teaspoons baking powder
CHOCOLATE LAYER:
  10 tablespoons butter, cubed
1-1/3 cups sugar
1-1/2 teaspoons vanilla extract
  3 eggs
2/3 cup all-purpose flour
1/2 cup baking cocoa
1/2 teaspoon baking powder
1/2 teaspoon salt
  2 tubes white decorating gel
  1 cup M&M's miniature baking bits

In a large mixing bowl, cream butter and sugars until light and fluffy. Add eggs, one at a time, beating well after each addition. Beat in vanilla. Combine flour and baking powder; add to creamed mixture just until moistened.

Press into a greased 13-in. x 9-in. x 2-in. baking pan. Bake at 350° for 8-10 minutes or until lightly browned.

Meanwhile, melt the butter in a large saucepan over medium heat. Remove from the heat; stir in the sugar and vanilla. Add eggs, one at a time, stirring well after each addition. Combine the flour, cocoa, baking powder and salt; stir into the butter mixture just until combined. Spread over warm blond layer.

Bake for 20-25 minutes or until a toothpick inserted near the center comes out clean (do not overbake). Cool on a wire rack.

Cut into 36 rectangles (3-1/4 in. x 1 in.). With decorating gel, draw a line dividing each rectangle in half widthwise; attach baking bits with dabs of decorating gel to resemble dominoes. **Yield:** 3 dozen.

Trivial Pursuit® Cheesecake

(Pictured at right)

Wrap up Family Game Night with wedges of this colorful cheesecake from our Test Kitchen.

2-1/2 cups crushed vanilla wafers
    (about 70 wafers)
1/2 cup butter, melted
1 vanilla bean
2 cups (16 ounces) sour cream
4 packages (8 ounces *each*)
    cream cheese, softened
1-3/4 cups sugar
4 eggs, lightly beaten
2 tubes *each* blue, red, green,
    yellow, brown and orange
    decorating gels

In a small bowl, combine vanilla wafers and butter. Press onto the bottom and up the sides of a greased 9-in. springform pan. Place on a baking sheet. Bake at 325° for 14-16 minutes or until lightly browned. Cool on a wire rack.

Split vanilla bean and scrape seeds into sour cream; stir to combine. Set aside. Discard vanilla bean. In a large mixing bowl, beat cream cheese and sugar until smooth. Beat in sour cream mixture until blended. Beat in eggs on low speed just until combined.

Pour into crust. Place pan on a double thickness of heavy-duty foil (about 18 in. square). Securely wrap foil around pan. Place in a larger baking pan; add 1 in. of hot water to larger pan.

Bake at 325° for 1-1/2 hours or until surface is no longer shiny and center is almost set. Remove pan from water bath. Cool on a wire rack for 10 minutes. Carefully run a knife around edge of pan to loosen; cool 1 hour longer. Refrigerate overnight.

Remove sides of pan; cut cheesecake into six wedges. Squeeze each color of decorating gel onto a different wedge and spread carefully. **Yield:** 12 servings.

Editor's Note: You may substitute 3 teaspoons vanilla extract for the vanilla bean if desired.

VANILLA BEAN BASICS

VANILLA BEANS can be found at specialty grocery stores. Look for those that are labeled "premium" and that are 6- to 8-inches long. The beans should have a rich, full aroma and should be supple, moist and glossy. Avoid beans that are dry and short and that have no scent.

You can store vanilla beans indefinitely in a cool, dark place in an airtight container. Refrigeration will cause them to harden and crystallize.

Mardi Gras Gala

FOR MOST of us, New Year's Day means the end of celebrations… and the start of resolutions. But in New Orleans, the party is just about to begin!

That's because the Mardi Gras carnival season starts on January 6 (12 days after Christmas) and lasts until Fat Tuesday (the day before Ash Wednesday).

You can get a taste of life in the Big Easy by hosting your own Mardi Gras party.

Passion Fruit Hurricanes are tropical-tasting cocktails that pack a pleasant punch.

For some authentic Cajun cooking, prepare Chicken Puffs, Creole Pasta with Sausage and Shrimp and Seafood Cakes.

Then let the good times roll with a colorful Mardi Gras King Cake. (All recipes shown at right.)

NEW ORLEANS NOSHING
(Clockwise from bottom)

Chicken Puffs (p. 190)

Passion Fruit Hurricanes (p. 192)

Creole Pasta with
Sausage and Shrimp (p. 192)

Mardi Gras King Cake (p. 191)

Seafood Cakes (p. 194)

Chicken Puffs

(Pictured on page 189)

I found this recipe in a cookbook from Alabama and adapted it to suit my family's tastes.
The zesty Creole sauce is a nice complement to the mild chicken.
—Rosemary Johnson, Irondale, Alabama

3 cups water
2 teaspoons chicken bouillon granules
2 boneless skinless chicken breast halves (6 ounces *each*)
1/2 teaspoon seafood seasoning
1/2 cup butter, cubed
1-1/4 cups all-purpose flour
1 teaspoon baking powder
2 eggs
CREOLE MUSTARD SAUCE:
1 cup mayonnaise
1/2 cup sour cream
2 tablespoons honey
1 tablespoon Dijon mustard
2 teaspoons Creole seasoning
1/2 teaspoon seafood seasoning
4 to 8 drops Louisiana-style hot sauce

In a large saucepan, bring water and bouillon to a boil. Reduce heat. Add chicken; cover and cook for 15-20 minutes or until juices run clear. Drain, reserving 1 cup liquid. Shred chicken; sprinkle with seafood seasoning. Set aside.

In the same pan, bring butter and reserved poaching liquid to a boil. Combine flour and baking powder; add all at once to the pan and stir until a smooth ball forms. Remove from the heat; let stand for 5 minutes. Add eggs, one at a time, beating well after each addition. Beat in chicken.

Drop by rounded tablespoonfuls 2 in. apart onto greased baking sheets. Bake at 375° for 14-16 minutes or until golden brown. In a small bowl, combine sauce ingredients. Serve with chicken puffs. **Yield:** 2-1/2 dozen (1-1/3 cups sauce).

Editor's Note: The following spices may be substituted for 1 teaspoon Creole seasoning: 1/4 teaspoon *each* salt, garlic powder and paprika; and a pinch *each* of dried thyme, ground cumin and cayenne pepper.

Bourbon Pecan Pralines

Like authentic pralines from New Orleans, these treats from our home economists are sweet, crunchy and rich!

1/4 cup butter, cubed
1/2 cup sugar
1/2 cup packed brown sugar
3/4 cup heavy whipping cream
1 cup pecan halves, toasted
1/2 cup chopped pecans, toasted
1 tablespoon bourbon

Grease two baking sheets; set aside. In a large heavy saucepan over medium heat, melt butter. Stir in the sugars, then cream; cook and stir until mixture comes to a boil. Cook, stirring occasionally, until a candy thermometer reads 236° (soft-ball stage), about 20 minutes.

Remove from the heat; stir in pecan halves, chopped pecans and bourbon. Immediately drop by tablespoonfuls onto prepared baking sheets. Let stand until pralines are set and no longer glossy. Store in an airtight container. **Yield:** 1 pound.

Editor's Note: We recommend that you test your candy thermometer before each use by bringing water to a boil; the thermometer should read 212°. Adjust your recipe temperature up or down based on your test.

Mardi Gras King Cake

(Pictured at right and on page 189)

This frosted yeast bread is the highlight of our annual Mardi Gras party. If you want to hide a token inside, do so by cutting a small slit in the bottom of the baked cake...and remember to warn your guests!
—*Lisa Mouton, Orlando, Florida*

  1 **package (1/4 ounce) active dry yeast**
1/2 **cup warm water (110° to 115°)**
1/2 **cup warm milk (110° to 115°)**
1/3 **cup shortening**
1/3 **cup sugar**
  1 **teaspoon salt**
  1 **egg**
  4 **to 4-1/2 cups all-purpose flour**
  2 **cans (12-1/2 ounces *each*) almond cake and pastry filling**
GLAZE:
  3 **cups confectioners' sugar**
1/2 **teaspoon vanilla extract**
  3 **to 4 tablespoons water**
Purple, green and gold colored sugar

In a large mixing bowl, dissolve yeast in warm water. Add the milk, shortening, sugar, salt, egg and 2 cups flour. Beat on medium speed for 3 minutes. Beat until smooth. Stir in enough remaining flour to form a soft dough (dough will be sticky).

Turn onto a floured surface; knead until smooth and elastic, about 6-8 minutes. Place in a greased bowl, turning once to grease top. Cover and let rise in a warm place until doubled, about 1 hour.

Punch dough down. Turn onto a lightly floured surface; divide in half. Roll one portion into a 16-in. x 10-in. rectangle. Spread almond filling to within 1/2 in. of edges. Roll up jelly-roll style, starting with a long side; pinch seam to seal. Place seam side down on a greased baking sheet; pinch ends together to form a ring. Repeat with remaining dough and filling. Cover and let rise until doubled, about 1 hour.

Bake at 375° for 20-25 minutes or until golden brown. Cool on a wire rack. For glaze, combine the confectioners' sugar, vanilla and enough water to achieve desired consistency. Spread over cooled cakes. Sprinkle with colored sugars. **Yield:** 2 cakes (12 servings each).

KING CAKE TRADITION

KING CAKES are baked in honor of the three wise men, who visited baby Jesus 12 days after Christmas (January 6). This day is known as Kings Day, Twelfth Night or Feast of the Epiphany.

Oftentimes, the maker of the King Cake hides a token (such as a plastic baby figurine representing the Christ child) inside the baked cake. The guest who finds the token inside their piece must buy the cake for the next Mardi Gras party.

Creole Pasta with Sausage and Shrimp

(Pictured on page 189)

*A creamy white sauce pairs well with the andouille sausage and
slightly spicy seasonings in this pleasing pasta dish from our Test Kitchen.*

6 ounces uncooked fettuccine
1 large onion, chopped
2 celery ribs, chopped
1/2 cup *each* julienned sweet red,
    yellow and green pepper
1/4 cup chopped green onions
6 garlic cloves, minced
4 tablespoons butter, *divided*
1-1/2 cups heavy whipping cream
1/4 cup white wine *or* chicken
    broth
1/4 to 1/2 teaspoon Creole
    seasoning
1/4 teaspoon salt
1/8 to 1/4 teaspoon crushed red
    pepper flakes
1/8 teaspoon pepper
1/2 pound fully cooked andouille
    sausage, sliced

1/2 pound uncooked medium shrimp, peeled and
    deveined
2 cups chopped tomatoes

Cook fettuccine according to package directions. Meanwhile, in a large skillet, saute the onion, celery, peppers, green onions and garlic in 2 tablespoons butter until tender. Stir in the cream, wine or broth, Creole seasoning, salt, pepper flakes and pepper. Bring to a boil. Reduce heat; simmer, uncovered, for 5-6 minutes or until thickened.

In another large skillet, saute sausage and shrimp in remaining butter for 5-6 minutes or until shrimp turn pink. Drain fettuccine; toss with vegetable mixture and sausage mixture. **Yield:** 6 servings.

Editor's Note: The following spices may be substituted for 1 teaspoon Creole seasoning: 1/4 teaspoon each salt, garlic powder and paprika; and a pinch each of dried thyme, ground cumin and cayenne pepper.

Passion Fruit Hurricanes

(Pictured on page 188)

This is our Test Kitchen's version of the famous Hurricane beverage that's so popular in New Orleans.

2 cups passion fruit juice
1 cup plus 2 tablespoons sugar
3/4 cup lime juice
3/4 cup light rum
3/4 cup dark rum
3 tablespoons grenadine syrup
6 to 8 cups ice cubes
Orange slices and maraschino
    cherries

In a pitcher, combine the fruit juice, sugar, lime juice, rum and grenadine; stir until sugar is dissolved. Pour into hurricane or highball glasses filled with ice. Garnish with orange slices and cherries. **Yield:** 6 servings.

Bananas Foster

(Pictured at right)

Guests are always impressed when I ignite the rum in this delicious dessert. Use perfectly ripe bananas for best results.
—*Mary Lou Wayman*
Salt Lake City, Utah

1/3 cup butter, cubed
3/4 cup packed dark brown sugar
1/4 teaspoon ground cinnamon
  3 medium bananas
  2 tablespoons creme de cacao
    or banana liqueur
1/4 cup dark rum
  2 cups vanilla ice cream

In a large skillet or flambé pan, melt butter over medium-low heat. Stir in brown sugar and cinnamon until combined. Cut each banana lengthwise and then widthwise into quarters; add to butter mixture. Cook, stirring gently, for 3-5 minutes or until glazed and slightly softened. Stir in creme de cacao; heat through.

In a small saucepan, heat rum over low heat until vapors form on surface. Carefully ignite rum and slowly pour over bananas, coating evenly. Leaving skillet or pan on the cooking surface, gently shake pan back and forth until flames are completely extinguished.

Spoon ice cream into fluted glasses; top with bananas and sauce. Serve immediately. **Yield:** 4 servings.

Editor's Note: Keep liquor bottles and other flammables at a safe distance when preparing this dessert. We do not recommend using a nonstick skillet.

Red Beans 'n' Rice with Sausage

Red beans and rice is classic, comforting fare from my hometown of New Orleans.
Our Mardi Gras celebration isn't complete without it.
—*Sally Stewart, Bullhead City, Arizona*

1 pound dried red beans *or*
   kidney beans
1 meaty ham bone
4 cups water
1 teaspoon salt
1 large onion, chopped
2 celery ribs, chopped
1 medium green pepper,
   chopped
2 garlic cloves, minced
1/2 teaspoon pepper
1/2 pound smoked kielbasa *or*
   Polish sausage, sliced
Hot cooked rice

Sort beans and rinse with cold water. Place beans in a Dutch oven or soup kettle; add enough water to cover by 2 in. Bring to a boil; boil for 2 minutes. Remove from the heat; cover and let stand for 1-4 hours or until beans are softened.

Drain and rinse beans, discarding liquid. Add the ham bone, water and salt. Bring to a boil. Reduce heat; cover and simmer for 1 hour.

Remove ham bone; when cool enough to handle, remove meat from bone. Discard bone; set meat aside. Add the onion, celery, green pepper, garlic and pepper to the bean mixture. Cover and cook on low for 30 minutes.

Add sausage and reserved ham. Cook, uncovered, for 15 minutes or until heated through, stirring occasionally. Serve with rice. **Yield:** 8 servings.

Seafood Cakes

(Pictured on page 189)

Ordinary crab cakes are fine, but my family prefers this version that also showcases scallops and shrimp.
—*Kimberlie Scott, Massena, New York*

1/2 pound uncooked scallops
1/4 pound uncooked medium
   shrimp, peeled and deveined
1/2 cup heavy whipping cream
1 egg yolk
1 tablespoon Dijon mustard
1/2 teaspoon salt
1/4 teaspoon cayenne pepper
5 cans (6 ounces *each*) lump
   crabmeat, drained
2 tablespoons minced chives
1/4 cup vegetable oil
Seafood cocktail sauce, optional

Place scallops and shrimp in a food processor; cover and pulse until chopped. Add the cream, egg yolk, mustard, salt and cayenne; cover and process until pureed. Transfer to a large bowl; fold in crab and chives. Refrigerate for at least 30 minutes.

With floured hands, shape mixture by 2 tablespoonfuls into 1/2-in.-thick patties. In a large skillet over medium-high heat, cook seafood cakes in batches in oil for 3-4 minutes on each side or until golden brown. Serve with seafood sauce if desired. **Yield:** 3 dozen.

New Orleans Jambalaya

(Pictured at right)

Jambalaya is a catch-all for meat and seafood, making it a favorite of my husband! It's sure to warm you up on a chilly day.
—Sabrina Hickey, Columbus, Ohio

1/2 teaspoon mustard seed
1/2 teaspoon coriander seeds
1/2 teaspoon whole peppercorns
1/2 teaspoon dill seed
1/2 teaspoon whole allspice
2 pounds boneless skinless chicken breasts, cut into 1-inch cubes
1 pound boneless skinless chicken thighs, cut into 1-inch cubes
1/2 pound boneless pork, cut into 1-inch cubes
1 medium onion, chopped
1 large green pepper, chopped
1 celery rib, chopped
2 garlic cloves, minced
2 tablespoons butter
1 tablespoon vegetable oil
1 pound smoked kielbasa *or* Polish sausage, cut into 1-inch slices
1 cup diced fully cooked ham
1 can (14-1/2 ounces) diced tomatoes, undrained
1 to 2 cups water, *divided*
1/2 cup tomato puree
2 tablespoons minced fresh parsley
2 teaspoons salt
3/4 teaspoon pepper
1/2 teaspoon dried thyme
1/2 teaspoon cayenne pepper
1/2 teaspoon chili powder
1/8 teaspoon apple pie spice
2 bay leaves
1/2 pound uncooked small shrimp, peeled and deveined
Hot cooked rice

Place the first five ingredients on a double thickness of cheesecloth; bring up corners of cloth and tie with kitchen string to form a bag. Set aside.

In a soup kettle, saute the chicken, pork, onion, green pepper, celery and garlic in butter and oil until meat is browned. Stir in the sausage, ham, tomatoes, 1 cup water, tomato puree, parsley, salt, pepper, thyme, cayenne, chili powder, apple pie spice, bay leaves and spice bag.

Bring to a boil. Reduce heat; cover and simmer for 1 hour, stirring occasionally. During the last 3 minutes, add shrimp and remaining water if necessary. Discard bay leaves and spice bag. Serve over rice. **Yield:** 16 servings.

Bayou Chicken

The chicken always turns out moist and tender whenever I prepare it this way.
—*Fran Dell, Las Vegas, Nevada*

1/2 cup all-purpose flour
1/2 teaspoon salt
1/4 teaspoon pepper
1/4 teaspoon paprika
 1 broiler/fryer chicken (3 to 4 pounds), cut up
 2 tablespoons butter
 2 tablespoons vegetable oil
1/2 pound sliced fresh mushrooms
1/4 cup chopped onion
 3 cans (15-1/2 ounces *each*) black-eyed peas, drained
1/2 teaspoon garlic salt
1/4 teaspoon herbes de Provence
1/2 cup white wine *or* chicken broth
 1 medium tomato, chopped

In a large resealable plastic bag, combine the flour, salt, pepper and paprika. Add chicken, a few pieces at a time, and shake to coat. In a large skillet, brown chicken in butter and oil on all sides. Remove and set aside.

In the same skillet, saute mushrooms and onion until onion is crisp-tender, stirring to loosen browned bits from pan. Stir in the peas, garlic salt and herbes de Provence. Transfer to an ungreased 13-in. x 9-in. x 2-in. baking dish.

Arrange chicken over pea mixture. Pour wine or broth over chicken; sprinkle with tomato. Cover and bake at 325° for 1-1/4 to 1-1/2 hours or until chicken juices run clear. **Yield:** 6 servings.

Editor's Note: Look for herbes de Provence in the spice aisle of your grocery store. It is also available from Penzeys Spices. Call 1-800/741-7787 or visit www.penzeys.com.

Baked Creole Shrimp

A friend shared this recipe with me after tinkering with different ways to prepare freshly caught shrimp. Here in the South, we bake the shrimp unpeeled.
—*Brenda Cox, Reidsville, North Carolina*

2-1/2 pounds uncooked medium shrimp, peeled and deveined
 1 cup butter, cubed
 2 medium lemons, thinly sliced
 3 tablespoons Worcestershire sauce
4-1/2 teaspoons Creole seasoning
 3 teaspoons pepper
1-1/2 teaspoons minced chives
1-1/2 teaspoons cider vinegar
1/2 teaspoon salt
1/2 teaspoon dried rosemary, crushed
1/2 teaspoon hot pepper sauce

Place shrimp in a 3-qt. baking dish. In a small saucepan, combine the remaining ingredients; bring to a boil over medium heat. Pour over shrimp.

Bake, uncovered, at 400°, for 15-20 minutes or until shrimp turn pink. Remove with a slotted spoon to a serving platter. **Yield:** 4-6 servings.

Editor's Note: The following spices may be substituted for 1 teaspoon Creole seasoning: 1/4 teaspoon each salt, garlic powder and paprika; and a pinch each of dried thyme, ground cumin and cayenne pepper.

Mardi Gras Gear

(Pictured at right)

COLORFUL, festive decorations are the perfect way to add authenticity to your gathering for Mardi Gras (French for Fat Tuesday).

You can find supplies in the official colors (green for faith; purple for justice; gold for power) on-line and at party stores.

Masks and Hats. For many, donning hats and feathered masks during Mardi Gras is the highlight of the carnival season. You can buy a bunch and set them out for guests to grab as they enter your party.

A Bounty of Beads. In New Orleans, people on floats throw out assorted beads to the parade watchers. In your home, hang beads from chandeliers, lay them on tables and wear them around your neck.

Doubloon Tokens. These double-sided toy coins are also thrown along the Mardi Gras parade route. Scatter them on tabletops at your party and encourage guests to take them home as party souvenirs.

In the photo at right, we created a "grab-and-go" costume station that would be perfect near the front door.

MARDI GRAS MASK INVITATION

WHAT better way to unveil your Mardi Gras plans than on a Mardi Gras mask! Purchase masks that allow you to write on the back and that fit into business-size envelopes.

Elegant Afternoon Tea

IRON your finest linens, dust off the china and polish your silver. Then invite a few girlfriends over for a tasteful tea…it's a fun-filled way to spend an afternoon!

Have hot Sunburst Spiced Tea ready as guests arrive. This delicious drink is fabulously flavored with orange and lemon zest and a blend of spices.

Finger sandwiches are synonymous with tea parties. So offer an appealing assortment, including Tuna Tea Sandwiches, Savory Cucumber Sandwiches and Nutty Chicken Sandwiches. (All recipes shown at right.)

A selection of sweets—like Blueberry Pecan Scones, Green Tea Citrus Sorbet, Pecan Sandies and Almond Petits Fours—round out the mid-afternoon menu.

LADIES' LUNCHEON
(Clockwise from top left)

Tuna Tea Sandwiches (p. 200)

Savory Cucumber Sandwiches (p. 203)

Nutty Chicken Sandwiches (p. 200)

Sunburst Spiced Tea (p. 204)

Tuna Tea Sandwiches

(Pictured on page 198)

A friend brought tuna sandwiches to a picnic years ago.
I never got the recipe from her, but these are close and just as delicious.
—Lisa Sneed, Bayfield, Colorado

1 can (6 ounces) light water-packed tuna, drained and flaked
1 to 2 tablespoons mayonnaise
1/4 teaspoon lemon-pepper seasoning
4 tablespoons soft goat cheese
4 slices multigrain bread, crusts removed
4 large fresh basil leaves

In a small bowl, combine the tuna, mayonnaise and lemon-pepper. Spread 1 tablespoon of goat cheese on each slice of bread. Spread two slices with tuna mixture; top with basil leaves and remaining bread. Cut in half or into desired shapes. **Yield:** 8 tea sandwiches.

Nutty Chicken Sandwiches

(Pictured on page 199)

Pineapple gives these chicken salad sandwiches a bit of sweetness, while pecans add a bit of crunch.
—Nancy Johnson, Laverne, Oklahoma

1 cup shredded cooked chicken breast
1 hard-cooked egg, chopped
1/2 cup unsweetened crushed pineapple, drained
1/3 cup mayonnaise
1/2 teaspoon salt
1/8 teaspoon pepper
1/4 cup chopped pecans, toasted
1/2 cup fresh baby spinach
8 slices white bread, crusts removed

In a small bowl, combine chicken, egg, pineapple, mayonnaise, salt and pepper. Cover and refrigerate at least 1 hour.

Just before serving, stir in pecans. Place spinach on four slices of bread; top with chicken salad and remaining bread. Cut each sandwich into quarters. **Yield:** 16 tea sandwiches.

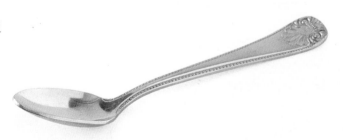

Almond Petits Fours

(Pictured at right)

Dainty, bite-sized cakes are often the highlight of a ladies' luncheon. Our home economists share their mouth-watering version here.

   1 **can (8 ounces) almond paste**
3/4 **cup butter, softened**
3/4 **cup sugar**
   4 **eggs**
   1 **cup cake flour**
1/4 **cup seedless raspberry**
     spreadable fruit
GLAZE:
4-1/2 **cups sugar**
2-1/4 **cups water**
 1/4 **teaspoon cream of tartar**
1-1/2 **teaspoons clear vanilla extract**
 1/4 **teaspoon almond extract**
   6 **cups confectioners' sugar**
Assorted food coloring

Line a 15-in. x 10-in. x 1-in. baking pan with parchment paper; coat the paper with nonstick cooking spray and set aside.

In a large mixing bowl, cream the almond paste, butter and sugar until light and fluffy. Add eggs, one at a time, beating well after each addition. Beat in flour. Spread evenly into prepared pan.

Bake at 325° for 12-15 minutes or until a toothpick inserted near the center comes out clean. Cool for 10 minutes before removing from pan to a wire rack to cool completely.

Cut cake in half widthwise. Spread jam over one half; top with remaining half. Cut into assorted 1-1/2-in. shapes.

In a large saucepan, combine the sugar, water and cream of tartar. Cook over medium-high heat, without stirring, until a candy thermometer reads 226°. Remove from the heat; cool at room temperature to 100°. Stir in extracts. Using a portable mixer, beat in confectioners' sugar until smooth. Tint some of glaze with food coloring.

Gently dip petits fours, one at a time, into warm glaze. Remove with a fork; allow excess glaze to drip off. (If glaze becomes too thick, stir in 1 teaspoon hot water at a time to thin.) Place petits fours on wire racks over waxed paper; let dry completely. **Yield:** 2-1/2 dozen.

Editor's Note: We recommend that you test your candy thermometer before each use by bringing water to a boil; the thermometer should read 212°. Adjust your recipe temperature up or down based on your test.

Blueberry Pecan Scones

(Pictured at far right, bottom)

These scones are great any time of year using fresh or frozen blueberries.
I serve them alone as a snack or as part of a meal.
— Priscilla Gilbert, Indian Harbour Beach, Florida

 2 cups all-purpose flour
 1/4 cup plus 1 tablespoon sugar, *divided*
 3 teaspoons baking powder
 3/4 teaspoon salt
 1/4 cup cold butter
 1 egg
 1/2 cup milk
 1-1/2 teaspoons vanilla extract
 1 cup fresh *or* frozen blueberries
 1/3 cup chopped pecans, toasted
 2 teaspoons grated lemon peel
 1 egg white, lightly beaten

In a large bowl, combine the flour, 1/4 cup sugar, baking powder and salt. Cut in butter until mixture resembles coarse crumbs. In a bowl, whisk the egg, milk and vanilla; add to crumb mixture. Stir in the blueberries, pecans and lemon peel just until moistened.

Turn dough onto a floured surface. With lightly floured hands, knead 6-8 times. Pat into an 8-in. circle; cut into eight wedges. Separate wedges and place 2 in. apart on a greased baking sheet.

Brush with egg white and sprinkle with remaining sugar. Bake at 375° for 18-22 minutes or until lightly browned. Serve warm. **Yield:** 8 scones.

Editor's Note: If using frozen blueberries, do not thaw before adding to batter.

SHAPING SCONES

WHEN preparing homemade scones, shape the dough into a circle on a floured surface. Cut it into wedges with a sharp knife.

Vanilla-Scented Tea

This mildly flavored tea from our Test Kitchen complements both sweet and savory items.

 4 cups water
 1 vanilla bean
 4 teaspoons English breakfast tea leaves *or* other black tea leaves

Place water in a large saucepan. Split vanilla bean and scrape seeds into water; add bean. Bring just to a boil.

Place tea leaves in a teapot. Pour vanilla water over tea leaves; cover and steep for 3 minutes. Strain tea, discarding leaves and bean. Serve immediately. **Yield:** 4 servings.

For one serving: Bring 1 cup water and 1-1/2 in. of seeded split vanilla bean just to a boil. Pour over 1 teaspoon tea leaves. Steep and strain as directed.

Lavender Mint Tea

(Pictured at right, top)

With wonderful mint, lavender, rosemary and honey, you won't miss the tea leaves in this hot beverage from our home economists.

1/4 cup thinly sliced fresh mint leaves
4 teaspoons dried lavender flowers
1/2 teaspoon minced fresh rosemary
4 cups boiling water
2 teaspoons honey, optional

In a large bowl, combine the mint, lavender and rosemary. Add boiling water. Cover and steep for 4 minutes. Strain tea, discarding mint mixture. Stir in honey if desired. Serve immediately. **Yield:** 4 servings.

Editor's Note: Dried lavender flowers are available from Penzeys Spices. Call 1-800/741-7787 or visit www.penzeys.com.

For one serving: Combine 1 tablespoon mint leaves, 1 teaspoon lavender and 1/8 teaspoon rosemary. Add 1 cup boiling water. Steep and strain as directed. Add honey as desired.

Savory Cucumber Sandwiches

(Pictured on page 199)

Italian salad dressing easily flavors this simple spread.
Serve it as a dip with crackers and veggies or use it as a sandwich filling.
—Carol Henderson, Chagrin Falls, Ohio

1 package (8 ounces) cream cheese, softened
1/2 cup mayonnaise
1 envelope Italian salad dressing mix
36 slices snack rye bread
1 medium cucumber, sliced

In a small mixing bowl, combine the cream cheese, mayonnaise and salad dressing mix until blended. Refrigerate for 1 hour.

Just before serving, spread over rye bread; top each with a cucumber slice. **Yield:** 3 dozen.

Pecan Sandies

These rich, nutty cookies pair well with tea, coffee and milk.
One batch never lasts long around our house!
—Leah Stewart, Lewisville, Arkansas

2/3 cup butter-flavored shortening
1/2 cup sugar
1/2 cup confectioners' sugar
1 egg
1 teaspoon vanilla extract
1-1/2 cups all-purpose flour
1/2 teaspoon cream of tartar
1/2 teaspoon baking soda
1/4 teaspoon salt
1/2 cup chopped pecans

In a small mixing bowl, cream shortening and sugars until light and fluffy. Beat in egg and vanilla. Combine the flour, cream of tartar, baking soda and salt; gradually add to creamed mixture. Stir in pecans.

Roll into 1-in. balls. Place 2 in. apart on ungreased baking sheets. Coat the bottom of a glass with nonstick cooking spray; flatten cookies with glass. Bake at 350° for 18-20 minutes or until edges are lightly browned. Cool for 1-2 minutes before removing to wire racks. **Yield:** 2 dozen.

Sunburst Spiced Tea

(Pictured on page 198)

Our home economists use oranges and lemon to lend a lovely citrus flavor to ordinary black tea.

2 medium oranges
1 medium lemon
4 cardamom seeds
4 whole cloves
4 teaspoons English breakfast tea leaves *or* other black tea leaves
4 cups boiling water

Using a citrus zester, remove peel from oranges and lemon in long narrow strips. (Save fruit for another use.) Place the peel strips, cardamom and cloves in a large bowl. With the end of a wooden spoon handle, crush mixture until aromas are released.

Add tea leaves and boiling water. Cover and steep for 6 minutes. Strain tea, discarding peel mixture. Serve immediately. **Yield:** 4 servings.

For one serving: Combine the zest of 1/2 orange, 1/4 lemon, 1 cardamom seed and 1 clove; crush as directed. Add 1 teaspoon tea leaves and 1 cup boiling water. Steep and strain as directed.

Teatime Party Favors

(Pictured at right)

THE TIME at the tea party will likely be fleeting. So send guests home with a memento of the special afternoon that they can cherish for years to come.

As you plan your party, be on the lookout for mismatched tea cup and saucer sets. You can find them at garage sales, flea markets, antique malls and even discount department stores. While shopping, also pick up vintage hankies.

At home, place each hanky in a sheer drawstring gift bag, allowing the corners to peek out. (You could also fill each gift bag with a sachet, tea bag or small picture frame.) Set each filled gift bag in a tea cup and pass them out as guests leave the party.

Green Tea Citrus Sorbet

Who says tea is only meant for sipping? Green tea cleverly stars in this sorbet from our Test Kitchen.

4 cups water, *divided*
8 individual green tea bags
1-1/2 cups sugar
2 tablespoons lemon juice
2 tablespoons lime juice

In a small saucepan, bring 2 cups water to a boil. Remove from the heat; add tea bags. Cover and steep for 5 minutes. Discard tea bags.

In a large saucepan, bring sugar and remaining water to a boil. Cook and stir until sugar is dissolved. Remove from the heat; stir in the juices and green tea.

Fill cylinder of ice cream freezer; freeze according to manufacturer's directions. Transfer sorbet to a freezer container; cover and freeze for 4 hours or until firm. **Yield:** 1-1/2 quarts.

Fun-Filled Fourth of July

YOU'LL want to flag the mouth-watering recipes in this chapter when planning a patriotic picnic for the Fourth of July.

Find freedom from the grill by offering a stars-and-stripes spread showcasing scrumptious sandwiches. Pesto Roast Beef Sub and Antipasto Focaccia Sandwiches are two such tried-and-true choices.

With cayenne pepper and assorted herbs, Three-Bean Salad features an explosion of flavors that adds a little spark to any outdoor event.

Guests will be in their glory when Fudgy Patriotic Brownies are passed around as the grand, finger-lickin'-good finale. (All recipes shown at right.)

PATRIOTIC PICNIC
(Clockwise from top)

Pesto Roast Beef Sub (p. 208)

Antipasto Focaccia Sandwiches (p. 214)

Fudgy Patriotic Brownies (p. 212)

Three-Bean Salad (p. 208)

Pesto Roast Beef Sub

(Pictured on page 207)

In this scrumptious sandwich, I dress up deli roast beef with a fast-to-fix pesto.
—*Patricia Kile, Greentown, Pennsylvania*

1 cup loosely packed basil leaves
2 tablespoons grated Parmesan cheese
1 tablespoon chopped dill pickle
1 tablespoon white wine vinegar
2 teaspoons Dijon mustard
1 garlic clove, peeled
1/4 cup olive oil
1 loaf (1 pound) unsliced French bread
1/2 pound thinly sliced deli roast beef
4 slices provolone cheese

1 medium tomato, thinly sliced
1-1/2 cups fresh baby spinach

For pesto, in a food processor, combine the basil, Parmesan cheese, pickle, vinegar, mustard and garlic; cover and process until chopped. While processing, gradually add oil in a steady stream; process until blended.

Cut the loaf of bread in half horizontally. Hollow out bottom half, leaving a 3/4-in. shell (discard removed bread or save for another use). Spread two-thirds of the pesto inside shell; layer with beef, cheese, tomato and spinach. Spread remaining pesto over cut side of bread top; place over sandwich. Cut into slices to serve. **Yield:** 6-8 servings.

Three-Bean Salad

(Pictured on page 206)

Fresh herbs and cayenne pepper provide the fantastic flavor in this marinated salad featuring fresh veggies and canned beans.
—*Carol Tucker, Wooster, Ohio*

1 can (15-1/2 ounces) great northern beans, rinsed and drained
1 can (15 ounces) garbanzo beans *or* chickpeas, rinsed and drained
1 can (15 ounces) black beans, rinsed and drained
1 medium tomato, chopped
1 medium onion, chopped
1 celery rib, chopped
1/3 cup *each* chopped green, sweet red and yellow pepper
1/2 cup water

3 tablespoons minced fresh basil *or* 1 tablespoon dried basil
2 tablespoons minced fresh parsley
2 tablespoons lemon juice
2 tablespoons olive oil
1-1/2 teaspoons minced fresh oregano *or* 1/2 teaspoon dried oregano
1/2 teaspoon salt
1/2 teaspoon pepper
1/4 teaspoon cayenne pepper

In a large bowl, combine the beans, tomato, onion, celery and peppers. In a small bowl, whisk the remaining ingredients; gently stir into bean mixture. Cover and refrigerate for 4 hours, stirring occasionally. **Yield:** 8 servings.

Grilled Steak and Portobello Stacks

(Pictured at right)

You don't need a special panini maker for these bistro-style sandwiches. They make take some time to prepare, but it's well worth it!
—Judy Murphy, Coeur d' Alene, Idaho

2 tablespoons plus 1/4 cup olive oil, *divided*
1 tablespoon herbes de Provence
1 beef tenderloin (1-1/4 pounds)
4 large portobello mushrooms
2 tablespoons balsamic vinegar
BALSAMIC ONION:
  1 large onion, halved and thinly sliced
4-1/2 teaspoons sugar
  1/2 teaspoon salt
  1/2 teaspoon pepper
  1 tablespoon olive oil
  2 tablespoons balsamic vinegar
HORSERADISH SAUCE:
  1/2 cup sour cream
1-1/2 teaspoons prepared horseradish
  1/4 teaspoon Worcestershire sauce
SANDWICHES:
  12 slices white bread
  1/4 cup butter, melted
  4 cups spring mix salad greens
  2 tablespoons red wine vinaigrette
  3/4 cup julienned roasted sweet red peppers

In a small bowl, combine 2 tablespoons oil and herbes de Provence. Rub over tenderloin; cover and refrigerate for 2 hours. Place mushrooms in a small bowl; toss with vinegar and remaining oil. Cover and refrigerate until grilling.

In a large skillet, cook the onion, sugar, salt and pepper in oil over medium heat for 15-20 minutes or until golden brown, stirring frequently. Remove from the heat; stir in vinegar. Set aside.

In a small bowl, combine the sauce ingredients. Cover and refrigerate until serving.

Grill tenderloin and mushrooms, covered, over medium heat for 8-10 minutes on each side or until meat reaches desired doneness (for medium-rare, a meat thermometer should read 145°; medium, 160°; well-done, 170°) and mushrooms are tender. Let tenderloin stand for 10 minutes.

Meanwhile, brush both sides of bread with butter. Grill over medium heat for 1 minute on each side or until browned. Toss salad greens with vinaigrette. Cut tenderloin and mushrooms into thin slices.

Divide mushrooms among four slices of bread. Layer with roasted peppers, greens and another slice of bread. Top each with onion mixture and beef. Spread sauce over remaining slices of bread; place over beef. Cut each sandwich diagonally in half. **Yield:** 4-8 servings.

Editor's Note: Look for herbes de Provence in the spice aisle of your grocery store. It is also available from Penzeys Spices. Call 1-800/741-7787 or visit www.penzeys.com.

Mini Burgers with the Works
(Pictured at far right)

I started preparing these mini burgers several years ago as a way to use up bread crusts in my freezer.
—Linda Lane, Bennington, Vermont

1/4 pound ground beef
3 slices process American cheese
4 slices white bread (heels of loaf recommended)
2 tablespoons Thousand Island salad dressing
2 pearl onions, thinly sliced
4 baby dill pickles, thinly sliced
3 cherry tomatoes, thinly sliced

Shape beef into 1-in. patties. Place on a microwave-safe plate lined with microwave-safe paper towels. Cover with another paper towel; microwave on high for 1 minute or until meat is no longer pink. Cut each slice of cheese into fourths; set aside.

Using a 1-in. round cookie cutter, cut out six circles from each slice of bread. Spread half of the bread circles with dressing. Layer with burgers, cheese, onions, pickles and tomatoes. Top with remaining bread circles; secure with toothpicks. Serve immediately. **Yield:** 1 dozen.

Editor's Note: This recipe was tested in a 1,100-watt microwave.

Grilled Chicken Pesto Sandwiches

Pesto and sweet red peppers really jazz up regular grilled chicken sandwiches.
—Lisa Sneed, Bayfield, Colorado

8 boneless skinless chicken breast halves (5 to 6 ounces each)
1/2 cup plus 2 tablespoons lemon juice, *divided*
1/4 cup plus 1 tablespoon olive oil, *divided*
2-1/4 teaspoons salt, *divided*
2-1/4 teaspoons pepper, *divided*
1-1/4 cups loosely packed basil leaves
1/4 cup shredded Parmesan cheese
1 garlic clove, peeled
1/4 cup pine nuts, toasted
8 hamburger buns, split
1/2 cup mayonnaise
8 slices provolone cheese
1-1/2 cups julienned roasted sweet red peppers

Flatten chicken to 1/4-in. thickness. In a large resealable plastic bag, combine 1/2 cup lemon juice, 1/4 cup oil, 2 teaspoons salt and 2 teaspoons pepper; add chicken. Seal bag and turn to coat. Refrigerate for 1 hour.

For pesto, place the basil, Parmesan cheese and garlic in a small food processor; cover and pulse until chopped. Add the pine nuts and remaining lemon juice, salt and pepper; cover and process until blended. While processing, gradually add remaining oil in a steady stream. Set aside.

Drain and discard marinade. Grill chicken, covered, over medium heat for 4-6 minutes on each side or until juices run clear. Grill buns, covered, for 2-3 minutes or until golden brown.

Spread 1 tablespoon mayonnaise over cut side of bun bottoms. Layer with chicken, provolone cheese and roasted red peppers. Spread pesto over cut side of bun tops; place over sandwiches. **Yield:** 8 servings.

Guacamole Appetizer Squares

(Pictured at right)

This cold appetizer pizza has appeared at family functions for many years. I know you'll love it, too.
—Laurie Pester, Colstrip, Montana

> 2 tubes (8 ounces *each*) refrigerated crescent rolls
> 1-1/2 teaspoons taco seasoning
> 1 package (1 pound) sliced bacon, diced
> 1 package (8 ounces) cream cheese, softened
> 1-1/2 cups guacamole
> 3 plum tomatoes, chopped
> 1 can (3.8 ounces) sliced ripe olives, drained

Unroll both tubes of crescent dough and pat into an ungreased 15-in. x 10-in. x 1-in. baking pan; seal seams and perforations. Build up edges. Prick dough with a fork; sprinkle with taco seasoning. Bake at 375° for 10-12 minutes or until golden brown. Cool completely on a wire rack.

In a large skillet, cook bacon over medium heat until crisp. Using a slotted spoon, remove to paper towels. In a small mixing bowl, beat cream cheese and guacamole until smooth.

Spread cream cheese mixture over crust. Sprinkle with bacon, tomatoes and olives. Refrigerate until serving. Cut into squares. **Yield:** about 3 dozen.

Family Traditions

ON Independence Day, we get the grill going early for barbecued smoked pork loins and get the corn ready for roasting. Love of country, family and food...what a good way to celebrate the Fourth of July!
—Loretta Ruda, Kennesaw, Georgia

Fudgy Patriotic Brownies

(Pictured on page 206)

A rich chocolate frosting makes these brownies really tasty. I always come home with an empty pan.
—Julie Moyer, Union Grove, Wisconsin

1 cup butter, cubed
4 squares (1 ounce *each*)
  unsweetened chocolate,
  chopped
2 cups sugar
1 teaspoon vanilla extract
4 eggs
1-1/4 cups all-purpose flour
1/2 teaspoon salt
1 cup chopped pecans
FROSTING:
1/4 cup butter, cubed
2 squares (1 ounce *each*)
  unsweetened chocolate,
  chopped
3 cups confectioners' sugar
5 to 6 tablespoons milk
1 teaspoon vanilla extract
Red, white and blue decorating icing

In a large saucepan, melt butter and chocolate over low heat; stir until smooth. Remove from the heat. Stir in sugar and vanilla. Add eggs, one at a time, stirring well after each addition. Combine flour and salt; stir into chocolate mixture until combined. Stir in pecans.

Spread into a greased 13-in. x 9-in. x 2-in. baking dish. Bake at 325° for 35-40 minutes or until a toothpick inserted near the center comes out clean. Cool on a wire rack.

For frosting, in a small heavy saucepan, melt butter and chocolate over low heat; stir until smooth. Remove from the heat. Stir in the confectioners' sugar, milk and vanilla until blended.

Frost brownies; score into 24 bars. Using a small star-shaped cookie cutter, lightly press a star outline in the center of each brownie. Outline stars with red, white and blue icing. **Yield:** 2 dozen.

BLT Pita Pockets

I often prepare sandwiches for dinner in summer when I want to keep my kitchen cool. Pita pockets are a nice change from regular bread.
—Stacie Lehnen, Youngsville, Pennsylvania

1 package (2.1 ounces)
  ready-to-serve fully cooked
  bacon
2 cups torn romaine
1-1/2 cups (6 ounces) shredded
  part-skim mozzarella cheese
1 large tomato, chopped
1/3 cup mayonnaise

3 pita breads (6 inches), warmed and halved
12 slices tomato

Microwave bacon according to package directions. Meanwhile, in a large bowl, combine the romaine, cheese and chopped tomato. Crumble bacon over the top; add mayonnaise and toss to coat. Line pita halves with tomato slices; fill each with 1/2 cup bacon mixture. **Yield:** 6 servings.

Sugar Cookie Fruit Pizzas

(Pictured at right)

*Purchased sugar cookies make a sweet
"crust" for colorful fruit pizzas.
Prepare them all year long with
a variety of fresh and canned fruits.*
—Marge Hodel, Roanoke, Illinois

1/2 cup sugar
  1 tablespoon cornstarch
1/2 cup unsweetened pineapple
    juice
1/4 cup water
  2 tablespoons lemon juice
  4 ounces cream cheese,
    softened
1/4 cup confectioners' sugar
1-3/4 cups whipped topping
 12 sugar cookies (3 inches)
  1 cup fresh blueberries
  1 cup chopped peeled kiwifruit
1/2 cup chopped fresh
    strawberries

For glaze, in a small saucepan, combine the sugar, cornstarch, pineapple juice, water and lemon juice until smooth. Bring to a boil; cook and stir for 2 minutes or until thickened. Transfer to a small bowl; refrigerate until cooled but not set.

In a small mixing bowl, beat cream cheese and confectioners' sugar until smooth; fold in whipped topping. Spread over tops of cookies. Arrange fruit on top; drizzle with glaze. Refrigerate for 1 hour or until chilled. **Yield:** 1 dozen.

PEELING A KIWIFRUIT

CUT off both ends from the fruit. Using a vegetable peeler, peel off the fuzzy brown skin. With a sharp knife, cut the fruit into slices, wedges or chunks.

Antipasto Focaccia Sandwiches

(Pictured on page 207)

Cooking for a crowd? Make these Italian-style sandwiches!
I love that they are prepared and refrigerated hours in advance.
—Robyn Cavallaro, Easton, Pennsylvania

1/2 pound Genoa salami, diced
1/2 pound deli ham, diced
1/2 pound pepperoni, diced
1 block (8 ounces) provolone cheese, diced
1 cup canned garbanzo beans *or* chickpeas, rinsed, drained and chopped
1 cup canned kidney beans, rinsed, drained and chopped
2 medium tomatoes, chopped
1/2 cup finely chopped red onion
1/2 cup sliced pepperoncinis

1/2 teaspoon coarsely ground pepper
1 cup Italian salad dressing
3 loaves (1 pound *each*) focaccia bread
3 cups torn leaf lettuce

In a large bowl, combine the first 10 ingredients; add salad dressing and toss to coat. Cover and refrigerate for 8 hours or overnight.

Cut each loaf of focaccia in half horizontally. Hollow out bottom halves, leaving 3/4-in. shells. Stir antipasto mixture; spoon into shells. Replace bread tops. Wrap sandwiches tightly in plastic wrap; refrigerate for at least 2 hours.

Just before serving, add lettuce to sandwiches. Cut into wedges. **Yield:** 3 sandwiches (6 servings each).

Green Bean Pasta Salad

I like to prepare this special pasta salad with fresh green beans and
homegrown dill. Serve chilled or at room temperature.
—Chris Snyder, Boulder, Colorado

8 ounces uncooked spiral pasta
1 pound fresh green beans, trimmed and cut into 1-inch pieces
1/4 cup olive oil
2 tablespoons white wine vinegar
1/8 teaspoon cayenne pepper
1 cup cubed fully cooked ham
4 green onions, thinly sliced
2 tablespoons minced fresh parsley
1 to 2 tablespoons snipped fresh dill *or* 1 teaspoon dill weed

Salt to taste
1 cup chopped walnuts, toasted

Cook pasta according to package directions. Meanwhile, place beans in a large saucepan and cover with water. Bring to a boil; cook, uncovered, for 8-10 minutes or until crisp-tender.

Drain pasta and beans; rinse in cold water. Place in a large bowl. In a jar with a tight-fitting lid, combine the oil, vinegar and cayenne; shake well. Drizzle over pasta mixture and toss to coat.

Add the ham, onions, parsley, dill and salt; toss to coat. Refrigerate until serving. Stir in walnuts just before serving. **Yield:** 10 servings.

Clever Beverage Coolers

(Pictured at right)

THIRST-QUENCHING beverages are a surefire way to keep guests cool at an outdoor summer gathering. But keeping refreshments cold in the sweltering sun can be a challenge.

If you don't have enough coolers to ice down drinks, use one of these innovative ideas.

Tabletop Ice Chest. Don't let the sun hamper your ability to chill out. A wicker picnic basket lined with a plastic liner or bag makes for a pretty and practical presentation. (See photo at top right.)

Frosty Fruit. Serving watermelon at your picnic? Don't get rid of the rind! Instead, hollow out the shell and fill it with ice and drinks as shown at right, middle. (Serve the sweet fruit for dinner.) This melon cooler is just the right size for a smaller group.

Buckets of Fun. A wheelbarrow and metal tub do double duty as basins for beverages on a patio (bottom right photo). Make sure both vessels are well-scrubbed and in good condition before using.

No matter how you choose to chill beverages, try to keep the containers in the shade. Also be sure to have plenty of ice on hand. And remember...the hotter it is, the more ice you'll need.

Thrill of the *Grill*

NO MATTER the season or occasion, people often head outside to cook great-tasting food on their grills. And it's no wonder…the food is always fabulous and the mess stays out of the kitchen!

Add a little sizzle to suppertime by preparing Apple-Butter Barbecued Chicken. The can-cooking method results in moist and tender, flavorful fare.

Looking to liven up ordinary side dishes? Check out Carrots on the Grill and Grilled Vegetable Medley. Then pass a basket of sliced Bacon Garlic Bread. (All recipes shown at right.)

From appetizers and sides to main dishes and even desserts, the dishes on the following pages provide everything you need for excellent outdoor dining.

BACKYARD YUMMIES
(Pictured above)

Apple-Butter Barbecued Chicken (p. 218)

Bacon Garlic Bread (p. 220)

Grilled Vegetable Medley (p. 219)

Carrots on the Grill (p. 219)

Apple-Butter Barbecued Chicken

(Pictured on page 217)

*I love cooking so much I sometimes think of recipes in my sleep and wake up
to write them down! This dream-inspired dish is my family's favorite way to eat chicken.*
— Holly Kilbel, Akron, Ohio

1 teaspoon salt
3/4 teaspoon garlic powder
1/4 teaspoon pepper
1/8 teaspoon cayenne pepper
1 roasting chicken (6 to 7 pounds)
1 can (11-1/2 ounces) unsweetened apple juice
1/2 cup apple butter
1/4 cup barbecue sauce

Combine the salt, garlic powder, pepper and cayenne; sprinkle over chicken.

Prepare grill for indirect heat, using a drip pan. Pour half of the apple juice into another container and save for another use. With a can opener, poke additional holes in the top of the can. Holding the chicken with legs pointed down, lower chicken over the can so it fills the body cavity. Place chicken on grill rack over drip pan.

Grill, covered, over indirect medium heat for 1-1/2 to 2 hours or until a meat thermometer reads 180°. Combine apple butter and barbecue sauce; baste chicken occasionally during the last 30 minutes. Remove chicken from grill; cover and let stand for 10 minutes. Remove chicken from can before carving. **Yield:** 6-8 servings.

REMOVING THE CAN FROM GRILLED CHICKEN

THE trickiest part of can cooking is removing the chicken from the grill. Carefully slide a wide grilling spatula under the can while grasping the chicken with tongs.

Remember, the liquid in the can is hot, so allow the chicken and can to cool slightly before removing the can. Using tongs or insulated gloves, grasp the can and gently twist the chicken slightly while pulling upward to release from the can.

To make this grilling method easier and safer, you may want to invest in a manufactured grill helper that holds or replaces the can. They can range in price from $7 to $20.

Carrots on The Grill

(Pictured at right and on page 217)

Family and friends are surprised when I tell them these carrots are prepared on the grill. This side complements any meaty entree.
—Carol Gaus, Elk Grove Village, Illinois

1/4 cup soy sauce
1/4 cup vegetable oil
  1 tablespoon minced fresh gingerroot
  1 tablespoon cider vinegar
  1 garlic clove, minced
  1 pound large carrots, halved lengthwise

In a large bowl, combine the soy sauce, oil, ginger, vinegar and garlic. Add carrots; toss to coat.

With tongs, place carrots on grill rack. Grill, covered, over medium heat for 15-20 minutes or until tender, turning and basting frequently with soy sauce mixture. **Yield:** 4-6 servings.

Grilled Vegetable Medley

(Pictured on page 217)

A simple-to-make marinade flavors a blend of vegetables in this recipe from our home economists.

  2 tablespoons Worcestershire sauce
  2 tablespoons olive oil
  2 tablespoons Dijon mustard
  1 teaspoon herbes de Provence
1/4 teaspoon pepper
  3 baby eggplants *or* 1 medium eggplant, cut lengthwise into 1/2-inch slices
  3 small yellow summer squash, cut lengthwise into 1/2-inch slices
  2 cups fresh sugar snap peas

In a large resealable plastic bag, combine the first five ingredients; add eggplant, squash and peas. Seal bag and turn to coat; refrigerate for 2 hours, turning once.

Drain and discard marinade. Place vegetables in a grill basket or disposable foil pan with slits cut in the bottom. Grill, covered, over medium heat for 5-7 minutes or until tender, stirring once. **Yield:** 4 servings.

Editor's Note: Look for herbes de Provence in the spice aisle of your grocery store. It is also available from Penzeys Spices. Call 1-800/741-7787 or visit www.penzeys.com.

Bacon Garlic Bread

(Pictured on page 217)

Guests at your next backyard barbecue will request our home economists' recipe for grilled garlic bread. Serve it as an appetizer or side dish.

1/3 cup butter, softened
1/3 cup mayonnaise
  4 bacon strips, cooked and crumbled
  5 garlic cloves, minced
  1 loaf (1 pound) French bread, halved lengthwise
  1 cup (4 ounces) shredded Italian cheese blend

In a small bowl, combine the butter, mayonnaise, bacon and garlic. Spread over cut sides of bread; reassemble loaf. Wrap in a large piece of heavy-duty foil (about 36 in. x 18 in.); seal tightly.

Grill, covered, over medium heat for 4-5 minutes on each side. Unwrap and separate bread halves. Sprinkle with cheese. Grill 5 minutes longer or until cheese is melted. **Yield:** 10-12 servings.

Ginger-Orange Pork Tenderloins

This fork-tender pork has a citrus, smoky flavor that my whole family loves. The combination of ingredients is unbeatable.
—Elaine Sweet, Dallas, Texas

1/2 cup orange juice concentrate
  2 tablespoons sherry *or* chicken broth
  2 tablespoons soy sauce
  1 tablespoon sesame oil
  2 tablespoons minced fresh thyme
  1 tablespoon minced fresh gingerroot
  3 garlic cloves, minced
  1 teaspoon pepper
  2 pork tenderloins (1 pound *each*)
GLAZE:
  1/4 cup orange juice concentrate
  2 tablespoons brown sugar
  2 tablespoons cider vinegar
  2 tablespoons molasses
  2 teaspoons minced fresh gingerroot
1/2 teaspoon salt
1/2 teaspoon pepper

In a blender or food processor, combine the first eight ingredients; cover and process until smooth. Pour into a large resealable plastic bag; add the pork. Seal bag and turn to coat. Refrigerate for 8 hours or overnight.

In a small saucepan, combine the glaze ingredients. Cook and stir over medium heat until thickened.

Prepare grill for indirect heat. Coat grill rack with nonstick cooking spray before starting the grill. Drain and discard marinade. Grill pork, covered, over indirect medium heat for 10-13 minutes on each side or until a meat thermometer reads 160°, brushing with glaze during the last 10 minutes. Let stand for 5 minutes before slicing. Serve with any remaining glaze. **Yield:** 6-8 servings.

Appetizer Pizzas

(Pictured at right)

To keep a summer kitchen cool, our home economists suggest preparing pizzas on the grill! A variety of ingredients tops flour tortillas for three terrific tastes.

9 flour tortillas (6 inches)
3 tablespoons olive oil

TRADITIONAL PIZZAS:
1/3 cup chopped pepperoni
3/4 cup shredded Colby-
   Monterey Jack cheese
1 jar (14 ounces) pizza sauce

MEDITERRANEAN PIZZAS:
1/2 cup chopped seeded tomato
1/3 cup sliced ripe olives
3/4 cup crumbled feta cheese
1/4 cup thinly sliced green onions
1 carton (7 ounces) hummus

MARGHERITA PIZZAS:
9 thin slices tomato
1 package (8 ounces) small
   fresh mozzarella cheese balls,
   sliced
1 tablespoon minced fresh basil
1 cup prepared pesto

Brush one side of each tortilla with oil. Place oiled side down on grill rack. Grill, uncovered, over medium heat for 2-3 minutes or until puffed. Brush tortillas with oil; turn and top with pizza toppings.

For Traditional Pizzas: Top three grilled tortillas with pepperoni and cheese. Cover and grill for 2-3 minutes or until cheese is melted. Cut into wedges; serve with pizza sauce.

For Mediterranean Pizzas: Top three grilled tortillas with tomato, olives, feta cheese and onions. Cover and grill for 2-3 minutes or until the cheese is heated through. Cut into wedges; serve with hummus.

For Margherita Pizzas: Top three grilled tortillas with tomato slices, mozzarella cheese and basil. Cover and grill for 2-3 minutes or until cheese is melted. Cut into wedges; serve with pesto. **Yield:** 9 appetizer pizzas.

Curried Salmon

(Pictured at far right)

Until our daughter shared this recipe, my husband and I swore we didn't like salmon.
But after one taste of this grilled version, we were converts!
—Carma Blosser, Livermore, Colorado

1/3 cup soy sauce
1/3 cup vegetable oil
1 teaspoon garlic powder
1 teaspoon curry powder
1 teaspoon lemon-pepper seasoning
1 teaspoon Worcestershire sauce
1/4 teaspoon Liquid Smoke, optional
6 salmon fillets (8 ounces *each*)

In a large resealable plastic bag, combine the soy sauce, oil, garlic powder, curry powder, lemon-pepper, Worcestershire sauce and Liquid Smoke if desired; add the salmon. Seal bag and turn to coat. Refrigerate for 1 hour.

Coat grill rack with nonstick cooking spray before starting the grill. Drain and discard marinade. Place salmon skin side down on rack. Grill, covered, over medium heat for 10-12 minutes or until fish flakes easily with a fork. **Yield:** 6 servings.

Grilled Peach-Berry Crisps

As dinner is winding down, put these individual fruit crisps from our
Test Kitchen on the grill. A scoop of cold ice cream is the crowning touch.

3 cups chopped peeled fresh peaches
1-1/2 cups fresh raspberries
3 tablespoons sugar
3 tablespoons plus 1/4 cup all-purpose flour, *divided*
1/4 teaspoon ground cinnamon
1/2 cup quick-cooking oats
2 tablespoons brown sugar
2 tablespoons cold butter
Vanilla ice cream, optional

In a large bowl, combine the peaches, raspberries, sugar, 3 tablespoons flour and cinnamon. Divide mixture evenly among four 4-1/2-in. disposable foil tart pans coated with nonstick cooking spray; set aside.

In a small bowl, combine the oats, brown sugar and remaining flour; cut in the butter until crumbly. Sprinkle over the filling.

Prepare grill for indirect heat. Grill crisps, covered, over indirect medium heat for 15-20 minutes or until filling is bubbly. Serve warm with ice cream if desired. **Yield:** 4 servings.

Grilled Pineapple with Lime Dip

(Pictured above, left)

This fruit appetizer was created by our home economists.
If desired, roll the pineapple wedges in flaked coconut before grilling.

1 fresh pineapple
1/4 cup packed brown sugar
3 tablespoons honey
2 tablespoons lime juice
LIME DIP:
　1 package (3 ounces) cream
　　cheese, softened
1/4 cup plain yogurt
　2 tablespoons honey
　1 tablespoon brown sugar
　1 tablespoon lime juice
　1 teaspoon grated lime peel

Peel and core the pineapple; cut into eight wedges. Cut each wedge into two spears. In a large resealable plastic bag, combine the brown sugar, honey and lime juice; add pineapple. Seal bag and turn to coat; refrigerate for 1 hour.

In a small mixing bowl, beat cream cheese until smooth. Beat in the yogurt, honey, brown sugar, lime juice and peel. Cover and refrigerate until serving.

Coat grill rack with nonstick cooking spray before starting the grill. Drain and discard marinade. Grill pineapple, covered, over medium heat for 3-4 minutes on each side or until golden brown. Serve with lime dip. **Yield:** 8 servings.

Tasty 'n' Tangy Baby Back Ribs

I doctor up bottled barbecue sauce with a blend of ingredients, including honey, mustard and red pepper flakes. Marinating the ribs makes them mouth-watering.
—Gladys Gibbs, Brush Creek, Tennessee

1 bottle (18 ounces) barbecue sauce
1 cup honey
1 can (6 ounces) tomato paste
1/2 cup white vinegar
1/2 cup lemon juice
1/4 cup soy sauce
1/4 cup Dijon mustard
2 tablespoons Worcestershire sauce
1 garlic clove, minced
1 teaspoon crushed red pepper flakes
1 teaspoon ground allspice
2 teaspoons coarsely ground pepper, *divided*

4 to 5 pounds pork baby back ribs
1 teaspoon salt

In a large saucepan, combine the first 11 ingredients. Add 1 teaspoon pepper. Bring to a boil. Reduce heat; simmer, uncovered, for 15 minutes. Remove from the heat; set aside 2 cups of sauce for basting.

Brush ribs with the remaining sauce; place in two large resealable plastic bags. Seal and turn to coat; refrigerate for 30 minutes.

Prepare grill for indirect heat, using a drip pan. Drain and discard marinade. Sprinkle both sides of the ribs with the salt and remaining pepper. Place on grill rack over drip pan. Grill, covered, over indirect medium heat for 1 hour, turning occasionally.

Baste ribs with some of the reserved sauce. Grill 15 minutes longer or until juices run clear and meat is tender, turning and basting occasionally. **Yield:** 4 servings.

Herb Beef Burgers

You can prepare these patties ahead of time and keep them covered in the fridge until ready to grill.
—Pat Habiger, Spearville, Kansas

1 medium tomato, seeded and chopped
1/3 cup canned chopped green chilies
1/4 cup chopped ripe olives
1/4 cup chopped onion
2 garlic cloves, minced
2 teaspoons chili powder
2 teaspoons Dijon mustard
1 teaspoon *each* minced fresh oregano, thyme, basil and parsley

1/2 to 1 teaspoon minced fresh dill
1/2 to 1 teaspoon grated lemon peel
1 pound ground beef
4 hamburger buns, split
Sliced tomato, lettuce leaves and sliced onion, optional

In a large bowl, combine the tomato, chilies, olives, onion, garlic, chili powder, mustard, herbs and lemon peel. Crumble beef over mixture and mix well. Shape into four patties.

Grill, covered, over medium heat for 5-7 minutes on each side or until no longer pink. Serve on buns with tomato, lettuce and onion if desired. **Yield:** 4 servings.

Planked Spicy Strip Steaks

(Pictured at right)

To infuse steaks with a sweet, smoky flavor, our home economists cook them on wood grilling planks. Simple seasonings are all you need.

> 2 maple grilling planks
> 4 New York strip steaks (about 12 ounces *each*), trimmed
> 1 tablespoon olive oil
> 3/4 teaspoon ground coriander
> 3/4 teaspoon chili powder
> 1/2 teaspoon ground allspice
> 1/2 teaspoon cayenne pepper

Soak grilling planks in water for 2-3 hours. Drizzle steaks with oil. Combine the coriander, chili powder, allspice and cayenne; rub over both sides of steaks. Grill, covered, over medium heat for 1-2 minutes on each side or until grill marks appear; remove.

Place planks on grill over direct medium heat. Cover and heat until planks create a light to medium smoke and begin to crackle (this indicates planks are ready), about 3 minutes. Turn planks over. Place steaks on planks. Grill, covered, for 15-20 minutes or until meat reaches desired doneness (for medium-rare, a meat thermometer should read 145°; medium, 160°; well-done, 170°). **Yield:** 4 servings.

Editor's Note: Steak may be known as strip steak, Kansas City steak, New York Strip steak, Ambassador Steak or boneless Club Steak in your region.

CEDAR PLANK POINTERS

YOU CAN purchase packages of grill-ready cedar, maple and cherry or apple wood planks at grocery, hardware, specialty and kitchen stores. Another option is to buy untreated planks at a lumberyard and cut them into 1-inch thick sections. (NEVER cook with wood that has been chemically treated.)

To prevent the wood from burning while grilling, first immerse the plank in water and let it soak for several hours or overnight. (You may have to weigh it down with a soup can.) For even more flavor, add white wine, beer, apple cider or fresh herbs to the water.

When ready to cook, dry off the plank and grill as the recipe directs. Remove the cooked food from the plank. Let the plank cool on the grill grate before removing.

The Appeal of Apples

WHETHER you eat them out of hand or use them in a recipe, crisp, juicy apples can be enjoyed in a variety of ways throughout the day.

Do you want to show family and friends they're the apple of your eye? Surprise them with a selection of sweets they're sure to fall for.

Apples pair well with ice cream topping and candies in Caramel-Crunch Apple Pie and Caramel Apple Dumplings.

Apple Coffee Cake Braid is an attractive fruity favorite that can be sampled around the clock. (Recipes shown at right.)

The following pages also offer innovative ideas for entrees, side dishes and salads.

AN APPLE A DAY
(Clockwise from top left)

Caramel-Crunch Apple Pie (p. 232)

Apple Coffee Cake Braid (p. 230)

Caramel Apple Dumplings (p. 228)

Caramel Apple Dumplings

(Pictured on page 226)

When our apples become ripe, it's not unusual for me to make as many as 30 of these fruity dumplings!
—Omaha Peterson, Kinta, Oklahoma

2-1/4 cups all-purpose flour
   2 teaspoons plus 1/4 cup sugar, *divided*
   1 teaspoon salt
   1 cup shortening
   2 eggs
1/4 cup water
   2 teaspoons white vinegar
   7 medium tart apples, peeled and cored
   7 tablespoons butter
1/4 teaspoon ground cinnamon
CARAMEL SAUCE:
   1 jar (12-1/4 ounces) caramel ice cream topping
1-1/2 cups packed brown sugar
   1 cup water
1/4 cup butter, cubed

In a large bowl, combine the flour, 2 teaspoons sugar and salt; cut in shortening until crumbly. In a small bowl, combine 1 egg, water and vinegar; gradually add to crumb mixture, tossing with a fork until dough forms a ball. Divide into seven portions.

On a lightly floured surface, roll each portion into a 7-in. square. Place an apple on each pastry square; place 1 tablespoon butter in the center of each. Combine cinnamon and remaining sugar; sprinkle over apples.

Bring up corners of pastry to the center; pinch the edges to seal. Beat the remaining egg; brush over pastry. Place in a greased 13-in. x 9-in. x 2-in. baking dish. Bake at 350° for 15 minutes.

Meanwhile, in a large saucepan, combine the sauce ingredients. Bring to a boil; cook and stir until smooth and blended. Pour over apples. Bake 35-40 minutes longer or until apples are tender and pastry is golden brown, basting occasionally with sauce. Serve warm. **Yield:** 7 servings.

Wasabi-Salmon Waldorf Salad

Looking to give a twist to typical Waldorf salad, I created this recipe featuring salmon, bacon and wasabi horseradish mayonnaise. It makes a hearty lunch salad.
—Patricia Harmon, Baden, Pennsylvania

   1 salmon fillet (4 ounces)
   2 large red apples, cut into 1/2-inch cubes
1/2 cup chopped cashews
   1 celery rib, chopped
   3 bacon strips, cooked and crumbled
1/2 cup wasabi horseradish mayonnaise
   1 tablespoon honey
1/8 teaspoon pepper
   4 lettuce leaves, optional

In a small skillet, bring 1 in. of water to a boil. Add salmon. Reduce heat; cover and simmer for 5-7 minutes or until fish flakes easily with a fork. Remove with a slotted spoon. Cool slightly; flake salmon.

In a large bowl, combine the salmon, apples, cashews, celery and bacon. In a small bowl, combine the mayonnaise, honey and pepper. Pour over salad and toss gently. Serve on lettuce leaves if desired. **Yield:** 4 servings.

Apple Nut Cake with Rum Sauce

(Pictured at right)

Special occasions call for wonderful recipes like this. A simple-to-make rum sauce nicely complements the apple cake.
—*Bettie De Boeuf, Lawrenceville, Illinois*

  4 **cups chopped peeled apples**
  2 **cups sugar**
  2 **eggs**
1/2 **cup vegetable oil**
  1 **teaspoon almond extract**
  2 **cups all-purpose flour**
  2 **teaspoons baking powder**
  1 **teaspoon salt**
  1 **teaspoon ground cinnamon**
1/2 **cup chopped pecans**
SAUCE:
1/2 **cup butter, cubed**
  1 **cup sugar**
  2 **tablespoons all-purpose flour**
1/8 **teaspoon salt**
  1 **cup water**
  2 **teaspoons vanilla extract**
1/2 **teaspoon rum extract**

In a large bowl, combine the apples and sugar. Let stand for 30 minutes.

In a small bowl, whisk the eggs, oil and almond extract. Add to apple mixture and toss to coat. Combine the flour, baking powder, salt and cinnamon; stir into apple mixture just until moistened. Stir in pecans.

Transfer to a greased 11-in. x 7-in. x 2-in. baking dish. Bake at 350° for 35-40 minutes or until a toothpick inserted near the center comes out clean.

For sauce, in a small saucepan, melt butter. Stir in the sugar, flour and salt until smooth. Gradually add water. Bring to a boil; cook and stir for 2 minutes. Remove from the heat; stir in extracts. Serve with warm cake. **Yield:** 9 servings (2 cups sauce).

Apple Coffee Cake Braid

(Pictured on page 227)

Holiday brunches at our house always feature this lovely braid.
The dough is prepared in a bread machine, giving me time to focus on other things.
— Trisha Kruse, Eagle, Idaho

3/4 cup warm milk (70° to 80°)
6 tablespoons butter, softened
1/2 cup packed brown sugar
1 egg, lightly beaten
1 teaspoon salt
3-1/4 cups bread flour
1 package (1/4 ounce) active dry yeast
FILLING:
2 cups thinly sliced peeled tart apples
1/3 cup packed brown sugar
1/3 cup raisins
2 teaspoons all-purpose flour
1-1/4 teaspoons apple pie spice
2 tablespoons butter, softened
GLAZE:
3/4 cup confectioners' sugar
1-1/2 to 3 teaspoons milk
1/2 teaspoon vanilla extract

In bread machine pan, place the first seven ingredients in order suggested by manufacturer. Select dough setting (check dough after 5 minutes of mixing; add 1 to 2 tablespoons of water or flour if needed).

For filling, in a large bowl, combine the apples, brown sugar, raisins, flour and apple pie spice; set aside. When cycle is completed, turn dough onto a lightly greased baking sheet. Roll into a 15-in. x 10-in. rectangle; spread butter down the center third of rectangle. Spoon filling over butter.

On each long side, cut 1-in.-wide strips to within 1 in. of filling. Starting at one end, fold alternating strips at an angle across filling; seal ends. Cover and let rise until doubled, about 40 minutes.

Bake at 350° for 30-35 minutes or until golden brown. Cool on a wire rack. Combine glaze ingredients; drizzle over coffee cake. **Yield:** 1 coffee cake.

Editor's Note: If your bread machine has a time-delay feature, we recommend you do not use it for this recipe.

COOKING WITH APPLES

TO REMOVE any contaminants on the skin of an apple, wash it thoroughly with soapy water and rinse it off before using. Cut out any bad or soft areas of the apple.

To prevent browning, dip peeled apple slices into one part citrus juice and three parts water.

Fruit Salsa

(Pictured at right)

Fruit Salsa is a nice change of pace from traditional tomato-based salsa. Kids love it with graham crackers.
—Kelly Harbaugh, York, Pennsylvania

  1 **quart fresh strawberries, chopped**
  2 **medium apples, peeled and chopped**
  2 **medium kiwifruit, peeled and chopped**
  2 **tablespoons brown sugar**
  2 **tablespoons apple jelly**
1/4 **cup orange juice**
Graham crackers

In a large bowl, combine the strawberries, apples and kiwi. In a small bowl, combine the brown sugar, jelly and orange juice; drizzle over fruit and toss gently to coat. Serve with graham crackers. **Yield:** 6 cups.

Apple-Stuffed Chicken Breasts

When my family asks me to serve chicken for dinner, I usually prepare these elegant stuffed chicken rolls.
—Lois Edwards, Citrus Heights, California

  6 **boneless skinless chicken breast halves (6 ounces *each*)**
  1 **teaspoon salt, *divided***
1/4 **teaspoon pepper**
1/2 **cup finely chopped onion**
  2 **garlic cloves, minced**
  3 **tablespoons butter, *divided***
  1 **medium apple, peeled and grated**
3/4 **cup soft bread crumbs**
1/4 **teaspoon dried basil**
1/4 **teaspoon dried rosemary, crushed**
1/4 **cup all-purpose flour**
1/2 **cup unsweetened apple juice**
  1 **tablespoon sherry *or* additional unsweetened apple juice**

Flatten chicken to 1/4-in. thickness. Combine 1/2 teaspoon salt and pepper; sprinkle over both sides of chicken. Set aside. In a small nonstick skillet, saute onion and garlic in 1 tablespoon butter until tender. Add apple; saute 1 minute longer. Stir in the bread crumbs, basil, rosemary and remaining salt; heat through.

Top each piece of chicken with 3 tablespoons apple mixture. Roll up and secure with toothpicks; coat with flour. In a large nonstick skillet, cook chicken in 1 tablespoon butter until browned on all sides. Remove and keep warm.

Stir apple juice and sherry or additional juice into pan, stirring to loosen any browned bits. Return chicken to pan. Bring to a boil. Reduce heat; cover and simmer for 15-20 minutes or until chicken juices run clear.

Remove chicken to a serving platter; discard toothpicks. Add remaining butter to pan juices; whisk until blended. Serve with chicken. **Yield:** 6 servings.

Caramel-Crunch Apple Pie

(Pictured on page 226)

This sweet apple pie will make you the hit of every party. Slices are even better
served warm with a scoop of vanilla ice cream.
—*Barbara Nowakowski, Mesa, Arizona*

28 caramels
2 tablespoons water
5 cups thinly sliced peeled tart
   apples (about 2 pounds)
1 unbaked pastry shell (9
   inches)
3/4 cup all-purpose flour
1/3 cup sugar
1/2 teaspoon ground cinnamon
1/3 cup cold butter
1/2 cup chopped walnuts

In a heavy saucepan, combine caramels and water. Cook and stir over low heat until melted; stir until smooth.

Arrange a third of the apples in pastry shell; drizzle with a third of the caramel mixture. Repeat layers twice. In a small bowl, combine the flour, sugar and cinnamon; cut in butter until crumbly. Stir in walnuts. Sprinkle over pie.

Bake at 375° for 40-45 minutes or until apples are tender (cover edges with foil during the last 15 minutes to prevent overbrowning if necessary). Cool on a wire rack for 1 hour. Store in the refrigerator. **Yield:** 6-8 servings.

Southwestern Apple Slaw

Three varieties of apples add color and crunch to this crowd-pleasing coleslaw.
—*Roxanne Chan, Albany, California*

1 *each* medium red, green and
   yellow apple, julienned
1-1/2 teaspoons lemon juice
4 cups shredded green cabbage
1 cup shredded red cabbage
1/4 cup chopped red onion
1 can (15 ounces) black beans,
   rinsed and drained
1 cup (4 ounces) shredded
   cheddar cheese
3 tablespoons mayonnaise
2 tablespoons cider vinegar
2 tablespoons apple juice
   concentrate
2 tablespoons vegetable oil
1 jalapeno pepper, seeded and
   chopped
1 tablespoon honey

1/4 teaspoon crushed red pepper flakes
1/4 teaspoon ground cinnamon
1 medium ripe avocado, peeled and diced
1/2 cup chopped walnuts, toasted
1 tablespoon minced fresh parsley

In a large bowl, toss apples and lemon juice. Add cabbage and onion. Stir in beans and cheese.

For dressing, in a small bowl, whisk the mayonnaise, vinegar, apple juice concentrate, oil, jalapeno, honey, pepper flakes and cinnamon. Pour over cabbage mixture and gently toss to coat. Cover and refrigerate for at least 1 hour.

Just before serving, stir in avocado. Sprinkle with walnuts and parsley. **Yield:** 10-12 servings.

Editor's Note: When cutting or seeding hot peppers, use rubber or plastic gloves to protect your hands. Avoid touching your face.

Delicious Stuffed Baked Apples

(Pictured at right)

Baked apples are always a welcome sight at the dinner table on frigid fall evenings. This dressed-up version also features raisins, cranberries and apricots.
—Glenda Ardoin, Hessmer, Louisiana

1/2 **cup golden raisins**
1/2 **cup dried cranberries**
1/4 **cup chopped dried apricots**
2-1/4 **cups cranberry-apple juice**
1/3 **cup cranberry juice**
     concentrate
  4 **large Golden Delicious apples**
1/3 **cup packed brown sugar**
3/4 **teaspoon ground allspice,**
     divided
1/4 **cup butter, melted**

In a small bowl, combine the raisins, cranberries and apricots. In a small saucepan, bring juice and concentrate to a boil. Pour over dried fruit; let stand for 15 minutes.

Meanwhile, core apples, leaving bottoms intact. Peel the top third of each apple; place in a greased 8-in. square baking dish.

Drain fruit mixture, reserving juice. Stir brown sugar and 1/2 teaspoon allspice into fruit; spoon into apples. Drizzle with butter. Pour 3/4 cup reserved juice around apples.

Cover and bake at 350° for 50 minutes. Uncover; bake 10-15 minutes longer or until tender. Meanwhile, in a small saucepan, bring remaining reserved juice and allspice to a boil; cook until liquid is reduced to 1/4 cup. Serve with baked apples. **Yield:** 4 servings.

BEST BAKED APPLES

FIRM-FLESHED APPLES are best for baking whole. Varieties include Empire, Fuji, Golden Delicious, Jonagold, Rome Beauty and Royal Gala.

Grandma's Apple Pie

You'll elicit oohs and aahs every time you serve slices of this classic apple pie.
The crisp crust is a nice contrast to the tender apples.
—Carole Davis, Keene, New Hampshire

Pastry for a double-crust pie
   (9 inches)
   6 to 7 cups thinly sliced peeled
      tart apples (about 2-1/2
      pounds)
   1 tablespoon lemon juice
   1 cup sugar
   2 tablespoons all-purpose flour
   1/2 teaspoon ground cinnamon
Dash ground nutmeg
   2 tablespoons butter, cubed
Milk
Additional sugar

Line a 9-in. pie plate with bottom pastry; trim pastry even with edge of plate. Set aside.

In a large bowl, toss apples with lemon juice. Combine the sugar, flour, cinnamon and nutmeg. Arrange half of the apples in pastry shell; sprinkle with half of the sugar mixture. Repeat layers. Dot with butter.

Roll out remaining pastry to fit top of pie; place over filling. Trim, seal and flute edges. Cut slits in pastry. Brush with milk and sprinkle with additional sugar.

Cover edges loosely with foil. Bake at 425° for 20 minutes. Remove foil; bake 30-35 minutes longer or until crust is golden brown and filling is bubbly. Serve warm if desired or cool on a wire rack. **Yield:** 6-8 servings.

Apple Cider Quick Bread

This moist, tasty quick bread is packed with apple flavor and aromatic spices.
Whole wheat flour and wheat germ add a boost of nutrition.
—Nancy Zimmerman, Cape May Court House, New Jersey

1-1/2 cups all-purpose flour
   1/2 cup whole wheat flour
   1/2 cup packed brown sugar
   3 tablespoons toasted wheat
      germ
   2 teaspoons baking powder
   1 teaspoon ground cinnamon
   1/2 teaspoon salt
   1/2 teaspoon baking soda
   1/2 teaspoon ground nutmeg
   2 eggs, lightly beaten
   1 egg white
   1/2 cup apple cider *or*
      unsweetened apple juice
   1/4 cup plain yogurt
   1/4 cup vegetable oil
   1 teaspoon vanilla extract
   1 cup shredded peeled tart apple
   1/3 cup golden raisins
   1 teaspoon grated orange peel

In a large bowl, combine the first nine ingredients. In a small bowl, combine the eggs, egg white, cider, yogurt, oil and vanilla. Stir into dry ingredients just until moistened. Fold in the apple, raisins and orange peel.

Transfer to a greased 9-in. x 5-in. x 3-in. loaf pan. Bake at 350° for 50-55 minutes or until a toothpick inserted near the center comes out clean. Cool for 10 minutes before removing from pan to a wire rack. **Yield:** 1 loaf.

Cinnamon Apple Muffins

(Pictured at right)

Even the finicky eaters in my family love these lovely muffins. The sweet butter is a tasty accompaniment.
—Louise Gilbert
Quesnel, British Columbia

1-1/2 cups all-purpose flour
1/2 cup sugar
1-3/4 teaspoons baking powder
1/2 teaspoon salt
1/2 teaspoon ground cinnamon
1/8 teaspoon ground nutmeg
1 egg
1/2 cup milk
3 tablespoons vegetable oil
3 tablespoons unsweetened applesauce
1 medium McIntosh apple, peeled and grated
TOPPING:
1/4 cup packed brown sugar
1 tablespoon all-purpose flour
2 tablespoons cold butter
1/2 cup quick-cooking oats
CINNAMON-HONEY BUTTER:
1/2 cup butter, softened
1/4 cup honey
1/2 teaspoon ground cinnamon

In a large bowl, combine the flour, sugar, baking powder, salt, cinnamon and nutmeg. In another bowl, whisk the egg, milk, oil and applesauce. Stir into dry ingredients just until moistened. Fold in apple. Fill greased or paper-lined muffin cups half full.

For topping, in a bowl, combine brown sugar and flour; cut in butter until crumbly. Add oats. Sprinkle over muffins. Bake at 350° for 18-22 minutes or until a toothpick comes out clean. Cool for 5 minutes before removing from pan to a wire rack.

In a small mixing bowl, beat the butter, honey and cinnamon until blended. Serve with warm muffins. Refrigerate leftover butter. **Yield:** 1 dozen.

Apple Nutmeg Rolls

Cinnamon and nutmeg add nice spice to these pinwheel rolls that are chock-full of apple chunks.
Frozen bread dough lends to its fast preparation.
—*Sue Ann Bunt, Painted Post, New York*

1 loaf (1 pound) frozen bread
   dough, thawed
2 tablespoons butter, softened
1/4 cup packed brown sugar
1/4 cup finely chopped walnuts
1 teaspoon ground cinnamon
1/2 teaspoon ground nutmeg
2 cups finely chopped peeled
   tart apples
ICING:
1/2 cup confectioners' sugar
2-1/2 teaspoons milk

On a lightly floured surface, roll dough into a 14-in. square. Spread with butter. In a bowl, combine the brown sugar, walnuts, cinnamon and nutmeg; add apples and toss to coat. Sprinkle over dough to within 1/2 in. of edges.

Roll up jelly-roll style; pinch seam to seal. Cut into 12 slices. Place cut side down in a greased 11-in. x 7-in. x 2-in. baking dish. Cover and let rise in a warm place until doubled, about 40 minutes.

Bake at 350° for 25-30 minutes or until golden brown. Combine icing ingredients until smooth; drizzle over warm rolls. **Yield:** 1 dozen.

Maple Sweet Potato-Apple Bake

When making this casserole, I use tart apples to offset the sweetness of the maple syrup and brown sugar.
—*Katie Sloan, Charlotte, North Carolina*

5 medium sweet potatoes
   (about 2-1/2 pounds), peeled
4 large apples, peeled
7 tablespoons maple syrup,
   divided
6 tablespoons butter, *divided*
1/2 cup coarsely chopped pecans
2 tablespoons cornstarch
1 tablespoon grated orange peel
1 teaspoon ground cinnamon
1/2 teaspoon salt
1/4 teaspoon ground nutmeg
3 tablespoons orange juice
TOPPING:
1 cup packed brown sugar
1 teaspoon ground cinnamon
3 tablespoons cold butter
1 cup chopped pecans

Cut sweet potatoes and apples into 1/4-in. slices. Place sweet potatoes in a Dutch oven; cover with water. Bring to a boil; reduce heat. Cover and simmer for 3-4 minutes or until crisp-tender; drain. Place in a greased 13-in. x 9-in. x 2-in. baking dish; set aside.

In a large skillet, saute apples in 2 tablespoons syrup and 2 tablespoons butter for 4-5 minutes or until crisp-tender. Layer over sweet potatoes; sprinkle with pecans.

In a small bowl, combine the cornstarch, orange peel, cinnamon, salt and nutmeg. Melt remaining butter; whisk in orange juice and remaining syrup. Stir into cornstarch mixture until well blended. Pour over pecans.

In a small bowl, combine brown sugar and cinnamon. Cut in butter until mixture resembles coarse crumbs; stir in pecans. Sprinkle over the casserole. Cover and bake at 375° for 45 minutes. Uncover; bake 15-20 minutes longer or until bubbly. **Yield:** 8-10 servings.

Pork with Apples 'n' Hazelnuts

(Pictured at right)

If pork tenderloin is on sale, I buy several with this recipe in mind. Round out the meal with rolls and a salad.
—Lorraine Caland, Thunder Bay, Ontario

   1 **pork tenderloin (1 pound), cut into 1/4-inch slices**
   1 **tablespoon olive oil**
   1 **small onion, chopped**
   1 **medium apple, cut into wedges**
   1 **medium carrot, julienned**
 1/2 **cup chicken broth**
   1 **cup heavy whipping cream**
   2 **tablespoons red wine vinegar**
   2 **tablespoons Dijon mustard**
   1 **tablespoon tomato paste**
Dash salt and pepper
   2 **tablespoons chopped hazelnuts**

In a large skillet, cook pork in oil over medium heat for 2-3 minutes on each side or until juices run clear. Remove and keep warm.

In the same pan, saute the onion, apple and carrot for 1 minute. Add broth; cook and stir for 5 minutes or until liquid is evaporated.

Stir in the cream, vinegar, mustard, tomato paste, salt and pepper. Bring to a boil. Reduce heat; simmer, uncovered, for 3-5 minutes or until sauce is slightly thickened. Return pork to the pan; stir to coat. Sprinkle with hazelnuts. **Yield:** 3-4 servings.

ALL ABOUT APPLES

EVERYONE knows that "an apple a day keeps the doctor away." That's because apples are rich in vitamins A, B1, B2 and C. They also contain numerous minerals, such as calcium, phosphorous, magnesium and potassium.

Although apples are available year-round, they each have their own peak season. Select apples that are firm and have a smooth, unblemished skin that is free from bruises.

Store unwashed apples in the refrigerator away from other vegetables with strong aromas. Apples can be refrigerated for up to 6 weeks.

One pound (about 3 medium apples) yields 2-3/4 cups sliced.

A Haunting Halloween

AS THE clock ticks closer to the witching hour of Halloween, get into the spirit by hosting a gloomy gathering.

You don't have to turn as white as a ghost at the thought of planning a mouth-watering menu. Just turn to the creepy cuisine featured here!

You're sure to cause a stir when you entice ghouls and goblins inside your haunt for steaming cups of Witches' Brew with Broomsticks.

Don't forget about the "spooktacular" sweets. Ghastly Pear Ghosts are a spine-tingling twist to traditional caramel apples. With cake and pudding mixes, Mini Pumpkin Cakes are alarmingly easy to prepare. (All recipes are shown at right.)

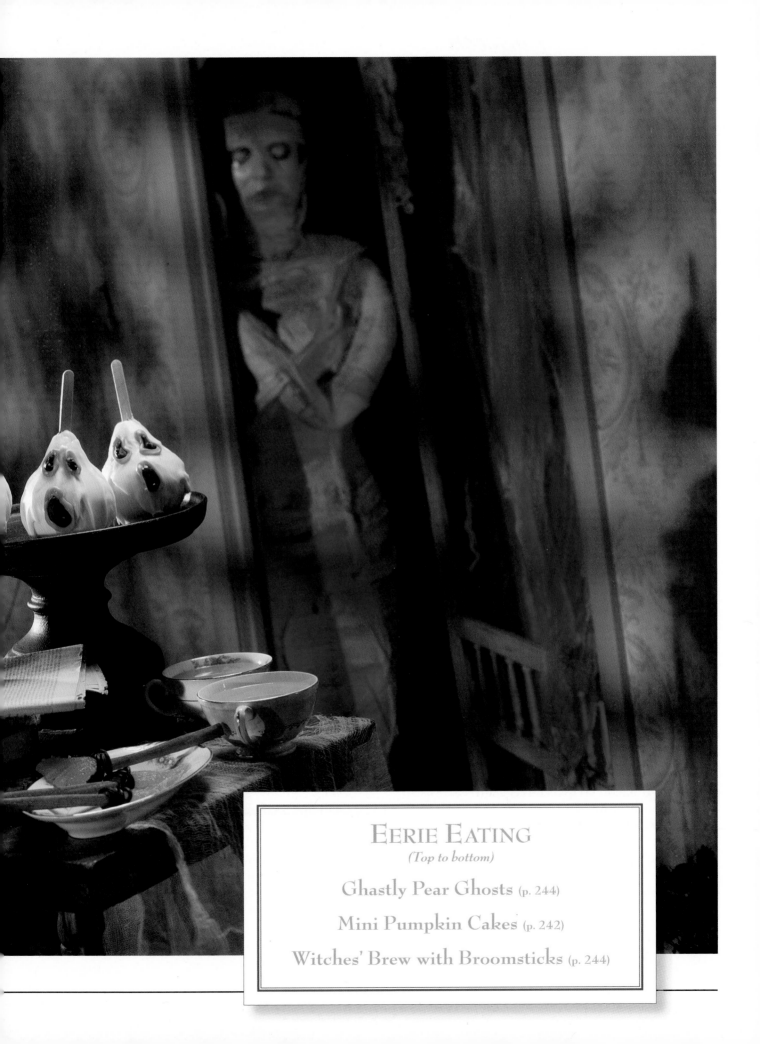

EERIE EATING
(Top to bottom)

Ghastly Pear Ghosts (p. 244)

Mini Pumpkin Cakes (p. 242)

Witches' Brew with Broomsticks (p. 244)

Witches' Hat Biscuits

(Pictured at far right)

These flaky biscuits have a delicious pumpkin flavor that appeals to everyone.
The honey butter adds a bit of sweetness to every bite.
—Billie Moss, Walnut Creek, California

2 cups all-purpose flour
1/4 cup sugar
3 teaspoons baking powder
1-1/2 teaspoons ground cinnamon
1/2 teaspoon salt
1/4 teaspoon baking soda
1/4 teaspoon ground nutmeg
1/2 cup cold butter
3/4 cup canned pumpkin
1/2 cup buttermilk
1/2 cup chopped walnuts
HONEY BUTTER:
1/2 cup butter, softened
1/2 cup honey
1/2 teaspoon grated orange peel

In a large bowl, combine the flour, sugar, baking powder, cinnamon, salt, baking soda and nutmeg. Cut in butter until mixture resembles coarse crumbs. Stir in pumpkin and buttermilk just until moistened. Stir in walnuts.

Turn dough onto a lightly floured surface; knead 8-10 times. Pat or roll out to 1/2-in. thickness; cut with a floured 3-1/4-in. witches' hat biscuit cutter. Place 1 in. apart on a greased baking sheet. Bake at 425° for 8-12 minutes or until golden brown.

Meanwhile, in a small bowl, combine the honey butter ingredients. Serve with warm biscuits. **Yield:** 1 dozen.

Spooky Spinach Salad

Sunflower kernels add fun crunch to this colorful spinach salad.
—J. Abrams, Surrey, British Columbia

4 cups torn romaine
2 cups fresh baby spinach
2 cups sliced fresh mushrooms
1 medium sweet orange pepper, julienned
6 bacon strips, cooked and crumbled
1/2 cup sunflower kernels
1/2 cup crumbled feta cheese
DRESSING:
1/2 cup plus 1 tablespoon olive oil
1/3 cup cider vinegar

2 teaspoons honey
2 garlic cloves, peeled
1/4 teaspoon salt
1/4 teaspoon paprika
1/8 teaspoon pepper

In a large salad bowl, combine the romaine, spinach, mushrooms, orange pepper, bacon, sunflower kernels and feta cheese.

In a blender, combine the dressing ingredients; cover and process until thick and well blended. Drizzle desired amount over salad; toss to coat. Serve immediately. Refrigerate leftover dressing. **Yield:** 6 servings (about 3/4 cup dressing).

Ravin' Good Stew

(Pictured at right)

*This stew is loaded with ingredients.
So it's sure to fill up little
ghosts and goblins before they
head out trick-or-treating.*
—Shirley Smith, Yorba Linda, California

1 can (29 ounces) pear halves
3 pounds beef stew meat, cut
   into 1-inch cubes
3 tablespoons vegetable oil
2 medium onions, chopped
3 tablespoons butter
1/3 cup all-purpose flour
1 tablespoon ketchup
2 teaspoons salt
1 teaspoon grated lemon peel
1/2 teaspoon dried thyme
1/2 teaspoon pepper
1/4 teaspoon ground cinnamon
1/8 teaspoon ground cloves
2-3/4 cups chicken broth
1/2 cup white wine *or* additional
   chicken broth
1 bay leaf
2 medium sweet potatoes,
   peeled and cubed
3 tablespoons golden raisins
2 tablespoons minced fresh
   parsley

Drain pears, reserving juice; chop pears and set aside. In a
Dutch oven, brown beef in oil in batches; drain and set
aside. In the same pan, saute onions in butter for 5 minutes. Stir in the flour, ketchup, salt, lemon peel, thyme,
pepper, cinnamon and cloves until blended.

Gradually stir in the broth, wine or additional broth and
reserved pear juice. Add bay leaf and beef. Bring to a boil.
Reduce heat; cover and simmer for 1 hour.

Add sweet potatoes; cover and simmer 30 minutes longer
or until potatoes and beef are tender. Stir in raisins and
pears; heat through. Discard bay leaf. Garnish with parsley.
Yield: 10 servings.

Mini Pumpkin Cakes

(Pictured on page 238)

*I saw these cute cakes at a local grocery store and decided to
make my own version at home. They're a hit at any fall gathering.*
—*Jennifer Dorff, Waukesha, Wisconsin*

1 package (18-3/4 ounces) spice
   cake mix
1 package (3.4 ounces) instant
   vanilla pudding mix
1 teaspoon ground cinnamon
4 eggs
1 cup canned pumpkin
1/2 cup milk
1/2 cup vegetable oil
3/4 cup chopped walnuts
ORANGE GLAZE:
7-1/2 cups confectioners' sugar
2/3 cup plus 2 tablespoons water
1 teaspoon maple flavoring
Red and yellow food coloring
GARNISH:
3 cups confectioners' sugar
3 tablespoons water
Green food coloring
4 Tootsie Rolls (2-1/4 ounces
   and 6 inches *each*), cut into
   2-inch pieces

In a large mixing bowl, combine the first seven ingredients. Beat on low speed for 30 seconds; beat on medium for 2 minutes. Fold in walnuts. Spoon 1/2 cupfuls into 12 greased miniature fluted tube pans. Bake at 350° for 20-25 minutes. Cool for 10 minutes before removing from pans to wire racks to cool completely.

In a large mixing bowl, beat the confectioners' sugar, water and maple flavoring until smooth. Tint orange with red and yellow food coloring. Place wire racks with cakes over waxed paper. Spoon half of the glaze evenly over tops and sides of cakes, letting excess drip off. Let stand until glaze is set. Repeat with remaining glaze.

In a small mixing bowl, beat confectioners' sugar and water until smooth; tint green. Cut a small hole in the corner of a pastry or plastic bag; insert a #4 round pastry tip. Fill bag with green frosting. Pipe vines on the pumpkins. For stem, insert a Tootsie Roll piece in the center of each pumpkin. **Yield:** 1 dozen.

Family Traditions

MAKING "mummies" for Halloween treats was a fun and easy activity for my niece several years ago. To make them, she spread white frosting over Twinkies, leaving a small unfrosted area at one end for the face. For the eyes, she dotted on tube frosting…or added mini chocolate chips and mini M&M's. —*Sandi Pichon, Slidell, Louisiana*

Gruesome Greek Dip

(Pictured at right, bottom)

Guests will not be able to stop eating this savory dip. The orange color makes it natural for a Halloween party.
— Gina Wilson, Austin, Texas

1 can (4 ounces) small shrimp, rinsed and drained
3 tablespoons lemon juice, *divided*
1 teaspoon Greek seasoning
1 package (8 ounces) cream cheese, cubed
3/4 cup crumbled feta cheese
1/2 cup chopped roasted sweet red peppers, drained
1 garlic clove, peeled
1 tablespoon minced fresh parsley
Baked pita chips

In a small bowl, combine the shrimp, 1 tablespoon lemon juice and Greek seasoning; set aside. In a food processor, combine the cheeses, red peppers, garlic and remaining lemon juice; cover and process until smooth. Stir into shrimp mixture.

Transfer to a serving bowl. Cover and refrigerate until serving. Just before serving, stir dip and garnish with parsley. Serve with pita chips. **Yield:** 2-1/2 cups.

Spicy Pumpkin Seeds

(Pictured above, top)

We look forward to fall in anticipation of making these spicy pumpkin seeds.
— Carolyn Hayes, Johnston City, Illinois

2 cups pumpkin seeds
2 tablespoons vegetable oil
1 teaspoon Worcestershire sauce
1/8 to 1/4 teaspoon hot pepper sauce
1/2 teaspoon salt
1/2 teaspoon paprika
1/4 teaspoon ground cumin
1/4 teaspoon cayenne pepper

In a small bowl, toss pumpkin seeds with oil, Worcestershire sauce and hot pepper sauce. Combine the salt, paprika, cumin and cayenne; sprinkle over seeds and toss to coat.

Line a 15-in. x 10-in. x 1-in. baking pan with foil; grease the foil. Spread pumpkin seeds in pan. Bake, uncovered, at 250° for 45-50 minutes or until lightly browned and dry, stirring occasionally. Cool completely. Store in an airtight container. **Yield:** 2 cups.

Ghastly Pear Ghosts

(Pictured on page 239)

Our Test Kitchen home economists came up with these treats as an alternative to traditional caramel apples. Wrap them up and give as gifts at your Halloween party.

6 medium ripe Bosc pears
6 Popsicle sticks
2 packages (14 ounces *each*) caramels
1/4 cup water
6 cups white candy coating disks
2 tablespoons plus 2 teaspoons shortening, *divided*
1/2 cup semisweet chocolate chips
1/2 cup orange candy coating disks

Line a baking sheet with waxed paper and grease the paper; set aside. Wash and thoroughly dry pears; insert a Popsicle stick into the top of each.

In a microwave-safe bowl, melt caramels with water; stir until smooth. Dip each pear into caramel mixture; turn to coat. Place on prepared pan; let stand until set.

In a microwave-safe bowl, melt white candy coating with 2 tablespoons shortening. Dip pears into coating. Return to pan; let stand until set.

In two separate microwave-safe bowls, melt chocolate chips and orange candy coating; stir 1 teaspoon shortening into each. Decorate ghost faces; let stand until set. **Yield:** 6 servings.

Witches' Brew with Broomsticks

(Pictured on page 239)

While growing up, my boys enjoyed helping me make this beverage with "broomsticks." Now I use the recipe with my grandchildren.
—Paula Marchesi, Lenhartsville, Pennsylvania

8 orange candy slices
8 cinnamon sticks (5 inches)
8 pieces black shoestring licorice (10 inches)
1/2 cup water
1/3 cup red-hot candies
6 cups milk
3/4 cup instant chocolate drink mix

For broomsticks, on a lightly sugared surface, roll each orange slice into a 1/4-in.-thick triangle. With wet scissors, snip bottoms of triangles to resemble broom bristles. Wrap pointed end of each around a cinnamon stick. Coil a licorice piece around the top of each orange slice to secure to cinnamon stick; set aside.

In a large saucepan, bring water and red-hots to a boil, stirring frequently until dissolved. Whisk in milk and chocolate drink mix. Cook, uncovered, over medium heat until hot. Pour into cups or mugs. Serve with broomstick stirrers. **Yield:** 8 servings.

Stained Cheesecloth Curtains

(Pictured at right)

GIVE your house a haunting Halloween feel with these coffee-stained, cheesecloth drapes.

Crumple cheesecloth and place it in a bucket of strong coffee. Soak until desired color. Wring out to remove excess coffee. Hang on an old clothesline to dry.

To create darker streaks and spots, place some of the coffee in a spray bottle and spray it on the cheesecloth as it dries.

For a well-worn look, use scissors to cut ragged openings in the dried cheesecloth.

Hang the disintegrated drapes over doors and windows. Or use them as tattered tablecloths.

HAUNTING HALLOWEEN DECOR

IT'S surprisingly simple to turn any room in your home into a haunted haven. In addition to the Stained Cheesecloth Curtains (above), purchase bags of spiderwebs and stuffed black crows. Don't toss out those dead plants…they add a little life to the spooky scene! Many craft and Halloween party stores carry a selection of spooky, life-size Halloween figures (like the mummy bride shown at right).

REFERENCE INDEX

Use this index as a guide to the many helpful hints, food facts, decorating ideas and step-by-step instructions throughout the book.

GENERAL RECIPE INDEX

This handy index lists every recipe by food category, major ingredient and/or cooking method.

Here's *Your* Chance To Be Published!

Send us your special-occasion recipes and you could have them featured in a future edition of this classic cookbook.

YEAR AFTER YEAR, the recipe for success at every holiday party or special-occasion celebration is an attractive assortment of flavorful food.

So we're always on the lookout for mouth-watering appetizers, entrees, side dishes, breads, desserts and more…all geared toward the special gatherings you attend or host throughout the year.

Here's how you can enter your family-favorite holiday fare for possible publication in a future *Holiday & Celebrations Cookbook*:

Print or type each recipe on one sheet of 8-1/2" x 11" paper. Please include your name, address and daytime phone number on each page. Be specific with directions, measurements and the sizes of cans, packages and pans.

Please include a few words about yourself, when you serve your dish, reactions it has received from family and friends and the origin of the recipe.

Send to "Celebrations Cookbook," 5925 Country Lane, Greendale WI 53129 or E-mail to *recipes@reimanpub.com*. Write "Celebrations Cookbook" on the subject line of all E-mail entries and *include your full name, postal address and phone number on each entry.*

Contributors whose recipes are printed will receive a complimentary copy of the book…so the more recipes you send, the better your chances of "being published!"